English G 2000

B1

für das 5. Schuljahr
an Realschulen

Cornelsen

English G 2000
Band B1

Im Auftrag des Verlages herausgegeben von
Prof. Hellmut Schwarz, Mannheim

unter Mitwirkung von
Wolfgang Biederstädt, Köln

Erarbeitet von
Barbara Derkow Disselbeck
Allen J. Woppert

unter Mitarbeit von
Wolfgang Biederstädt, Köln • Joachim Blombach, Herford • Mervyn Whittaker, Bad Dürkheim • Herbert Willms, Herford *sowie* Helga Estor, Darmstadt • Martina Kretschko, Dresden

in Zusammenarbeit mit der Englischredaktion
Cedric J. Sherratt (Projektleitung), Dr. Karl Brehmer (verantwortlicher Redakteur), Kirsten Bleck, Susanne Döpper , Elke Lehmann, Rebecca Robb, Uwe Tröger, Dr. Gunther Weimann *sowie* Claudia Rothe, Corinna Böwing (Assistenz)

Beratende Mitwirkung
Rolf Aalbers, Kempen • Isolde Arnold, Leipzig • Franz-Josef Brüggemann, Rheda-Wiedenbrück • Dr. Jens Peter Green, Oldenburg • Gerhard Großnann, Rastatt Prof. Dr. Liesel Hermes, Karlsruhe • Bernd Jost, Salzbergen • Dr. Dieter Krohn, Hannover • John Loram, Engen • Horst Mücke, Schüttorf • Dr. Marita Schocker-Ditfurth, Kirchzarten • Michael Semmler, Lünen • Prof. Franz Vettel, Heppenheim Gerd Vogel, Heuchlingen *sowie* Karen Shipley, Kingsway High School, Chester

Illustration
David Barnett, Oadby, Leicester
sowie Linda Rogers Associates, London: Roger Fereday; Gabriele Heinisch, Berlin; Skip G. Langkafel, Berlin

Layout und technische Umsetzung
Jutta Debo, Susanne Meyer

Für die freundliche Unterstützung danken wir Chester City Council und der Kingsway High School, Chester.

Zusatzmaterialien zum vorliegenden Schülerbuch:

Workbook mit Einführungskurs (Bestellnummer 351831),
ohne Einführungskurs (351815)
2 Cassetten zum Schülerbuch (Lehrerfassung 351858)
2 CDs zum Schülerbuch (Lehrerfassung 351874)
Auf weitere Bestandteile wird im Handbuch für den Unterricht (351807) verwiesen.

Cornelsen online

http://www.cornelsen.de

1. Auflage €
Druck 12 11 10 9 Jahr 07 06 05 04

Alle Drucke dieser Auflage sind inhaltlich unverändert und können im Unterricht nebeneinander verwendet werden.

Druck: CS-Druck CornelsenStürtz, Berlin

ISBN 3-464-35179-3 – broschiert
ISBN 3-464-35178-5 – gebunden

Bestellnummer 351793 – broschiert
Bestellnummer 351785 – gebunden

Gedruckt auf säurefreiem Papier, umweltschonend hergestellt aus chlorfrei gebleichten Faserstoffen.

Contents

° fakultativ

Dein Englischbuch enthält folgende Teile:

UNITS	die sieben Kapitel des Buches
TOPICS	besondere Themen wie z.B. „britisches Geld"
LANGUAGE SUMMARY (S)	eine Zusammenfassung der Grammatik jeder Unit
VOCABULARY (V)	das Wörterverzeichnis zum Lernen der neuen Wörter
DICTIONARY (D)	das alphabetische Wörterverzeichnis zum Nachschlagen
LISTS	Listen: **Names** (Namen), **Grammatical terms** (grammatische Begriffe), **Sounds** (Laute), **Classroom phrases** (Redewendungen für das Klassenzimmer)

Jede Unit besteht aus vier Teilen:

'LEAD IN'	die erste Doppelseite einer Unit; Einstieg in das neue Thema
▶ A: A-SECTION	der neue Lernstoff mit ersten Übungen
▶ P: PRACTICE	Übungen, Sprachspiele und Aktivitäten
▶ T: TEXT	eine spannende oder lustige Geschichte

In den Units findest du diese Überschriften und Symbole:

ACTIVITY	Aufgaben, bei denen du etwas tust – z.B. malen oder basteln.
GAME	Spiele für zwei, für eine Gruppe oder für die ganze Klasse – natürlich auf Englisch.
PROJECT	Allein, zu zweit oder in der Gruppe kannst du hier Nachforschungen anstellen, Fotos und Bilder sammeln, malen usw., um dann ein Poster oder etwas anderes zu machen.
▶▶▶ NOW YOU	Hier kannst du über dich selbst sprechen oder schreiben.
▶ Looking at language	Hier sammelst du Beispiele, mit denen du deine eigene Grammatikübersicht erstellen kannst.
LISTENING	Hier gibt es Hörtexte auf Cassette/CD und dazu Aufgaben im Buch.
SOUNDS	Hier geht es um die Aussprache von Lauten, Wörtern und Sätzen.
REVISION	Hier wird wiederholt – damit du nichts vergisst.
WORD WATCH	Unter dieser Überschrift geht es immer um Wörter. Hier findest du Übungen wie **Word link** (Wortverbindung), **Odd word out** (Das unpassende Wort raus), **The fourth word** (Das vierte Wort).
WORKING WITH THE TEXT	Unter dieser Überschrift gibt es Aufgaben zum Text.
◆◆	Partnerarbeit
❖	Gruppenarbeit
1	schwierigere Übung

WELCOME!

English in Germany

KENYA
THIS SIGN IS ON THE EQUATOR
EQUATOR
NANYUKI
ALTITUDE 6389FT
PANAM

ACTIVITY

BOXER-SHORTS
REINE SEIDE
Das Super-Outfit: T-Shirt und Jeansjacke
Musik Café mit LIVE Musik!
Fitness-Training für Männer und Frauen
Sun Travel
LAST MINUTE FLÜGE!
I speak a little English. And you?

Hello. What's your name?

ALEXANDER Hello.
DILEK Hello. What's your name?
ALEXANDER My name is Alexander.

DILEK Where are you from?
ALEXANDER I'm from Berlin. And where are you from?
DILEK I'm from Berlin, too. My mum and dad are from Turkey*.

▶▶▶ **NOW YOU**

Song **Good morning**

Can you count?

1	one [wʌn]	**6**	six [sɪks]	**11**	eleven [ɪ'levn]
2	two [tu:]	**7**	seven ['sevn]	**12**	twelve [twelv]
3	three [θri:]	**8**	eight [eɪt]	**13**	thirteen [ˌθɜ:'ti:n]
4	four [fɔ:]	**9**	nine [naɪn]	**14**	fourteen [ˌfɔ:'ti:n]
5	five [faɪv]	**10**	ten [ten]	**...**	

10
9
8
7
6
5
...

ALEXANDER How old are you?
DILEK I'm twelve.

▶▶▶ **NOW YOU**

* Weitere Ländernamen findest du auf der hinteren Umschlaginnenseite.

Can you spell?

Alphabet song

DILEK Can you spell your name, please?
ALEXANDER A – L – E – X – A – N – D – E – R.

▶▶▶ **NOW YOU**

The letter number box

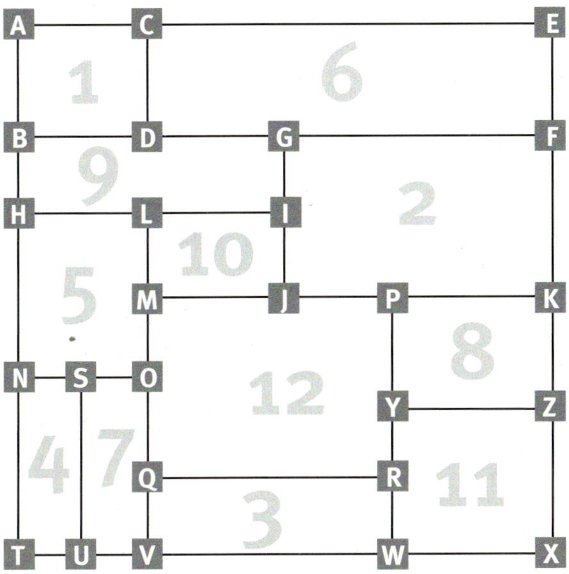

ALEXANDER Box number one is ACDB.
DILEK Box number two is GFK …
YOU …
TEACHER And box number 13?

What's this in English?

ALEXANDER It's a classroom.

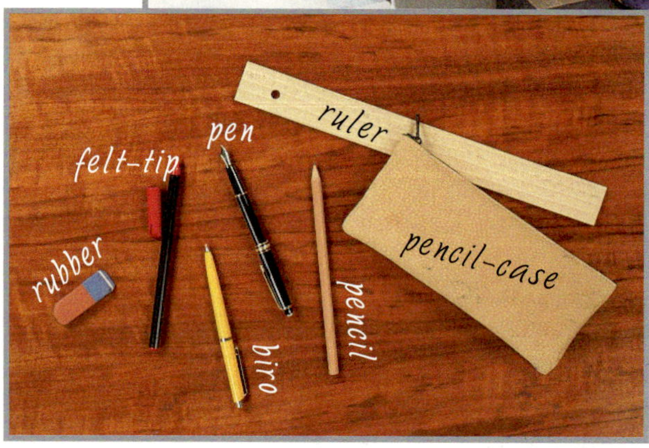

DILEK What's this in English?
ALEXANDER It's a biro.

▶▶▶ **NOW YOU**

Find the classroom words.

What colour is it?

ALEXANDER What colour is your felt-tip?

DILEK It's red.

▶▶▶ **NOW YOU**

Song **I'm a blue chameleon**[1]

Words by B Derkow Disselbeck
Music by J Blombach

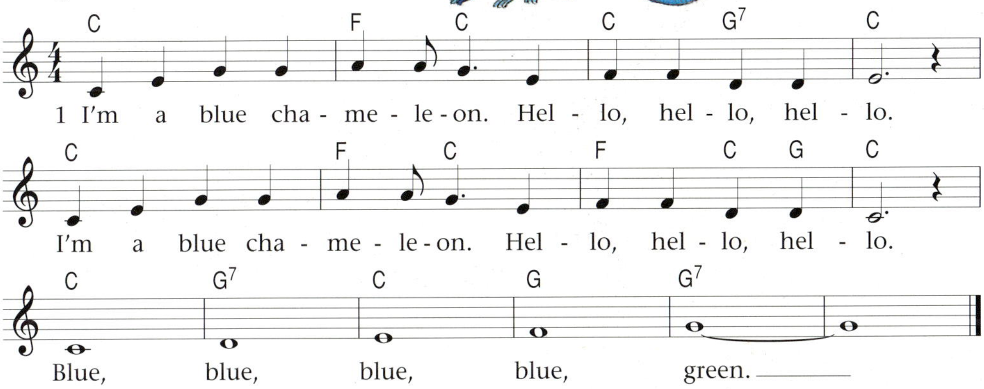

[1] chameleon [kə'mi:liən] *Chamäleon*

2 I'm a green chameleon …

3 I'm a red …

4 I'm a yellow …

5 I'm a white chameleon.
Goodbye, goodbye, goodbye.

How many words can you make?

I
a
are
…

1 UNIT 1 Hello, Form 7 CH!

This is Jenny Snow.
She's eleven.
She's from Chester,
a town in England.
Her sister Sally is thirteen.

This is Nick Baker, and this is Debbie Baker.
Nick and Debbie are twins.
They're eleven.
They're from Chester, too.

This is Sita Gupta, and this is her brother Sanjay. Sita is eleven and Sanjay is fourteen. They're from Chester.

This is Ben Scott. He's eleven, too. He's from Ashton.

▶▶▶ **NOW YOU** and your form

CLAUDIA This is Jens. He's … . He's from … .
JENS This is Katja. She's … . She's from … .
KATJA …

ACTIVITY
Start a scrapbook.

▶ 1

MISS HUNT Good morning, boys and girls. Welcome to Kingsway High School. I'm Miss Hunt. I'm new in Chester. I'm from Nottingham. I'm your form teacher.

FORM 7CH Good morning, Miss Hunt.

▶ 2

MISS HUNT What's your name?

JENNY My name is Jenny Snow.

MISS HUNT How old are you, Jenny?

JENNY I'm eleven.

MISS HUNT And what's *your* name?

DEBBIE I'm Debbie Baker. And this is Nick. He's my brother.

MISS HUNT Oh, you're Nick Baker.

NICK Yes, Miss Hunt.

▶ 3

MISS HUNT And what's your name?

BEN I'm Ben Scott.

MISS HUNT Where are you from, Ben?

BEN I'm from Ashton. It's a village near Chester. But my mum is from Berlin. She's German. I'm not German, I'm British, I'm ...

MISS HUNT Yes, thank you, Ben.

▶ 4

MISS HUNT And what's your name?

SITA I'm Sita, Sita Gupta.

MISS HUNT Sita ... what a nice name.

SITA Thank you. It's Indian.

MISS HUNT And where are you from, Sita?

SITA I'm from Chester.

→ S 1: 1a (p. 126)
→ P 1, 2, 3, 12

5 SONG Hi there, hi there

▶▶▶ NOW YOU and your form

▶ 6

SANJAY Hi, Sita.
SITA Hi. Oh Sanjay, this is Debbie, and this is Nick. They're my new friends. They're in 7CH, too.
SANJAY Hello, Debbie. Hello, Nick. Oh! You're twins!
NICK Yes, we're twins.

▶ 7

SITA Nick, Debbie, this is Sanjay. He's my brother.
DEBBIE You're lucky, Sita! Let's swap.
NICK Oh, ha ha, Debbie. Very funny.

▶ Looking at language

Find forms on pages 14 and 15 like:

I'm *we're*
you'… …
… …

→ S 1: 2a, b (p. 127)
→ P 4, 5, 13

▶ 8

DEBBIE Oh, no! Where are my pencils?
JENNY Here, Debbie. Here are your pencils. And here are your felt-tips.
DEBBIE Thank you, Jenny. And here are my rulers, but where are my biros?
JENNY Here are two blue biros, under the chair.
MISS HUNT OK, boys and girls. Open your books at page five, please.
DEBBIE Oh, no. Where are my books?

9 ▶ What's on the floor?

1 two biros
2 two f…
3 six p…
4 …

→ S 1: 1b (p. 126)
→ P 6

▶ 10

I'm not a teacher!
I'm a tortoise.

I'm not thirteen!
I'm eleven.

… a girl!
I'm a boy.

… in Year 7!
I'm in Year 10.

We aren't twins!
We're sisters.

… in Year 10!
We're in Year 7.

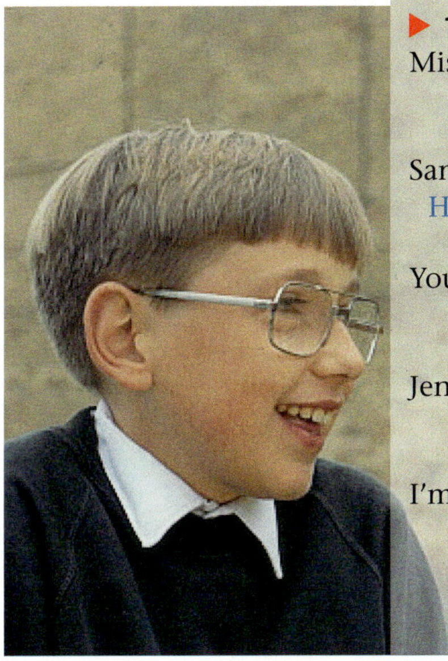

▶ 11

Miss Hunt is from Berlin.
She isn't from Berlin!
She's from Nottingham.
Sanjay is from Nottingham.
He isn't from Nottingham!
He's from Chester.
Your name is Tim.
It isn't Tim!
It's Ben.
Jenny and Sally are twins.
They aren't twins!
They're sisters.
I'm very clever.
You aren't clever.
You're silly, Nick!

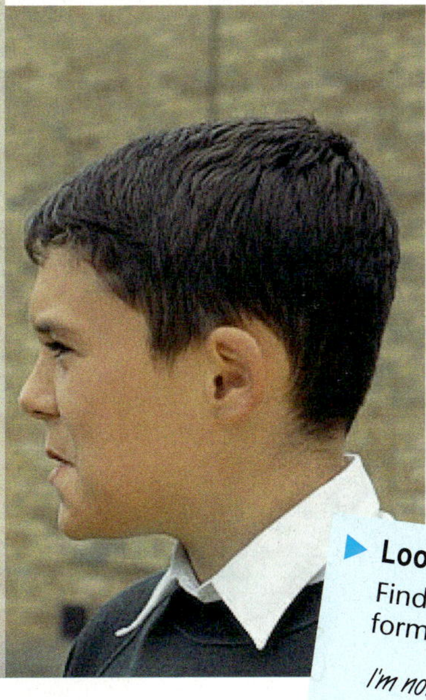

▶ Looking at language

Find the negative short forms in A10 and A11.

I'm not ... *we* ...
you ... ...
... ...

→ S 1: 2c (p. 127)
→ P 7, 8, 11

▶ 12

TRUNDLE: Is Debbie Baker nice?
JENNY: Yes, she is.
TRUNDLE: Is Nick nice, too?
JENNY: Yes, he is, Trundle.
TRUNDLE: Are Nick and Debbie brother and sister?
JENNY: Yes, they are.

▶ 13

TRUNDLE: Jenny, are you in Year 7 now?
JENNY: Yes, I am.
TRUNDLE: Are Nick and Debbie your friends?
JENNY: Yes, they are.
TRUNDLE: Am I your friend, too?
JENNY: Yes, Trundle, you are. Now shhhh!

▶ 14

TRUNDLE: Jenny, how old are Nick and Debbie? Are they twelve?
JENNY: No, they aren't. They're eleven.
TRUNDLE: Are you and Sally twelve?
JENNY: No, of course we aren't. Are you a silly tortoise, Trundle?
TRUNDLE: No, I'm not. I'm a very clever tortoise.

▶ Looking at language

Find the questions and short answers.

Is Debbie Baker nice? – Yes, she is.
...
Are they twelve? – No, they aren't.
...

→ S 1: 2d, e (p. 128)
→ P 9, 10

1 ▶ This is ...

1 This is *Ben*. He'*s from Ashton*. 2 This is *Sally*. She... . 3 This is ... 4 ... 5 ...

◆◆ 2 ▶ Ashton?

Now you and your partner.

◆◆ 3 ▶ A questionnaire

a *Copy the questionnaire into your exercise book. Talk to your partner. Complete the questionnaire.**

	My name:	*My partner:*
	Milena	*?*
how old?	*11*	*?*
from ...?	*Croatia*	*?*

b *Now tell your form.*

* Ländernamen findest du auf der hinteren Umschlaginnenseite.

4 ▶ At Kingsway High School

Use we're/they're.

DEBBIE	Jenny and Sita are in my form. *Jenny and Sita* are my new friends.
	Jenny and Sita are in my form. *They're* my new friends.
JENNY	Sally and I are sisters. *Sally and I* are at Kingsway High School.
NICK	Debbie and I are eleven. *Debbie and I* are twins.
BEN	The twins are eleven. *The twins* are nice.
SITA	My brother and I are from Chester. *My brother and I* are British.
MISS HUNT	Debbie and Nick are twins. *Debbie and Nick* are in my form.

5 ▶ This is ...

Use he's/she's/it's/they're.

This is Sita Gupta. *She's* in Form 7CH.

This is my village. ... near Chester.

This is my mum. ... from Germany.

This is my dad. ... British.

This is Debbie, and this is Nick. ... in Form 7CH, too.

This is Jenny Snow, and this is Sally Snow. ... sisters.

This is Sanjay Gupta. ... in Year 10.

6 SOUNDS The plural

a *Listen to the cassette/CD and say the plural.*

biro • desk • bin • girl
group • name • teacher • book

b *Make two groups.*

[-s]	[-z]
desks, …	biros, …

c *Say:*

The S in snakes[1]
Is the S in books,
Is the S in groups,
Is the S in desks,
Is the S in snakes.

Buzz buzz rulers,
Buzz buzz rubbers,
Buzz buzz sisters,
Buzz buzz brothers.

[1] snake [sneɪk] *Schlange*

◆◆ 7 ▶ Right! Wrong!

Make sentences and talk to your partner.

Ben and Nick
Trundle
Debbie
Sanjay and Sita
Miss Hunt
Chester
I
My teacher

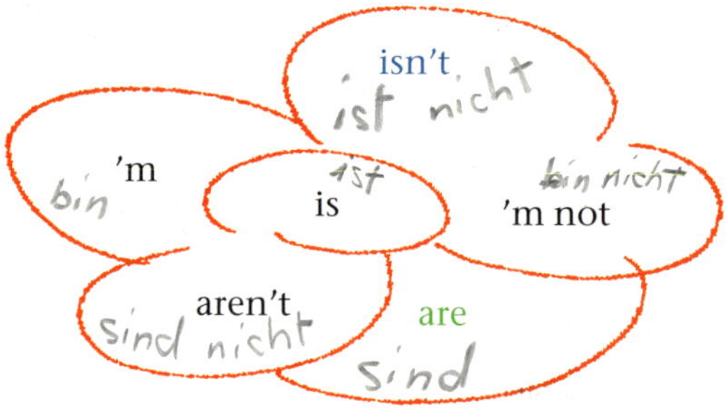

a tortoise
a teacher
twelve
green
in England
from India
German
eleven

YOU Ben and Nick are from India.
YOUR PARTNER Wrong. Ben and Nick aren't from India.
Trundle isn't a teacher.
YOU Right.
...

8 ▶ I'm not a tortoise!

a *Copy the chart and complete it.*

	Trundle	Sita	You
11?	✗	✓	?
12?	✓	✗	?
boy?	✗	✗	?
girl?	✗	✓	?
tortoise?	✓	?	?
British?	✓	?	?
German?	✗	?	?
in Year 7?	✗	?	?
in Year 5?	✗	?	?

b *Use* I'm – I'm not; he's – he isn't; she's – she isn't.

Trundle isn't eleven. He's twelve.
He isn't a ...
Sita is ...
I'm/ I'm not ...

9 ▶ Questions and answers

Match the answers to the questions.

a
1 Is Nick your brother, Debbie?
2 Are you in Form 7CH, Jenny?
3 Is your name Indian, Sita?
4 Are Jenny and Sally sisters?
5 Are you and Debbie twins, Nick?
6 Is Miss Hunt your form teacher, Ben?

– Yes, she is.
– Yes, he is.
– Yes, they are.
– Yes, we are.
– Yes, it is.
– Yes, I am.

b
1 Are you and Sally twins, Jenny?
2 Are you silly, Trundle?
3 Is your mum British, Ben?
4 Are Debbie and Jenny sisters?
5 Is Sanjay in your year, Nick?
6 Am I your friend?

– No, I'm not.
– No, they aren't.
– No, he isn't.
– No, we aren't.
– No, she isn't.
– No, you aren't.

10 ACTIVITY Red cards, blue cards

Write the words on red cards.

Trundle • Jenny • Ben • Debbie
Miss Hunt • Sita • Sanjay • Nick
you • I • ...

Write the words on blue cards.

German* • British • eleven • twelve
thirteen • fourteen • a girl • a boy
a teacher • a tortoise • in Form 7CH
from Chester • ...

LISA Is Miss Hunt a tortoise?
CHRISTIAN Of course she isn't. Miss Hunt is a teacher.

CHRISTIAN Are you German?
LISA Yes, I am.

11 LISTENING

a

b

c

d

e

f

1 *Look at the pictures.*
2 *Now listen to the cassette/CD.*
3 *Listen again. Write the numbers 1, 2, 3, 4, 5 and 6 in your exercise book. Now match the numbers to the letters.*

WORD WATCH

12 ▶ Odd word out

a
1 red, yellow, biro, green → *biro*
2 British, German, Chester, Indian
3 welcome, desk, board, chair
4 felt-tip, rubber, pencil, biro
5 I, you, she, the
6 teacher, tortoise, girl, boy
7 Nick, Debbie, Jenny, Sally
8 mum, sister, teacher, dad

◆◆ **b** *Write one* Odd word out *and ask your partner.*

13 ▶ Word groups

Make two groups: people *and* the classroom.

biro • board • book • boy
brother • chair • dad • desk
felt-tip • friend • girl • mum
pencil • ruler • school bag • sister
teacher • twins

people	the classroom
sister	desk
teacher	teacher

* Weitere Ländernamen und deren Adjektive findest du auf der hinteren Umschlaginnenseite.

Home from school!

WORKING WITH THE TEXT

1 ▶ What's wrong here?
Correct the mistakes.

Debbie and Nick are home from Ashton. The new school is silly. Debbie and Nick aren't in the same form. They're in Form 7CB. Jenny Snow is in Form 7CB, too. Debbie is her new friend. Miss Hunt is the form teacher in 7CB. She's a German teacher. She isn't very nice.

The kids in Form 7CB are great. Sita Gupta and Debbie and Nick are friends, too. Sanjay Gupta is thirteen. He's in Year 9. He's a nice boy. His mum and dad are from Germany.

Debbie and Nick are home from <u>school</u>. The new school is <u>great</u>. …

2 ▶ Now your story for your scrapbook
You're home from your new school. Write a story.

My school – great / Form … / my friend – same form / his/her name – … / his/her mum and dad – from … / form teacher – very nice / girls and boys – great

My school is great. I'm in Form …

TOPIC 1 English in the classroom

1 GAME Let's swap
Swap things with your partner.
Look at the picture.

2 ● What can you see in your classroom?
Copy the network. Use words, not pictures. Fill in: bin, board, poster, …

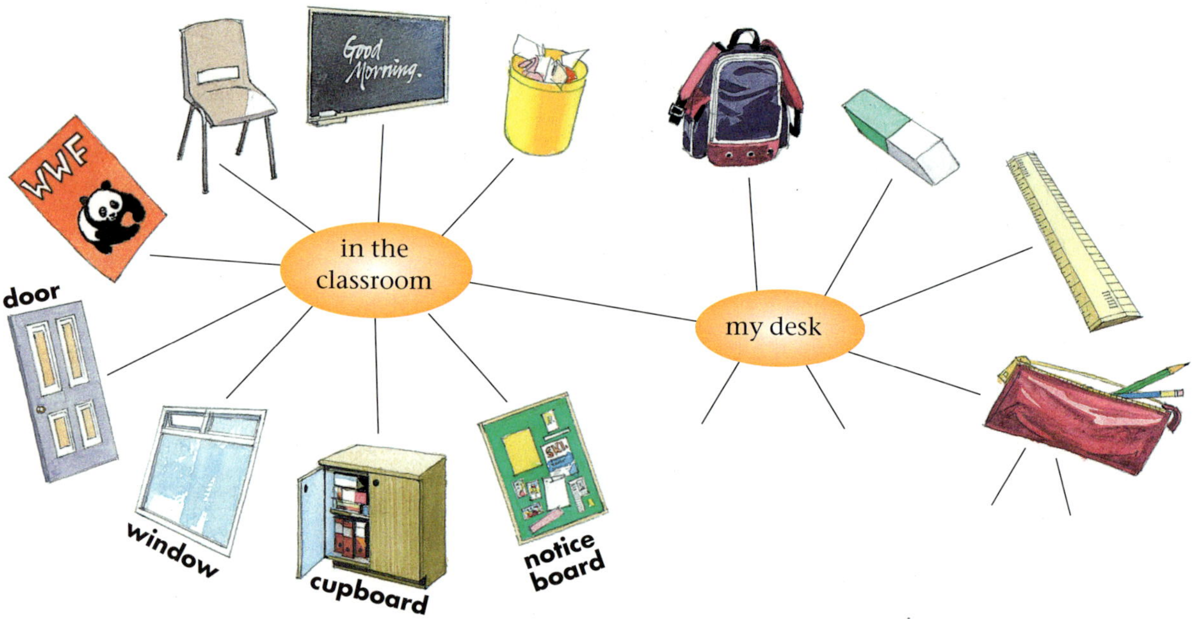

3 ● What can you hear in the classroom?

a *What can you hear in your classroom? Find more sentences.*

❖ **b** *Now you are the teacher. Look at the picture.*

4 What can you say in your classroom?*

1 Can I say it in German?
2 Can I help?
3 Sorry?
4 Can I open the window, please?
5 Can I go to the toilet?
6 Sorry, I haven't got my homework.

5 GAME

Say it in English, please.

Team A:	Kann ich helfen?
Teacher:	Say it in English, please.
Team B:	Can I help?
Team B:	Ruhe bitte!
Teacher:	Say it in English, please.
Team A:	...

6 PROJECT

Make English ladders for your classroom wall.

Can you find more sentences – or new ladders?

* Die folgenden und weitere *classroom phrases* findest du auf Seite 184.

UNIT 2 My family and my pets

Here I am with my grandma.
She's great. Ben Scott

Here's my family – my grandpa, my brother Sanjay, my mum and my dad.
Sita Gupta

This is my sister Sally with our cat. Her name is Marmalade. And here I am with my tortoise. His name is Trundle.
Jenny Snow

Here are Mum and Dad with Nick and our dog, Lulu.

And here are Aunt Helen and Uncle Paul. Debbie Baker

▶▶▶ NOW YOU

Bring a family photo to school and write about it.

This is my brother/... /...
His name is ...
He's ...

Pets Pets Pets

I'm a happy rabbit.
My name is Sue.
I'm a happy rabbit,
And who are you?

I'm a yellow budgie.
My name is Blue.
I'm a yellow budgie,
And who are you?

I'm a little hamster.
My name is Boo.
I'm a little hamster,
And who are you?

▶▶▶ **NOW YOU** for your scrapbook
Write a new verse about a pet.

hamster cat rabbit goldfish tortoise dog

silly funny little yellow happy German

I'm a silly dog.
My name is Koo.
...

Pooh Koo Moo Roo Shooh Woo

▶ 1

Jenny is home from school with her new friends.
And here's her mum.

MRS SNOW Oh! Hello! Who are you?
DEBBIE I'm Debbie, Debbie Baker. Are you Mrs Snow?
MRS SNOW Yes, I am.
NICK Oh, is your mum a nurse, Jenny?
JENNY Yes, that's right. Hi, Mum. This is Nick and this is Ben.
MRS SNOW Hello, Nick. Hello, Ben.
JENNY Tea, Mum?

▶ 2

Now Debbie, Nick and Ben are with Jenny and Sally in their garden.

SALLY This is our cat.
DEBBIE What's her name?
JENNY Her name is Marmalade. And this is my tortoise.
BEN A tortoise? Is this its cage?
JENNY Not *its* cage, Ben. *His* cage. Trundle is a 'he'.

▶ Looking at language

Look at A1 and A2 and complete:

I	*my*	*we*	...
you	...	*you*	...
he	...	*they*	...
she	*her*		
it	...		

→ S 2: 1 (p. 129)
→ P 1, 2

▶ 3

NICK I've got a dog.
DEBBIE *You've* got a dog? She's *our* dog, Nick.
NICK OK, Debbie, *we've* got a dog. She's great. Her name is Lulu.
BEN That's nothing. My friends have got two dogs. They're champions!
NICK And they've got three cats and six budgies, right? And they're champions, too?
BEN Ha ha, Nick. Very funny.

▶ 4

→ S 2: 2a (p. 129)
→ P 3, 4, 13

5 ▶ Hamster or tortoise?

Jenny ✗ hamster ✓ tortoise	Jenny hasn't got a hamster. But she has got a tortoise.	**Ben** ✗ pet ✓ computer	Ben hasn't got a pet. But he has got a computer.
Nick ✗ budgie ✓ dog	Nick … a budgie. But he … a dog.	**Sally** ✗ rabbit ✓ cat	Sally … a rabbit. But she … a cat.
Trundle ✗ basket ✓ cage	Trundle … a basket. But he … a cage.	**Lulu** ✗ cage ✓ basket	Lulu … a cage. But she … a basket.

▶ 6

▶▶▶ NOW YOU

Talk about pets.

I've got a cat. He's black and white. His name is Benjamin.

I haven't got a goldfish. But my friend has got a goldfish. It …

▶ Looking at language

Find the positive and negative forms of *have got*.

I've got	*I haven't got*
you' …	…
…	…

→ S 2: 2b (p. 130)
→ P 5, 6

▶ **7**

At the *Step in India* restaurant …

MR GUPTA Have you got problems, Sita?
SITA Well … all my friends have got pets, and I haven't got a pet.
MR GUPTA All your friends? What about Jenny? Has she got a pet?
SITA Yes, she has got a tortoise.
MR GUPTA And Debbie and Nick? Have they got a pet?
SITA Yes, they've got a dog.
MR GUPTA Well, Sita, we've got a pet, too.
SITA Oh, have we got a pet?
MR GUPTA Yes, the goldfish in the restaurant.
SITA Oh, Dad …

▶ **8**

Now Jenny is with Debbie, Nick and Ben.

JENNY Have you got a red felt-tip, Debbie?
DEBBIE No, I haven't.
JENNY Of course you've got a red felt-tip. Look.
DEBBIE Oh, you're right. Sorry. Yes, I have, Jenny. Here.
JENNY Thanks.
BEN Have you got a garden, Nick?
NICK Yes, we have.
DEBBIE Jenny, have Sita and her family got a garden?
JENNY No, they haven't.
BEN And have you got a swimming-pool?
NICK No, of course we haven't.
BEN But *I've* got a swimming-pool.
DEBBIE Jenny, has Sita got a pet?
JENNY No, she hasn't.
DEBBIE What about Sanjay? Has he got a pet?
JENNY No, he hasn't.
NICK But he *has* got a girlfriend. Poor Debbie!
DEBBIE Ha ha, Nick. Very funny!

▶ **Looking at language**

Find the questions and short answers.

Have you got …?
– No, I haven't. / Yes, I have.
Has she got …?
– No, she … . / Yes, she has.
…

▶▶▶ **NOW YOU** and your partner

a *Copy the questionnaire into your exercise book. Ask questions.*

A Malte, have you got a dog?
B No, I haven't.
A Have you got a hamster?
B Yes, I have. I've got two hamsters.

Have you got a …	*No*	*Yes*	*Number*
cat?	?	?	?
dog?	?	?	?
hamster?	?	?	?
silly brother?	?	?	?
nice teacher?	?	?	?

b *Now tell your form.*

Malte hasn't got a dog, but he has got two hamsters.

→ S 2: 2c, d (p. 130/131)
→ P 7, 8

▶ 9

BEN Where's your dad, Jenny?
JENNY He isn't here. My parents aren't together. They're divorced.
BEN Oh, I'm sorry.
JENNY Oh, that's OK. My dad has got a new wife. Her name is Tracy. They've got a house in Great Barrow.

▶ 10

DEBBIE Funny, my dad has got an uncle in Great Barrow.
BEN *I've* got three uncles and two aunts. I haven't got a grandpa. But I've got a grandma and an Oma.
NICK & DEBBIE An Oma???

→ S 2:3 (p. 131)
→ P 9, 10

▶ 11

This is Ben's family. Ben's dad is Richard Scott. Ben's mum is Karin Scott. Ben's uncles are Edward Simpson, David Scott and Bernd Bauer. Ben's aunts are Claire Simpson and Stefanie Zimmer-Bauer.
The Scotts' family tree is in Ben's room.

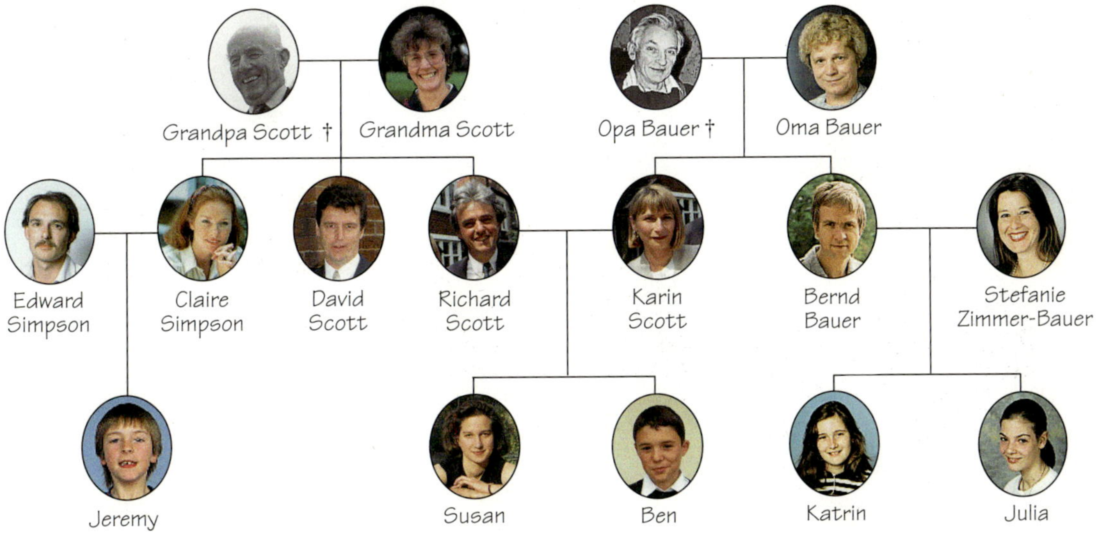

▶ 12

Ben Scott: My family
I have got two grandmothers. Oma Bauer is my mother's mother. She is in Berlin. And … is my father's mother. She has got a room in our house in Ashton. Oma Bauer's husband and Grandma Scott's husband – my two grandfathers – are dead. My mother's name is … . My father's name is Richard. I have got a sister. Her name is … . She is not in Ashton. She is in America.
Aunt Claire and Uncle Edward are in Bristol with my cousin … . Uncle … is not married. He is in Scotland. Uncle Bernd is in Berlin with Aunt … and my two cousins, … and … .

▶▶▶ **NOW YOU** for your scrapbook
Make a family tree for your family. Write about it.

→ S 2:4 (p. 131/132)
→ P 11, 12, 14, 15

1 ▶ Jenny is my new friend

a *Use* my/your/his/her/its.

1 SITA Jenny is my new friend. … mum is a nurse.
2 DEBBIE Sita is lucky. … brother is nice.
3 NICK Ben is in my form. … mum is German.
4 JENNY The new cage is in the garden. … tortoise is in it.
5 DEBBIE Your mum is very nice, Jenny. … sister is nice, too.
6 BEN My school is great. … name is Kingsway High School.
7 SITA This is my brother. … name is Sanjay.

b *Use* our/your/their.

1 We're twins. *Our* name is Baker.

2 ▶ My form

a *Use the right words.*

Ben Scott: My form
I'm in Form 7CH at (her, my, your) new school.
Miss Hunt is (our, her, their) form teacher.
She's OK.
Nick and (its, his, my) sister Debbie are in (my, your, their) form. They're twins.
(Her, Their, Your) name is Baker.
Jenny Snow and Sita Gupta are in (their, its, our) form, too. Sita is very nice. (Her, My, His) brother is in Form 10PW. (My, Their, His) name is Sanjay.

b *Now you. Write three or four sentences about your form. You can put them in your scrapbook.*

3 ▶ Make sentences with *have got*/*has got*.

1 Jenny	twins
2 The Scotts	basket
3 Mr and Mrs Baker	dog
4 Trundle	garden
5 Marmalade	cat
6 Debbie and Nick	cage
7 Sally and Jenny	sister
8 Sally	tortoise

1 Jenny *has got* a tortoise.
2 The Scotts *have got* a garden.
3 …

4 ▶ I've got ...

a *Make a network and say what you've got.*

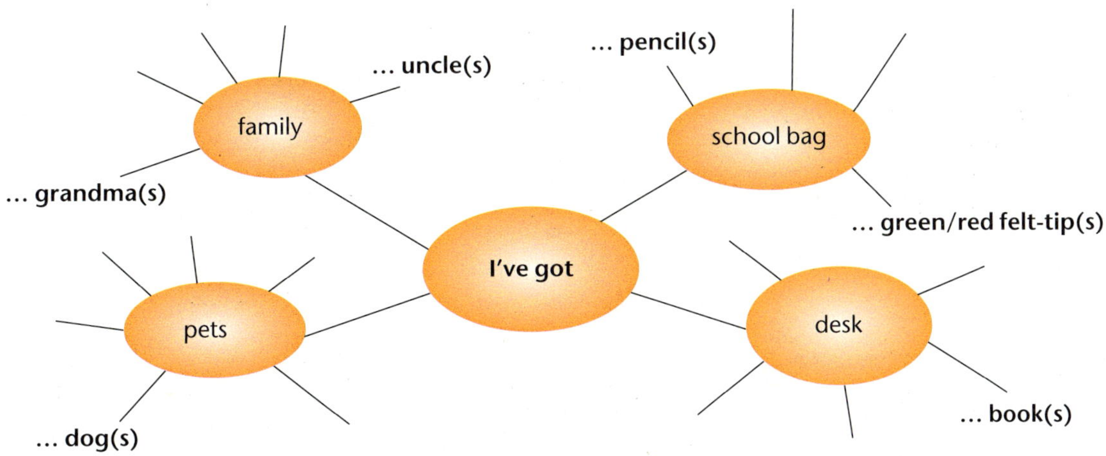

I've got two grandmas, a brother and a mother. I've got two cats and a hamster. I've got ... in my school bag. I've got ... on my desk.

◆◆ **b** *Swap networks with your partner. Tell your form about his or her network:*
He/She has got ...

5 ▶ Miss Hunt has got a computer

a *Copy the chart into your exercise book. Complete it.*

	computer	*pet*	*garden*
Miss Hunt	✓	✗	✓
the twins	✗	✓	✓
Ben	✓		
the Snows	✗		

b *Say what they've got and what they haven't got.*
Use have got – haven't got; has got – hasn't got.

1 Miss Hunt *has got* a computer. She *hasn't got* a pet. But she ... a garden.
2 The twins *haven't got* a computer. But ... .
3 Ben ...
4 The Snows ...

6 SOUNDS

a *Listen to the cassette/CD and say the words.*

[ɪ]
English • his • in • it
morning • kid • kitchen • sister
six • window

[iː]
be • green • he • people
please • see • she • speak
tea • thirteen

b *Listen to the cassette/CD and say the sentences.*

1 Good morning, Miss Hunt.
2 Is this your felt-tip?
3 Debbie and Nick are twins.
4 English is great!
5 Can you see the little village?
6 The pencils are in the green bin.
7 He's my new teacher.
8 He's British, but she's Indian.
9 Speak English, please.
10 She isn't twelve. She's thirteen.

◆◆ 7 ▶ Have Debbie and Nick got a dog?

With a partner: ask questions and give short answers.

Has	Debbie and Nick	got a	cage?
Have	Jenny		dog?
	Sita		sister?
	Ben		brother?
	Jenny and Sally		restaurant?
	Sanjay		tortoise?
	the Guptas		cat?
	Trundle		girlfriend?
	you		boyfriend?

Have Debbie and Nick got a dog?
– Yes, they have.
Has Jenny got a restaurant?
– No, she hasn't.
Has Trundle got a girlfriend?
– I don't know.

❖ 8 ▶ The question game

LISA I've got a blue pencil-case. – Max, have you got a blue pencil-case, too?

MAX Yes, I have. – Marco, have you got a blue pencil-case, too?

MARCO No, I haven't. But … a blue *sweatshirt*. – Laura, … you got a blue sweatshirt, too?

LAURA No, I haven't. But I've got a *red* sweatshirt. – Maik, …?

9 ▶ The alphabet, the song

Read out loud.

the alphabet, the song, the hamster, the Indian name, the black cat, the old dog, the English book, the German school, the answer, the aunt and the brother, the clever uncle

10 ▶ An aunt and an uncle

a *Read out loud.*

An aunt and an uncle,
A sister, a brother.
An English name,
A German mother?
A pen and a pencil,
A box and a book.
An 'a' or an 'an'?
– Look!

b *Use* a *or* an.

1 I've got *an* aunt and … uncle in England.
2 I haven't got … exercise book.
3 'Sita' is … Indian name.
4 Ben has got … great computer.
5 I've got … good friend in Chester.
6 Have you got … desk in your room?
7 Trundle is … old tortoise.

11 ▶ Jenny's tortoise is silly

Make new sentences. Use 's *or* s'.

1 Jenny has got a silly tortoise. → *Jenny's* tortoise is silly.
2 The Scotts have got a nice garden. → … garden is nice.
3 Sanjay has got a nice girlfriend. → … girlfriend is nice.
4 Ben Scott has got a German grandma. → … grandma is German.
5 Sita has got an Indian name. → … name is Indian.
6 The twins have got a great dog. → … dog is great.
7 Marmalade has got a basket in the kitchen. → … basket is in the kitchen.

12 LISTENING Families

a *Look at the families here. Imagine you're in the family. Tell your form about it:*
I've got three brothers and a mum and a dad. I've got a grandma, too.

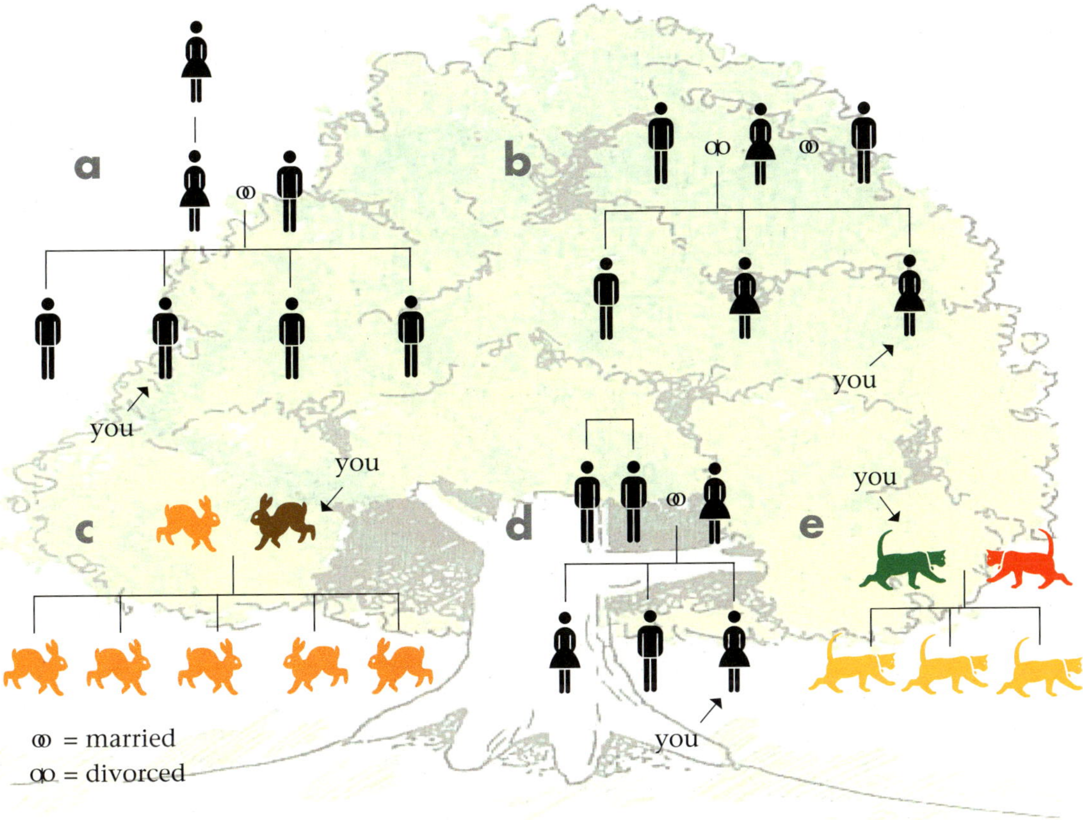

b *Now listen to the texts. Match the numbers to the letters.*

WORD WATCH

13 ▶ The fourth word

1 cat – basket tortoise – *cage*	4 I – my we – ?	7 desk – on cupboard – ?
2 black – white right – ?	5 dad – mum grandpa – ?	8 11 – number K – ?
3 he – his they – ?	6 yes – no hello – ?	9 I – am she – ?

14 ▶ Word partners

Match the words.

aunt • brother • *dad* • grandpa
husband • married • mother

divorced • father • grandma • *mum*
sister • uncle • wife

15 ▶ Who is it?

1 Your mother's or your father's mother.
– Oh, it's my *grandmother*.
2 Your mother's or your father's sister.
– It's my … .
3 Your mother's or your father's father.
4 Your mother's or your father's brother.

A cool new friend

Ben is lonely. He hasn't got a lot of friends. His dad is an engineer and his mum a professor, so they're often out. And his sister Susan is in America.

Of course he has got Grandma Scott. Grandma Scott is great. But today she isn't in her room. She's out, too. Ah well, Ben has got his computer.

C1B1 Poor Ben!
BEN Oh! Who are you?

C1B1 My name is C1B1. Hello!
BEN Hello, C1B1. Where are you from?
C1B1 I'm from your cool computer. I'm cool, too.
BEN Yes, you are. But who are you really?
C1B1 I'm C1B1. Really!

GRANDMA Who's there? Ben?
BEN Hello, Grandma. I've got a new friend.
C1B1 Good afternoon, Mrs Scott.
GRANDMA Good afternoon. Er, Ben, where *is* your friend?
BEN Here, Grandma, in the computer.

GRANDMA In the computer?
BEN Yes, Grandma. Look.
C1B1 How are you, Mrs Scott?
GRANDMA Fine, thank you.
Er, who *is* he, Ben ?
What's his name?
C1B1 My name is C1B1.
GRANDMA Funny name!
C1B1 Well, 'Grandma' is a funny name, too.
GRANDMA You're right, C1B1. Ben, your new friend is really cool.

BEN Grandma is great!
C1B1 dnA 1B1C si taerg, oot!
BEN What?!

WORKING WITH THE TEXT

1 ▶ Answer the questions

1 Has Ben got a lot of friends?
2 Is Grandma Scott in her room?
3 Where's his sister Susan?
4 Who's Ben's new friend?
5 Where's C1B1?
6 Is C1B1 great?
7 What's C1B1's funny sentence really?
8 Have you got a computer?

2 ▶ Computer virus!

Ben's computer has got a virus.
Please correct C1B1's wrong sentences.

Hello, Ben. are How you? lonely you Are? out Grandma is. too your And out, are parents. here But I'm! in Look your computer. C1B1 new I'm friend your. Hey, Ben. a got You've name silly. Ben the bin – ha ha ha! Ben poor Oh! Sorry, name a funny got haven't you.

TOPIC 2 Numbers

1 ● One, two, three

1	one [wʌn]	11	eleven [ɪ'levn]	21	twenty-one [ˌtwenti'wʌn]	101	a hundred **and** one
2	two [tuː]	12	twelve [twelv]	22	twenty-two [ˌtwenti'tuː]	200	two hundred
3	three [θriː]	13	thir**teen** [ˌθɜː'tiːn]	30	thirty ['θɜːti]	1000	**a** thousand ['əˈθaʊznd]
4	four [fɔː]	14	fourteen [ˌfɔː'tiːn]	40	**for**ty ['fɔːti]		
5	five [faɪv]	15	fifteen [ˌfɪf'tiːn]	50	fifty ['fɪfti]		
6	six [sɪks]	16	sixteen [ˌsɪks'tiːn]	60	sixty ['sɪksti]		
7	seven ['sevn]	17	seventeen [ˌsevn'tiːn]	70	seventy ['sevnti]		
8	eight [eɪt]	18	eighteen [ˌeɪ'tiːn]	80	eighty ['eɪti]		
9	nine [naɪn]	19	nineteen [ˌnaɪn'tiːn]	90	ninety ['naɪnti]		
10	ten [ten]	20	twenty ['twenti]	100	**a** hundred [ə'hʌndrəd]		

2 GAME Buzz

A One
B Two
C *Buzz*
D Four
E Five
F *Buzz*
G Seven
H Eight
I *Buzz*
etc

3 *Listen to* Trundle's Number Rap. *Can you say it?*

Trundle's Number Rap

1 2 3 4
Here is Trundle at the door.

5 6 7 8
And, as always, he is late.

9 10 9 10
Back to one and now again.

4 ● Telephone numbers

What's your telephone number?
What's your friend's telephone number?

ACTIVITY
Make a poster: Our form's telephone numbers.
You can copy your friends' numbers into your scrapbook.

5 ● 5 x 0 (Five times nought)

6 GAME Snakes and ladders[1]

a *Draw a board on cardboard.*
Cut it out.
Write the numbers 1 to 100.
Draw the snakes and the ladders.
Colour the board.

b *Bring a dice and counters to school. Throw the dice, move your counter.*
Go up ↑ the ladders and down ↓ the snakes.

A A four. 75, 76, 77, 78 …
Oh, no! Down the snake.
B A three. 67, 68, 69 …
Great! Up the ladder!

[1] snakes and ladders [ˌsneɪks_ən ˈlædəz]
Schlangen und Leitern

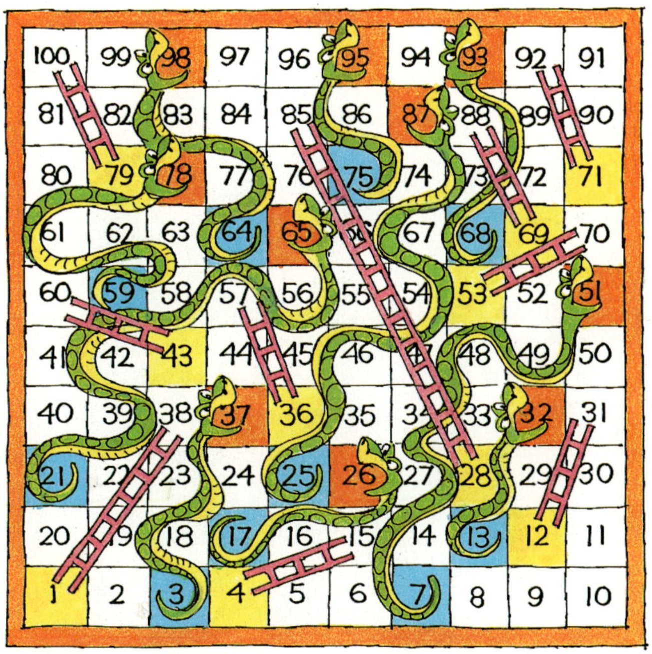

UNIT 3 Around the house

This is the Snows' house. It has got a small garden, but it hasn't got a garage.

This is the Bakers' house. It has got a garden and a garage.

This is the Guptas' restaurant, Step in India. The Guptas have got a flat over the restaurant.

This is the Scotts' house. It has got a big garage for two cars and a big garden.

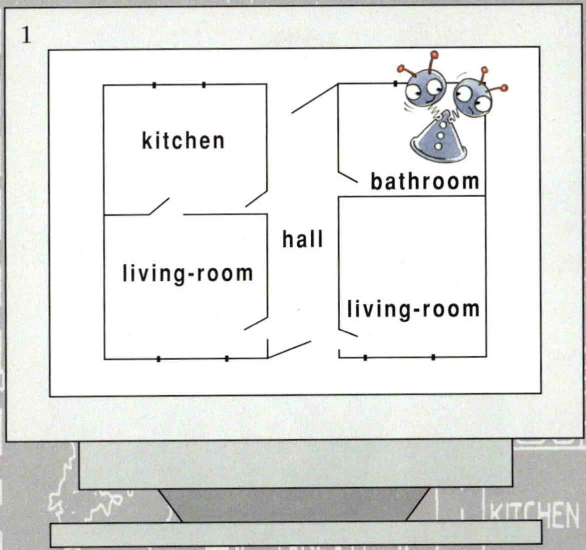

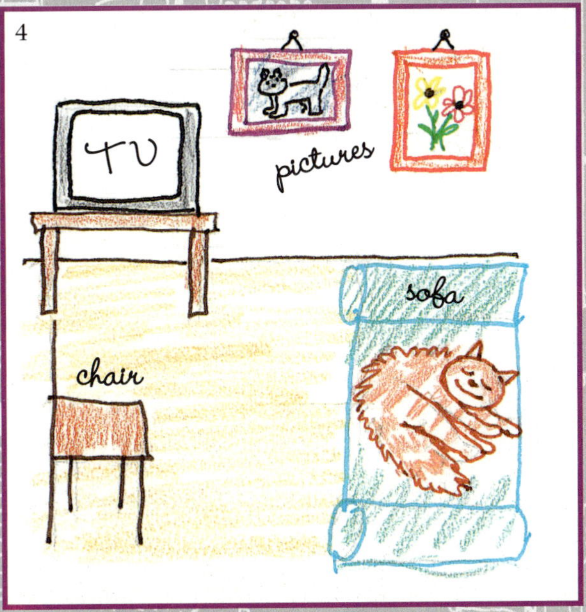

Match pictures 1, 2, 3 and 4 to the photos on page 40.

I think number 1 is the Scotts' house. C1B1 is in the bathroom.
I think number 2 is the ... house. I can see ... .

ACTIVITY for your scrapbook
Draw a room in your flat or house. Tell your partner what you've got in the room. → P 12

1

MRS BAKER	Nick! Debbie!
NICK	Yes, Mum?
MRS BAKER	It's late. Please help me.
NICK	OK, Mum.
MRS BAKER	Debbie! Your room isn't very tidy.
DEBBIE	Oh, Mum.

2

NICK	Debbie, come here and help me.
DEBBIE	But my film ... it's really good.
NICK	No, it isn't. It's boring. Come and help me, please. Let's tidy up ... and clean the bathroom.
DEBBIE	Oh go away, Nick!
MRS BAKER	Debbie! Go upstairs and help Nick. Now!

ACTIVITY

Listen to the rap on the cassette/CD and move to the music.

Raise your arms – and up and down.

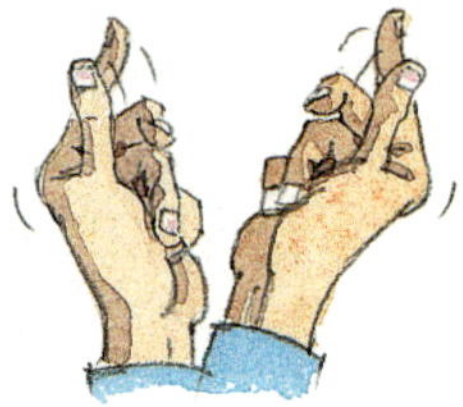
Snap your fingers.

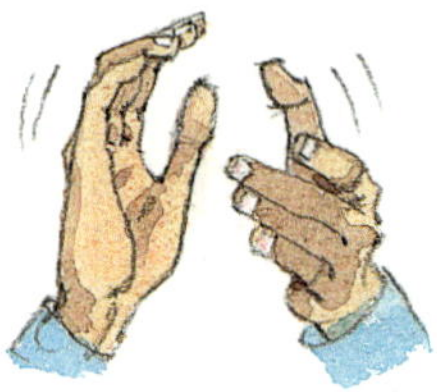
Clap your hands.

Close your eyes.

GAME Robot[1] Right, Robot Wrong

A Robot Right, put the pencil on the floor.

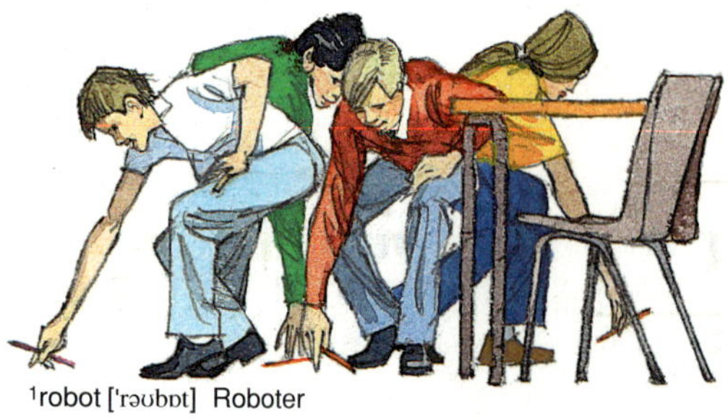

A Robot Wrong, sit down.

[1]robot ['rəʊbɒt] Roboter

→ S 3: 1, 2a (p. 132)
→ P 1

▶ 3

Oh, Lulu! Don't do that! You silly dog. Don't take my school bag. Put it on the floor! Come here. Now, please. And don't go into the living-room! You're dirty. And don't run upstairs. Downstairs, now! Go to your basket in the kitchen.

▶ **Looking at language**

Collect sentences from pages 42 and 43 like:

Please help me. ...
Don't do that! ...

→ S 3: 2b (p. 132)
→ P 2

▶▶▶ **NOW YOU**

Write a list of don'ts for your parents, your brother or sister, or your pet.

Don't come into my room.
Don't take my ...
Don't use my ...
Don't wear my ...
Don't draw ...
Don't open ...
...

▶ 4

Debbie and Nick are upstairs now. Nick is in the bathroom. But where's Debbie?

MR BAKER Debbie, Nick, come and help me in the kitchen.
DEBBIE Sorry Dad, we're cleaning the bathroom.
NICK Debbie! *I'm* cleaning the bathroom. *You're* reading a book.
DEBBIE Shhh ...
MR BAKER Oh! Debbie! Nick! They're here!

▶ 5

▶ 6

At the Snows' house Jenny and Sally are helping their mum, too. Sally is cleaning the bathroom. Jenny is tidying up her room. Mrs Snow is working in the kitchen. She's washing Sally's pullover.

▶ **Looking at language**

Find sentences in A4 and A6 like:

I'm cleaning the bathroom.

...

Sally ... the bathroom.

...

Jenny and Sally ... their mum, too.

▶▶▶ **NOW YOU**

Look at the verbs:

is listening to
is drawing
is cleaning
is helping
is going
is tidying up
is working
is reading
is playing

Close your eyes and imagine what your mother/father/brother/sister/pet is doing now.

Open your eyes and say what they're doing.

Tim: I think my mother is reading a book now.
Lea: I think my father is ...

→ S 3: 3a (p. 133)
→ P 3

▶ 7

It's six o'clock now. Jenny and Sally are packing for a weekend with their dad. Well, Sally is packing ...

MRS SNOW Jenny, Sally, where are you?

SALLY We're upstairs. I'm packing, but Jenny isn't packing. I think she's reading.

JENNY No, I'm not reading! I'm packing, too.

→ S 3: 3c (p. 133)
→ P 4

▶ 8

MARMALADE You aren't packing, Trundle!

TRUNDLE No, Marmalade, *I'm* not packing. Sally and Jenny are packing. I'm sitting here and writing a letter.

MARMALADE Boring! Bye bye!

→ S 3: 3b (p. 133)
→ P 5

9

MR SNOW	Hello, Wendy.
MRS SNOW	Hello, Ron.
MR SNOW	Where are the girls? Are they packing?
MRS SNOW	Yes, they are.
MR SNOW	Or are they playing?
MRS SNOW	No, they aren't, Ron. They're packing.

10

MR SNOW	Hi, Sal.
SALLY	Hi, Dad. Is Tracy waiting in the car?
MR SNOW	No, she isn't. She's at home. Where's your sister? Is she packing?
SALLY	No, she isn't.
MR SNOW	Is she reading?
SALLY	Yes, she is.
MR SNOW	Oh no.
SALLY	Jenny, Dad is waiting!

Looking at language

Collect present progressive questions and short answers:

Are they packing? – Yes, ...

...

What are you doing?

...

→ S 3: 3d (p. 134)
→ P 6, 10, 11

11

JENNY	Hi, Mum. We're here. How are you?
MRS SNOW	Fine.
JENNY	What are you doing?
MRS SNOW	I'm making dinner. What about you?
JENNY	I'm reading, Sally and Tracy are watching TV and Dad is washing the dishes.
MRS SNOW	Jenny, why aren't you helping your dad?
JENNY	Oh, he's fine. Mum, what's Trundle doing?
MRS SNOW	He's sleeping.
JENNY	And Marmalade? What's she doing?
MRS SNOW	She's sleeping, too. Listen, Jenny – the pets are fine and I'm fine, OK? Now go and help your dad ... and have a nice weekend. Bye now.
JENNY	Bye, Mum.

NOW YOU and a partner

Write a telephone dialogue. Use these or other words.

sit, run, watch TV, sleep, write, make tea, clean, listen to, play with

YOU	Hi, ... What are you doing?
YOUR PARTNER	I'm ... .
YOU	And what about your parents? What are they doing?
YOUR PARTNER	They're ... .
YOU	And what about your sister/brother? What's she/he ...?
YOUR PARTNER	She's/He's ... .
YOU	And what's your ... doing?
YOUR PARTNER	...

Now act the dialogue with your partner.

→ S 3: 3e (p. 134)
→ P 7, 8, 9, 13

1 ▶ Come here, please

Put in the right verb: come • listen to • look at • make • open • use • write

1 *Come* here, please.
2 … your name on the board, please.
3 … a blue biro, please.
4 … your books at page 44, please.
5 … the picture in your books, please.
6 … a poster for the classroom, please.
7 … your teacher, please.

2 ▶ Don't do that in the classroom!

Look at the pictures. Make sentences.

1 
write

2 
listen to

3 
read

4 
speak

5 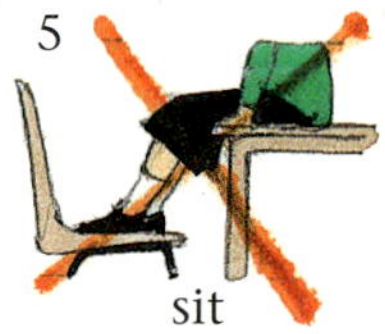
sit

1 *Don't write* in your books. 2 … your walkman. 3 … comics.
4 … German. 5 … on the desk.

3 ▶ Jenny is drawing a tortoise

Say what the people are doing. Use: clean • draw • listen to • play • tidy up • work

1 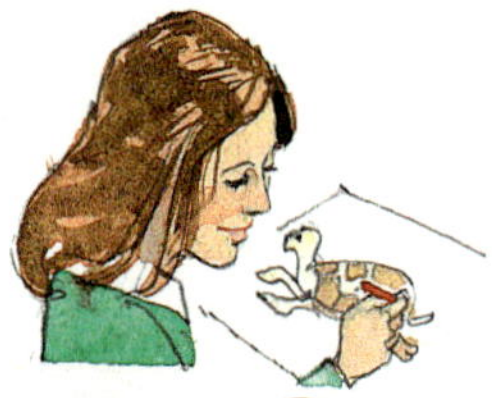

2 

3 

4 

5 

6 

1 Jenny *is drawing* a tortoise.
2 Debbie and Nick are … the living-room.
3 Sanjay … a CD.
4 Ben and his grandma … a computer game.
5 Sally and her mum … in the garden.
6 Trundle … his cage.

4 ▶ That isn't right!

Find and correct the mistakes.

1 
Nick is helping his mother.

2 
Mrs Baker is cleaning the floor.

3 
Lulu is playing with a hamster.

4 
Mr and Mrs Baker are reading comics.

1 Nick *isn't helping* his mother. *He's helping* his father.
2 Mrs Baker … the floor. … a window.
3 Lulu … a hamster. … a cat.
4 Mr and Mrs Baker … comics. … books.

5 ▶ Sorry, Mum

Make sentences.
Mind the spelling!

1 Sorry, Mum. *I'm making* tea.
2 Sorry. We're … stickers.
3 …

◆◆ 6 ▶ Spot the difference

a *Work with a partner. Partner A: look at picture A. Partner B: look at picture B. Write down what the people in your pictures are doing.*

b *Ask questions and find out the differences.*

A Is Lulu playing with a pullover in your picture?
B Yes, she is.
Is Mrs Baker opening the door in your picture?
A No, … . She's … .
Are Debbie and Jenny …?
B …

❖ 7 ▶ What am I doing?

Mime an activity in front of your form: 'What am I doing? Guess!'

A What am I doing?
B Are you …?
A Yes, I am./No, I'm not.

8 ▶ Sorry?

What are your friends saying? Ask questions with who/what/where.

1 FRIEND ★ is going downstairs.
YOU Sorry? *Who* is going downstairs?
2 FRIEND I'm going to the ★ now.
YOU Sorry? … are you going?
3 FRIEND ★ is going there with me.
YOU Sorry? … is going there with you?
4 FRIEND I'm wearing my ★.
YOU Sorry? … are you wearing?
5 FRIEND I'm reading a great ★.
YOU Sorry? …?
6 FRIEND My sister is playing in the ★.
YOU Sorry? …?

9 ▶ At the Step in India restaurant

Look at the picture. What are the people doing?

1 What's Mr Gregg doing? – He's *reading* a book.
2 What … Sita …? – She … the kitchen.
3 … Mrs Gupta …? – She … to the kitchen.
4 … Sanjay …? – He … Miss Hunt.
5 … the boy and girl …? – They … a picture.
6 … Mr Gupta …? – He … the floor.

10 LISTENING Who's who?

1 *Copy the card on a piece of paper.*
2 *Listen to the questions and fill in the boxes – write short answers, not sentences.*
3 *Collect the cards and give them out to your form.*
4 *Now – who's who?*

11 SOUNDS

a *Listen to the cassette/CD and say the words.*

[æ] black, happy, married, rabbit
[e] dead, friend, letter, spell
[ə] problem, German, mother, together
[eɪ] cage, great, name, today

b *Put the words in the right group.*

about • again • brother • game
hamster • help • husband
Indian • make • pack • page
pencil • school bag • take • wait

[æ]	[e]	[ə]	[eɪ]
hamster	again	about	game
…	…	…	…

WORD WATCH

12 ▶ Trundle's dream house

a *Complete the text about Trundle's dream house.*

Trundle's dream house has got four rooms, a hall and a garage. The garage is green. The hall is …
The living-room is over the bedroom.
The kitchen is under the …

b *Draw your dream house. (You can draw it in your scrapbook.) Colour the rooms. Now write about it.*

13 ▶ Word link

Match the verbs to the nouns.

bathroom • board • box • cage
car • cassettes • CDs • cupboard
door • floor • garage • radio
room • teacher • window

clean	open	listen to
the bathroom	the box	cassettes
the board	…	…
…		

The tree house

It's Saturday at the Bakers' house. Mr and Mrs Baker, Aunt Helen and Uncle Paul are sitting in the living-room. They're talking and talking. It's very boring. So Debbie and Nick and their cousins Hannah and Zack are in the garden.

DEBBIE Nick, have you got the rope? OK, pull!
HANNAH Let's pull together, Nick.
NICK Thanks, Hannah. Up, up … and here it is. Now, let's put your piece of wood there.
HANNAH OK.
NICK Debbie, one more piece of wood, please, for the floor.
ZACK Here, Debbie.
DEBBIE Thank you, Zack. Nick, the rope!
NICK Here.

Now the children are making the walls and the roof.

HANNAH Here, Nick?
NICK No, don't put the piece of wood there, Hannah. That's the door.
HANNAH Here?
NICK No, not there, that's the window. Yes, there. That's right.

It's five o'clock now.

NICK OK, Debbie, come up.
DEBBIE Great!
ZACK What about me, Debbie?
DEBBIE No, Zack, you're too small.
ZACK No, I'm not. Oh please, Debbie.
DEBBIE Oh, OK. But be careful!

Now the four children are in the tree house. Debbie and Nick are at the window – they're playing.

NICK Wheeee … we're flying.
ZACK No, we aren't, Nick.
DEBBIE Yes, we are, Zack. Look, there are the old city walls …
NICK … and there's the river …
DEBBIE … and the cathedral. Careful! We're very near the roof!
NICK And there's the river again. Wheee …

ZACK Hannah, Hannah, we *are* flying now. The tree house is moving!
HANNAH Don't be silly, Zack.
DEBBIE Oh no! Zack is right. The tree house *is* flying … down!

The tree house isn't a tree house now. It isn't in the tree, and it isn't a house. It's just old wood again.

WORKING WITH THE TEXT

Read the sentences. Then write them in the right order.

- Debbie, Nick and their cousins are making a tree house in the garden.
- They're playing a game: the tree house is flying.
- The tree house isn't a tree house now.
- Mr and Mrs Baker, Aunt Helen and Uncle Paul are talking in the living-room.
- The children are in the tree house.
- The tree house is moving down.

3

TOPIC 3 The time and date

1 ● What time is it?

a

It's eight **o'clock**.

It's **quarter past** eight.

It's **half past** eight.

It's **quarter to** nine.

It's **five past** eight.

It's **ten past** eight.

It's **twenty-five to** nine.

It's … .

Read out the times.
4.00, 3.15, 6.30, 2.45, 1.30, 10.00, 11.00, 8.15, 12.15, 7.30
6.20, 3.50, 11.25, 4.35, 7.10, 11.55, 1.10, 2.25, 12.05, 8.55, 9.20

b

It's eight o'clock.

It's eight o two.

It's eight thirty.

It's … .

Read out the times.
10.22, 11.49, 12.30, 9.50, 4.44, 2.17, 6.06, 1.35, 8.51, 9.03,
7.45, 1.29, 3.12, 12.04, 8.30

◆◆ 2 ● When's …?

Work with a partner.

YOU Let's watch 'Highlander'.
YOUR PARTNER OK. When is it?
YOU It's at 4.25.

TV Times

3.50 to 5.30 Kids' TV:
3.50 Cartoon
4.00 Budgie the little helicopter
4.25 Highlander
4.55 The pet show
5.30 Home and away
6.00 The computer show

3 ● A calendar

9th April *Say* the ninth of April

1998 *Say* nineteen ninety-eight
2020 *Say* two thousand and twenty

on 31st October, 2020
Say on the thirty-first of October, two thousand and twenty

What's the date?

1st	**first**	**12th**	**twelfth**
2nd	**second**	13th	thirteenth
3rd	**third**	14th	fourteenth
4th	**fourth**	…	
5th	**fifth**	**20th**	**twentieth**
6th	sixth	21st	twenty-first
7th	seventh	22nd	twenty-second
8th	**eighth**	23rd	twenty-third
9th	**ninth**	…	
10th	tenth	30th	thirtieth
11th	eleventh	31st	thirty-first

▶▶▶ **NOW YOU** and a partner
Look at the calendar and ask questions.

What day is 1st May, 2020?
– It's a … .
What's the date today/tomorrow/next Monday/…?
– It's 4th May, 1999/… .
When's your birthday?
– It's on 1st April/…

4 ● Secret agent's[1] calendar

	1	2	3	4	5	6
A	1	2	3	4	5	6
B	7	8	9	10	11	12
C	13	14	15	16	17	18
D	19	20	21	22	23	24
E	25	26	27	28	29	30
F	31	-st	-nd	-rd	-th	Jan
G	Feb	Mar	Apr	May	Jun	Jul
H	Aug	Sep	Oct	Nov	Dec	quarter
I	half	to	past	o'clock	o	morning
J	afternoon	evening	night	in the	on	at

Secret message[2] for Agent XYZ:
Come J6 A2 I5 A4 J4 J1 J5 D5 F4 G3.

– Agent ABC

Can you read the secret message?

▶▶▶ **NOW YOU** and a partner
Write a message for your partner.

[1] secret agent [ˌsiːkrət_ˈeɪdʒənt] *Geheimagent/in*
[2] secret message [ˌsiːkrət ˈmesɪdʒ] *geheime Nachricht*

UNIT 4 Happy birthday!

March

M	T	W	T	F	S	S
–	1	2	3	4	5	6
7	8	9	10	11	12	13
14	15	16	17	18	19	20
21	22	23	24	25	26	27
28	29	30	31			

It's 5th March. Debbie and Nick are dreaming about their birthday. It's next Saturday.

Debbie is dreaming about ...

My dream birthday

Nick is dreaming about ...

▶▶▶ NOW YOU

And what's your dream birthday?

Write a list – for your scrapbook.

ACTIVITY

Make a birthday calendar for your form. Add the names and birthdays of your favourite film/sports/pop stars.

Happy birthday!

January
3rd Julia
18th Kevin Costner
27th Markus

▶ 1

NICK Mum, next Saturday is our birthday.
MRS BAKER Yes, Nick.
DEBBIE Can we have a birthday party?
MRS BAKER Yes, of course you can.
NICK Ugh! Not a birthday party, Debbie. Mum, can we go to a film? They've got 'Rambo 15' at the Odeon.
MRS BAKER No, you can't. You can't go to 'Rambo 15' – it isn't for children.
NICK Oh Mum!
MR BAKER I've got an idea! Debbie can have a party for her friends. And Nick can have a video.
MRS BAKER A party for Debbie and a film for Nick …
NICK Great, Dad!

▶ **Looking at language**
Collect sentences with *can/can't*:

Debbie can have a party for her friends. …
Can we have a birthday party?
– Yes, of course … .
…

▶ 2

DEBBIE Let's make invitation cards, Nick.
NICK Oh Debbie, must we really make invitation cards?
DEBBIE Yes, we must.
NICK We can tell our friends about the party …
DEBBIE No. Invitation cards are nice.

▶ 3

Now Nick and Debbie are making the invitation cards for next Saturday.

DEBBIE Can you draw a birthday cake with twelve candles on it, Nick?
NICK Yes, of course I can! Can you?
DEBBIE No, I can't. Here, you can draw the pictures on the cards.
NICK And what can *you* do?
DEBBIE I can write the time and date on the cards.

▶▶▶ NOW YOU

◆◆ **a** *Ask your partner. Make notes.*

Can you … ? – Yes, I can./No, I can't.

draw

make tea

play football

ride a bike

write

sing

b *Make a window and fill it in.*

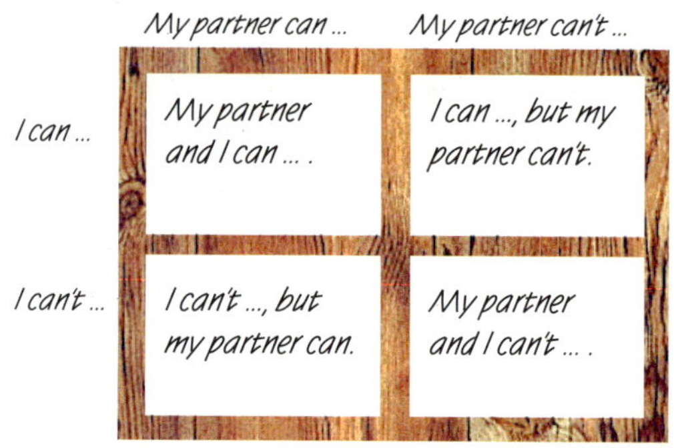

c *Now tell your form.*

→ S 4: 1 (p. 134/135)
→ P 1, 2, 3

▶ 4

Jenny, Sita and Ben are looking for birthday presents for Debbie and Nick. Ben has got lots of ideas, but …

BEN A box of chocolates?
JENNY Boring.
BEN A biro?
SITA Boring.
BEN A watch?
JENNY Watches are expensive.
SITA Look, what a nice scarf.
JENNY But scarves are expensive, too. Look.
SITA What about the calendar? That's cheap.
JENNY Yes, it's cheap, but calendars are very …
SITA … very …
BEN … boring!

Boxes

Lots of boxes in classes
and classes in boxes.
Lots of boxes and scarves
and scarves in boxes.
And lots of boxes in boxes in boxes.

▶▶▶ NOW YOU and your partner

It's your friend's birthday next week.
What's a good present?
Write a dialogue like this and act it.

YOU It's …'s birthday next week. Let's look for a present.
YOUR PARTNER What about …?
YOU Yes, that's nice.
YOUR PARTNER OK. That's our present.

→ S 4: 2a (p. 136)
→ P 4

▶ 5

The children are still looking for a present for Debbie and Nick.

BEN What about a mouse? Or two mice – one for Debbie and one for Nick?
JENNY Don't be silly, Ben. They've got a dog.
SITA What are Nick's hobbies, Ben?
BEN His hobby is football, but he has got a football.
JENNY Thank you, Ben!
BEN Hey, I've got an idea. Let's make a video.
SITA A video?
JENNY But we haven't got a camcorder.
BEN You haven't, but I have. Let's go.

→ P 11, 15

▶ 6

Jenny, Sita and Ben are making the video for Debbie and Nick's birthday. Sita and Jenny are the stars. Ben is the director.

'Sita, stand in front of the man with the dog.'

'No, don't stand there, go back and sit under the tree.'

'No, sit on the bench.'

'Jenny, sit next to the woman with the book.'

'No, sit between the bench and the tree.'

'No, stand behind the tree.'

▶ 7

Now Sita is the director: 'Ben, stand next to the men with the football. Oh, no, don't stand there, stand next to the women on the bench. And now – back ... back ... back ...'
Oh no! Ben is in the bin!

▶▶▶ **NOW YOU** and two partners

Imagine you've got a camcorder. Make a video. One of you is the director, two are the stars.

Stand on the chair, Pia.
Uwe, sit under the desk.
...

stand
sit

in
on
under
next to
behind
in front of
between

→ S 4: 2b (p. 136)
→ P 5, 12, 16

* In the sentence 'I is the 9th letter in the alphabet.'

▶ 8

MARMALADE Jenny is a film star now.
TRUNDLE Oh, really?
MARMALADE Yes, she's in Ben's video.
TRUNDLE But she can't act.
MARMALADE No, but she can sing.
TRUNDLE I can sing, too. And I can dance.
MARMALADE Well, I can climb.
TRUNDLE Aren't we clever, Marmalade?
MARMALADE Yes, we are. Let's make a video, too.

▶ 9

TRUNDLE Look at me, Marmalade. I'm dancing.
MARMALADE Very good, Trundle.
TRUNDLE Be careful with the camcorder, Marmalade.
MARMALADE Yes, Trundle. Now dance!
TRUNDLE OK. – Look, there are Jenny and Sita. Can you see them?
MARMALADE Hey, Jenny, look at us. We're making a video, too.
TRUNDLE She can't hear you.
MARMALADE But I can hear her.
TRUNDLE She's listening to Ben.
MARMALADE Why is she listening to him?
TRUNDLE Because he's the director, Marmalade.

RAP

→ S 4: 3 (p. 136)
→ P 6, 7, 8, 17

▶ **10**

It's 4 o'clock on 12th March. Mr and Mrs Baker are in the kitchen. Nick and Debbie are in the living-room. Nick is putting his film in the video recorder. There are lots of sandwiches on the table. And there's a birthday cake. There are candles on the cake. Debbie is counting them.

▶ **11**

DEBBIE Nick, there aren't twelve candles on the cake. There are only eleven! Look.

NICK You're right, Debbie. Mum, is there one more candle in the kitchen?

MRS BAKER Yes, there is.

NICK And Mum, is there lots of cola?

MRS BAKER No, there isn't! There's orange juice. – Oh, there are people at the door. Your friends are here.

→ P 9, 10

SONG Happy birthday — Music by M J Hill

▶ **12**

The kids are in the living-room. They're watching Sita, Jenny and Ben's video. There are lots of nice pictures of Chester, but the really great part is 'Ben in the bin'. All the kids are laughing – well, not *all* the kids.

→ P 13, 14, 18

1 ▶ The birthday party

Complete Debbie and Nick's questions and their mum and dad's answers. Match them.

1 Mum, *can* you make hamburgers and chips for our birthday?
2 … I watch 'Rambo 15' at the party?
3 … our friends come at 4 o'clock?
4 Dad, … you sing for our friends?
5 … we play football at the party?
6 … Sita's brother come to the party?
7 … Jenny's sister come, too?

a Yes, they … . That's a good time.
b No, I *can't*! But I can make a nice cake.
c Yes, I … . 'Happy birthday' or 'Tea for two'?
d Yes, she … .
e Yes, of course he … .
f No, you … . Football isn't a party game.
g No, you … . That isn't a film for children.

2 ▶ Can Trundle fly?

Make questions with can *and give short answers.*

draw • fly • play football
read • ride bikes • sing

Can Trundle *fly?*
– No, he can't.

… Sanjay … ?
– Yes, … .

3 ▶ Sorry, I can't

a *What are the answers? Use* can't *and* must.

1 NICK Sorry, I *can't*. I *must tidy up* my room.
2 DEBBIE Sorry, I … . I … invitation cards.
3 SANJAY Sorry, … . I … in the restaurant.
4 JENNY … . … dinner.
5 C1B1 …

b *Say why they can't ride their bikes with Ben.*

1 Nick *can't ride* his bike with Ben. He *must tidy up* his room.
2 Debbie … her bike with Ben. She …
…

4 SOUNDS The plural

Listen to the plural forms on the cassette/CD and put the words in the right group.

[-s]	[-z]	[-ɪz]
baskets bikes ...	bookshelves ...	cages ...

baskets • bikes • bookshelves • cages
cakes • cards • cats • desks
families • hobbies • houses
invitations • pages • pieces • rabbits
scarves • tortoises • watches

5 GAME What can you see?

a *Look at the picture for two minutes. Then close your book and make a list: what's in the picture?*

My list: boxes, books, ...

b *Swap lists with your partner. Now make a list together. Who are the champions?*

6 ▶ Can you help me?

Complete the sentences with me *or* us.

1 **BEN** I've got a new game. Can you play with ..., Grandma?
2 **DEBBIE** It's our birthday next week. Can you make a cake for ..., Mum?
3 **SITA** I've got a problem with my homework. Can you help ..., Sanjay?
4 **TRUNDLE** Marmalade and I are dancing. Can you see ..., Jenny?
5 **ZACK** I can't sleep, Dad. Can you sing a song with ...?
6 **MRS SNOW** Jenny, Sally, where are you? Can't you hear ...?

7 ▶ Don't ask me – ask them

Look at the picture. Then complete the sentences with him, her *or* them.

1 Mum is in the living-room. Ask … .
2 Aunt Helen is in her room. Ask … .
3 Hannah and Zack are in the garden. Ask … .
4 Uncle Paul is in the living-room. …
5 Jenny and Sally are at home. …
6 Sita and Sanjay are at home. …

8 ▶ I can't see them!

Complete the sentences with him, her, it *or* them.

1 Where's Nick? I can't see *him*.
2 Where's Debbie? I can't see … .
3 Where are Mum and Dad? I can't see … .
4 Where's my ruler? I can't see … .
5 Where are the children? …
6 Where are my pens? …
7 Where are Sita and Sanjay? …
8 Where's your brother? …
9 Where are the twins? …
10 Where are your books? …

9 GAME What's your word?

Write a word on a piece of paper.
Now draw lines for the letters on a second piece of paper.
Can your partner guess the letters?

T _ _ *T* _ _ _ _

Is there an 'A' in your word?
– No, there isn't.
Is there a 'T' in your word?
– Yes. There are two 'Ts'.
Is your word 'tortoise'?
– Yes, it is. Very good!

◆◆ 10 ▶ Spot the difference

Work with a partner. Partner A: look at picture A. Partner B: look at picture B. Say what you see. Use there's *and* there are. *Find out the differences.*

picture B

picture A

A There's a red cake in my picture.
B There's a green cake in my picture. There's a candle on the cake.
A There are …

WORD WATCH

11 ▶ Odd word out!

1 cake, juice, chips, hamburger
2 nice, good, boring, great
3 mice, tortoises, dogs, pets
4 kitchen, garden, bathroom, living-room
5 friend, brother, sister, cousin
6 July, Monday, November, March

12 ▶ The fourth word

1 football – play bike – ?	5 Wednesday – day February – ?
2 I – me she – ?	6 clean – dirty expensive – ?
3 child – children woman – ?	7 boxes – box scarves – ?
4 over – under in front of – ?	8 watch – TV listen to – ?

13 ▶ Word link

Read pages 54–57 again. Find all the two-word combinations with birthday.

happy birthday ... birthday birthday ...
birthday *cake* birthday ... birthday ... birthday ...

14 LISTENING The day of the mice

a *Oh no! The cat is away and there are 20 mice in the kitchen. In this picture, you can see only ten. Find them and say where they are:*

There's a mouse on the chair.
There are two mice ...

b *Now make a copy of the kitchen picture. Listen to the text and draw in the other mice. Here's how you can draw a mouse:* 

c *Now you can say where all twenty mice are.*

15 ▶ Have you got a cat?

❖ **a** *Copy the questionnaire into your exercise book. What pets have boys and girls in your form got? Ask five classmates.*

	cat	dog	hamster	rabbit	budgie	...
Jasmin	✓	✗	✗	✗	✓	?
Thomas	✗	✓	2	✗	✗	?
Moritz	?	?	?	?	?	?
Nora	?	?	?	?	?	?
...	?	?	?	?	?	?

b *Write five sentences like:*
Jasmin has got a cat and a budgie.
Thomas has got a dog and two hamsters.

◆◆ 16 ▶ What are they doing?

Work with a partner.
PARTNER A *Ask questions (= red).*
PARTNER B *Answer the questions (= green).*
A Is Ben making a video?
B No, he isn't. He's washing a pullover.

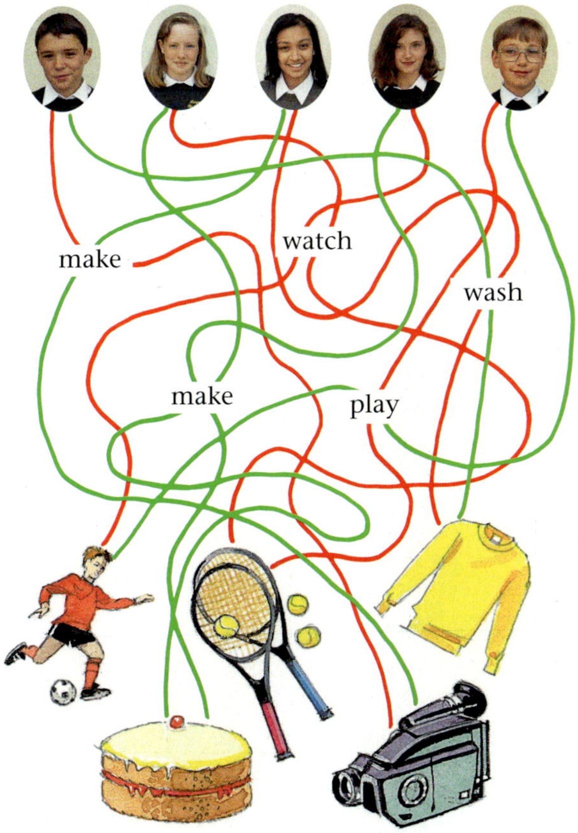

17 ▶ Who is he?

a *Complete the text with* he's *or* his.

Who is the boy?
... in my form. ... eleven. ... OK, but he hasn't got a lot of friends. ... mum is German, but ... dad is British. ... British, too.
... grandma has got a room in their house. ... sister is in America.
He isn't from Chester. ... from Ashton. Who is he?
Jenny Snow

b *Now you. Write a text about a boy in your form. But don't use his name. Your classmates must guess who he is. (You can put your text in your scrapbook.)*

18 ▶ Where are they?

Fill in there, their *or* they're.

Marmalade and Trundle:

M Where are Jenny and Sally? Are they in *their* rooms?
T No, they aren't ... . out.
M Are Jenny, Sita and Ben still looking for a present for ... friends?
T No, ... making a video. ... using Ben's camcorder. He's ... director.
M Are they making the video at Ben's house in Ashton?
T No, they aren't making it ... . making it in Chester.

Mr and Mrs Baker:

MRS B Where are Nick and Debbie?
MR B ... waiting for ... friends in the living-room.
MRS B Can I help? Where are the sandwiches and the cake?
MR B ... on the table in the living-room. The orange juice is ... . And ... are chocolates in the cupboard. Can you put them on the table?
MRS B OK. Ah, listen. I think ... friends are here. Yes, ... at the door.

Twelve little cakes

Mrs Snow is in the kitchen. She's making little cakes. And here are Jenny and Sally.

JENNY Hi, Mum. We're home.
SALLY Hi, Mum.
MRS SNOW Hello, girls. – Sally, put it down!
SALLY Oh, Mum. Can't I eat one cake now?
MRS SNOW No, you can't. The cakes aren't for you.
JENNY & SALLY What?!
MRS SNOW They're for Mrs Crick. It's her birthday today.
SALLY Mrs Crick? But she's a witch.
MRS SNOW Don't say that! Mrs Crick is very nice.

MRS SNOW I must go now. Take the cakes and go to Mrs Crick, please.
JENNY & SALLY Yes, Mum ...

Jenny and Sally are alone now – with the cakes.

JENNY Mrs Crick is very lucky.
SALLY Yes, she is. Twelve cakes for her! – Hey, let's eat one.
JENNY We can't do that. They aren't for us.
SALLY Don't be silly, Jenny. Mrs Crick can't eat twelve cakes.
JENNY Well ... OK.

JENNY Now there are eleven cakes. We can't give her *eleven*.
SALLY You're right. Let's eat one more.

Now there are ten cakes. And there are people at the door.

NICK Hi, Jenny. Hi, Sally.
DEBBIE Oh – cakes!
JENNY Yes, but they aren't for us. They're for Mrs Crick. It's her birthday.
BEN Ten cakes for …
SALLY … the witch!
JENNY Sally!
SALLY Oh, Mum can't hear us …

And then …

The next day, Mrs Snow is at the supermarket. Mrs Crick is there, too.

MRS CRICK Oh, Mrs Snow. Thank you for the little cake. You and your girls are very nice.
MRS SNOW Yes, … thank you. And happy birthday again, Mrs Crick.

WORKING WITH THE TEXT

1 ▶ Mrs Snow is making cakes

Match the two parts and make sentences.

1 Mrs Snow is making	are at the supermarket.
2 Today is	little cakes in the kitchen.
3 Jenny and Sally think Mrs Crick	have only got one cake.
4 At Mrs Crick's house the girls	are in trouble.
5 The next day, Mrs Snow and Mrs Crick	Mrs Crick's birthday.
6 Jenny and Sally	is a witch.

2 ▶ The other cakes

Write the missing dialogue between lines 10 and 11 on page 67. You can start like this:

JENNY Hi, Sita. Hi, Sanjay.
SANJAY Hi, Jenny. Hi, Sally. Oh – cakes!
SALLY … cakes – Mrs Crick / …
SITA … five cakes …
…

TOPIC 4 Money, money, money

1 ● Pounds and pence

British money	
	You say
1p	one p [piː]
45p	forty-five p
£1	one pound/a pound
£1.25	one (pound) twenty-five
£2	two pounds
£5.80	five (pounds) eighty

German money	
	You say
€ 0.50	fifty cents
€ 1.00	one euro/a euro
€ 1.25	one (euro) twenty-five
€ 2.00	two euros
€ 3.40	three (euros) forty

Say £89.30 27p £10 10p £1.50 13p
£3.65 £88.88 2p £11.25 99p

Say € 1.35 € 0.83 € 26.80
€ 4.98 € 0.49 € 2.50

2 ● How much is it?

The red felt-tip is sixty-five p.
The yellow pencil-case is … .

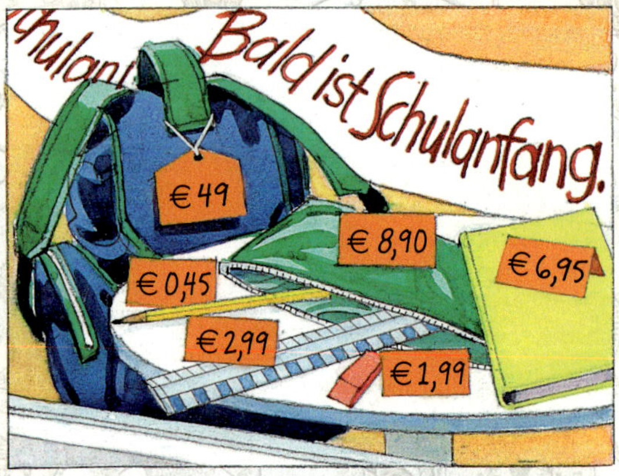

The yellow pencil is forty-five cents.
The blue ruler is … .

3 ● How much are the presents?

a You're in England. You're looking for presents for your family and friends in Germany. But you've only got £15. What can you buy?
Make a list and read it to a partner.

b *Ask your teacher for the exchange rate. How much are the things in the picture in euros?*

4 ● May I help you?

ASSISTANT	Good morning. May I help you?
CUSTOMER 1	No, thank you. I'm just looking.
ASSISTANT	Good afternoon. May I help you?
CUSTOMER 2	Yes, please. I'm looking for a present for my mother.
ASSISTANT	What about a picture? Here's a nice picture of Chester.
CUSTOMER 2	Very nice. How much is it?
ASSISTANT	Three pounds fifty.

►►► **NOW YOU** and a partner

A Good … . May I help you?
B Yes … . I'm … ./ No … . I'm … .
A What about …? Here's …
B … . How …?
A …

SONG Money, money

Money makes the world go around,[1]
the world go around, the world go around.
Money makes the world go around,
it makes the world go round.
A mark, a yen, a buck[2] or a pound,
a buck or a pound, a buck or a pound
is all that[3] makes the world go around.
That clinking, clanking sound[4]
can make the world go round.
Money, money, money, money, money,
money …

[1] Money makes the world go around [wɜːld] *Geld bewegt die Welt* [2] buck *(slang)* [bʌk] *Dollar*
[3] all that *alles, was* [4] that clinking, clanking sound ['klɪŋkɪŋ], ['klæŋkɪŋ] *das klirrende, klappernde Geräusch*

5 UNIT 5 Kingsway High School

The Kingsway High School uniform is green and black (or grey). All pupils must wear it.

Match the texts to the photos.

a In the picture pupils are eating in the school canteen in the lunch break.
b There are lessons in the morning and in the afternoon.
c The pupils are at Assembly. Assembly is at 10.50 every day.
d Here's the Kingsway drama group. Kingsway has got lots of groups and clubs.
e In the picture Year 7 girls are playing hockey. There are lots of other sports at Kingsway: football, volleyball and basketball.

These sentences can help you:

- Text ... goes with picture ... .
- Picture ... and text ... go together.

1

2

4

3

5

PROJECT for the unit

Work in groups of four. In the next weeks, collect information about your school:
- *number of girls, boys, teachers, forms*
- *school clubs and other groups*
- *lessons*

Take photos or draw pictures of:
- *your classroom*
- *other rooms*
- *your form*
- *your teachers*

Make a poster about your school with the pictures and information.

▶ 1
Jenny, Ben, Sita, Nick and Debbie go to Kingsway High School. Here are four pages from the Kingsway brochure.

KINGSWAY HIGH SCHOOL

WELCOME

▶ 2
Welcome to Kingsway High School. There are 640 pupils and 44 teachers at Kingsway. In the brochure there is a lot of information about our school.

THE SCHOOL DAY

▶ 3
School is every day from Monday to Friday. We start lessons at 8.45 and we finish at 3.30. There are three lessons in the morning and two in the afternoon. Morning break is at 11.05.

Lunch break is from 12.20 to 1.30. Pupils can buy lunch in the school canteen or bring sandwiches from home.

ACTIVITIES

▶ 4
After school, from 3.30 to 5.00, there are lots of clubs and activities. Pupils play badminton, tennis or do judo. Lots of pupils are in the computer club or the drama group. You can find the right club or group for you on the activities notice board!

▶▶▶ NOW YOU

We start lessons at … . We finish … .
There are … . Breaks are … . …

▶ 5

Here's a letter from Ben to his cousins in Berlin.

Timetable, Form 7CH

Monday

8.45–9.45	Geography
9.45–10.45	English
10.50–11.05	Assembly
11.05–11.20	Morning break
11.20–12.20	Music
12.20–1.30	Lunch break
1.30–2.30	Maths
2.30–3.30	Drama

5th May

Dear Katrin and Julia,

Thanks for your letter. I can try and answer your questions about my school.

I start school every morning at 8.45. On Mondays my first lesson is Geography. I like our teacher, Miss Hunt. Then I go to English, then we've got Assembly, then morning break. After the break I've got Music – not my favourite lesson! Lunch break is at 12.20. In the afternoon I've got Maths (super!) and Drama (OK).

I finish the day at 3.30. Well, not really – I do activities (computer club, football team) after school – and homework …

Is your school in Berlin very different? Can you tell me in your next letter?

Love,
Ben

▶▶▶ **NOW YOU**

Talk about your timetable for Monday. Use words from Ben's letter like:

My first lesson is …
Then I've got …

→ P 1, 18, 19

6 ▶ School activities

Sita plays chess, so she's in the chess club. The club meets in room 3 on Mondays after school.

Can you write or talk about Nick and Sally?

Nick collects stamps, so he's in the stamp club. The club (meet) in room 4 on … .

Sally (take) photos, so she's in the camera club. The club … .

→ S 5: 1a (p. 137)
→ P 2, 3, 4, 5, 6

▶ 7

Sita's brother Sanjay does judo. He's in the school team. Sita goes to all the matches. She watches her brother.

Debbie and Jenny are in the drama group.

Debbie acts, and Jenny sings and dances. Debbie can't dance – but she tries.

→ S 5: 1b (p. 138)
→ P 7, 8, 22, 23

▶ **Looking at language**

Collect the simple present forms from pages 72 and 73:

We start, …
Sita plays, …

▶ 8

MARMALADE They've got lots of activities at Kingsway! Have you got a hobby, Trundle?
TRUNDLE Yes, I have. I've got lots of hobbies. I like tennis and chess and books …
MARMALADE I don't like chess and I don't like books …
TRUNDLE And you don't like tennis, right?
MARMALADE Wrong! I love tennis.

→ P 9

▶ 9

Marmalade likes football, too. But Trundle hates it. Cats and tortoises are very different. Trundle likes books, but he doesn't like football. Marmalade likes tennis, but she doesn't like books. And she doesn't like music. Trundle loves music. Poor Marmalade!

▶▶▶ **NOW YOU** and a partner

Copy the chart and fill it in. Swap charts with your partner. Now tell your form about him/her:
Lisa likes English, but she doesn't like Geography. She …

	I like	*I don't like*
school lesson	?	?
activity	?	?
pop star	?	?
film star	?	?

→ S 5: 1c, d (p. 138)
→ P 10, 11, 12, 13, 16

10 ▶ Trundle's song

Words by B Derkow Disselbeck
Music by J Blombach

[1] (to) trundle along [ˌtrʌndəl‿əˈlɒŋ] *entlangzockeln* [2] as [æz] *während* [3] slow [sləʊ] *langsam* [4] sweet [swiːt] *süß, niedlich*

→ P 17

▶ 11

Ben's sister Susan is 18. She's an au pair with Brian and Carol Peterson in Shorewood, Wisconsin, in the USA. Here's a letter to her family in Ashton about her day.

25th May

Dear Mum, Dad and Ben,

I'm still very happy here in Shorewood. The Petersons are really nice, and I've got lots of friends.

How's my day? Well, I always get up at 6.30. Yes, that's right: I never get up before 7.30 at home – you know that!

I give the kids their breakfast and take Laurie and Linda to their schools and little Lenny to his kindergarten – in my car. That's right, I've got a car! The Petersons have got three, and I can use one of them.

School starts at 8.15 here, so I'm back at 8.30. Carol and Brian are at work then, and I clean the house and make lunch for little Lenny. He only goes to kindergarten in the mornings, so he's at home in the afternoons. I fetch him at 12 o'clock.

In the afternoons I play with Lenny. Then I usually fetch Linda from school at 3.30. Laurie – she's 16 – does lots of activities at school. So I often fetch her at 4.30 or 5. That's a problem. Brian and Carol are back at 6 and like a big dinner on the table. Of course I make dinner, too.

After dinner I sometimes help the girls with their homework. I always go to bed at 10 or 10.30.

Imagine you are Ben. Can you tell Grandma 10 things from Susan's letter?

▶▶▶ NOW YOU

a *Make five sentences about your day and tell your partner.*

I	always	get up at/before …
	usually	eat breakfast at …
	often	go to school at …
	sometimes	eat lunch at …
	never	eat dinner at …
		go to bed at/before …
		…

b *Write a letter about your day. Look at Susan's letter for ideas. Start like this:*

Dear …,
I usually get up at …
First I …

Finish your letter like this:
Yours,
…

→ S 5: 2 (p. 139)
→ P 14, 15, 20, 21, 24

1 ▶ Who am I?

a *Put the verbs in the sentences.*

finish • help • go (4x) • start • buy • play • do • eat

I go to school at 8.20. Lessons ... at 8.45. We ... to Assembly at 10.50. My friends and I ... games in the morning break. My friends ... lunch in the school canteen. But I ... sandwiches. Afternoon lessons ... at 3.30. After lessons I ... to clubs or I ... to our flat and ... my homework. Then my brother and I ... our parents in our restaurant.
Who am I?

b *Now write about your day. Then put your texts in a box. One pupil must take a text and read it to the group. Who is it?*

2 ▶ Supertrundle!

Fill in the right verbs: clean • fly • play • read • ride • take

1 On Mondays Trundle *takes* photos.

2 On Tuesdays he ... tennis.

3 On Wednesdays he ... the house.

4 On Thursdays he ... his plane[1].

5 On Fridays he ... lots of books.

6 On Saturdays he ... his bike.

[1] plane [pleɪn] *Flugzeug*

3 ▶ Mrs Scott comes from Germany

-s *or not?*

1 Mrs Scott (come) from Germany.
Mrs Scott comes from Germany.
2 Debbie and Jenny (like) drama.
Debby and Jenny like drama.
3 Mr and Mrs Scott (take) Ben to school.
4 Nick (collect) stamps. He (swap) them with pupils in the stamp club.
5 Sita and Sanjay (help) their parents.
6 Sita (play) chess in the chess club.
7 Debbie and Jenny (sing and act) in the drama club.
8 Ben (buy) lunch in the canteen.
9 The clubs (meet) after school.

4 ▶ Every weekend

Every weekend	Ben	help	her pupils' exercise books.
	Sita and Sanjay	plays	their rooms.
	Miss Hunt	cleans	his bike around Ashton.
	Debbie and Nick	reads	chess with her brother.
	Trundle	tidy up	their parents in the restaurant.
	Sita	rides	his cage.
	I	...	...

5 ▶ At Assembly

At Assembly, the teachers tell the pupils about their clubs. Put in the right form of the verbs.

Lots of pupils *take* photos. One girl in the camera club *takes* really good photos. A man here in Chester ... lots of them.

Mrs Cobb

buy • take (2x)

The chess club ... every Monday after school. We ... chess and ... videos of matches between the champions. We ... to matches at different schools, too.

Mrs Keller

go • meet • play • watch

The stamp club ... every Tuesday after school. We ... stamps and ... a lot about geography.

Mr Bond

learn • meet • swap

The drama group ... after school on Wednesdays.
The pupils ..., ... and ... . We ... videos of our plays, too.

Miss Hunt

act • dance • make
meet • sing

◆◆ 6 ▶ Ben buys lunch

a *Look at the chart. Then tell your partner about the people at Kingsway.*

A Ben buys lunch. What about Miss Hunt?
B She buys lunch, too. What about Debbie and Nick?
A ...

b *What about you? Tell your partner.*

Partner A

	Ben	Miss Hunt	Debbie and Nick	Sita and Sanjay
lunch	buys lunch	?	bring sandwiches	?
after lessons	plays football	?	go to clubs on Tuesdays and Wednesdays	?
after dinner	plays with his computer	?	watch TV	?

Partner B

	Ben	Miss Hunt	Debbie and Nick	Sita and Sanjay
lunch	?	buys lunch	?	bring sand-wiches
after lessons	?	meets with the drama group	?	go to clubs on Mondays and Fridays
after dinner	?	draws pictures	?	read or help their parents

7 SOUNDS The simple present, third person singular

Listen to the verb forms on the cassette/CD. What's the pronunciation of the ending? Put the verb form in the right group.

[-s]	[-z]	[-ɪz]
collects	…	…
…		

8 ▶ A week with Joe Bloggs

Say what Joe Bloggs does every week.

Monday	*play tennis*
Tuesday	*do judo*
Wednesday	*wash the dishes*
Thursday	*go to the supermarket*
Friday	*meet friends*
Saturday	*clean the flat*
Sunday	*sleep*

1 Every Monday he *plays* tennis.
2 Every Tuesday he … judo.
3 …

9 ▶ I collect stamps

NICK I *collect* stamps. I *don't collect* stickers.

DEBBIE & NICK We … uniforms to school. We … jeans.

SITA I … chess. I … card games.

BEN I … football. I … tennis.

JENNY & SALLY We … books. We … comics.

SITA & SANJAY We … to Kingsway High School. We … to Blacon High School.

10 ▶ What about …?

Make dialogues.

1 Ben likes computers. What about stamps?
– No, Ben *doesn't like* stamps.
2 Nick plays football. What about tennis?
– No, he … tennis.
3 Jenny reads books about pets. What about books about film stars?
– No, she … books about film stars.
4 Sita loves chess. What about football?
– No, … .
5 Debbie goes to the drama group. What about the judo club?
6 Lulu likes children. What about cats?
7 Marmalade climbs trees. What about walls?
8 Miss Hunt eats lunch at school. What about dinner?

◆◆ **11 ▶ My 'like/don't like' alphabet**

a *Copy the chart. Then write what you like and what you don't like. (You can put your chart in your scrapbook.)*

b *Now tell your partner:*
I like …, but I don't like … .

c *Swap charts with your partner. Now tell your form:*
My partner likes …, but he/she doesn't like … .

	I like	*I don't like*
A	*Asterix my aunt*	*afternoon lessons*
B	*my budgie*	*black*
C	*cakes*	–
D	*my dad*	*dogs*
E	*English*	–
F		

12 ▶ Trundle doesn't sleep in Jenny's room

Say what the Snows don't do. Use don't *or* doesn't.

1 **JENNY** My tortoise has got a cage in the garden. He *doesn't* sleep in my room.
2 **JENNY** Dad and Tracy *don't* like dogs.
3 **SALLY** Our cat is funny. She … eat mice.
4 **SALLY** My sister and I have got lots of CDs. We … listen to cassettes.
5 **JENNY** Sally and I listen to the radio before school. We … watch TV.
6 **MRS SNOW** Jenny tidies up the house for me, but she … clean the bathroom.
7 **JENNY** My room is very tidy, but Sally … make her bed before school.
8 **TRUNDLE** My cage is OK, but I … play there.

13 ▶ My friend Marmalade

Complete the sentences with the correct form of the verbs.

My friend Marmalade

I don't like (not like) cats, but Marmalade is different. She climbs (climb) trees, of course, but she (play) with me, too. Marmalade is lucky. She (not sleep) in the garden, she (sleep) in the Snows' house. Marmalade and I (do) lots of activities together. But not every day. My friend Millie the mouse (come) to my cage every Thursday afternoon. Marmalade (not come) then.
We've got a good friend, Lulu. She's Debbie and Nick's pet. Lulu (not come) to our house every day, but every second day. Then we (play) with her. Dogs (not like) cats, but – Marmalade is different!

14 ▶ They go to work at …

	always	usually	sometimes	never
Mr Waggly		7.30	7.45	before 7.20
Mrs Wiggly	8.00			
Mr & Mrs Woggly		8.25	8.20	after 8.30
Mr & Mrs Wuggly	7.30			

a *Make sentences about the people.*

1 Mr Waggly usually goes to work at 7.30. He … at 7.45. He never … .
2 Mrs Wiggly always … .
3 …

b *What about you and your family?*

15 ▶ Trundle often rides a bike

Write six sentences with always, never, often, sometimes *and* usually.
(Of course you can write silly sentences, too!) These words can help you:

eat • get up at • go to a • make • play • read
ride • sleep in a • watch • wear

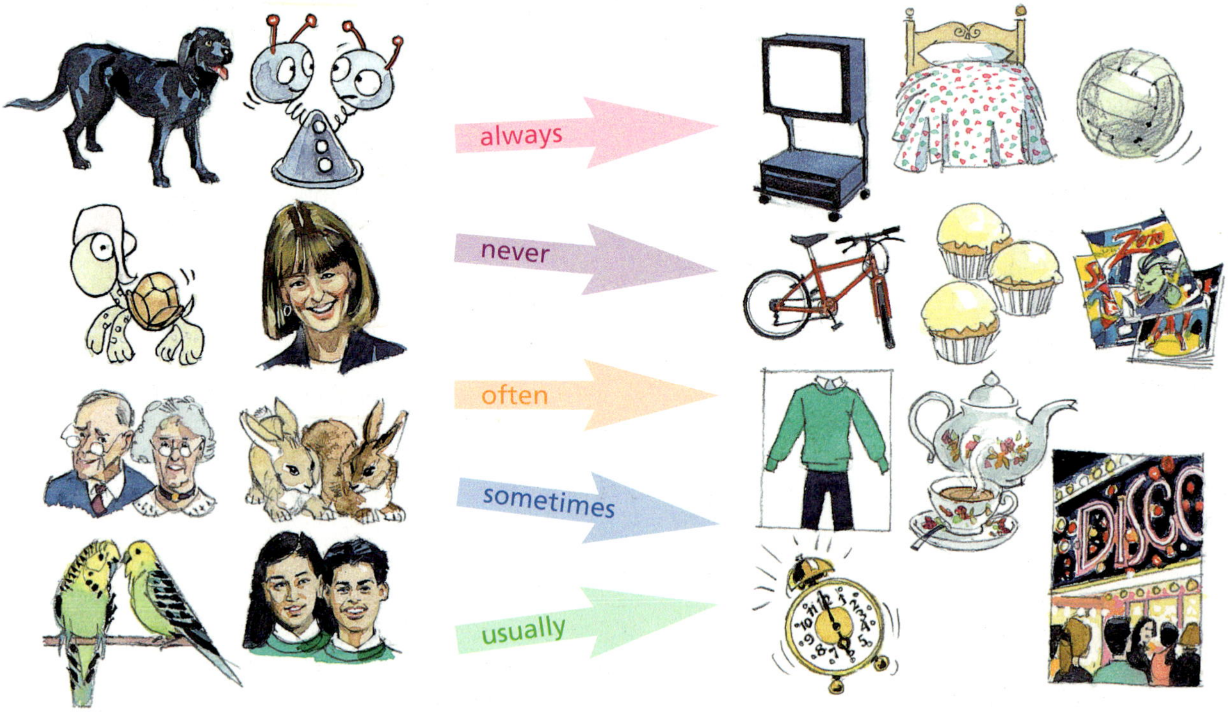

Trundle often rides a bike.
C1B1 always ...

16 ▶ An interview with Miss Hunt

a *Nick is doing an interview with Miss Hunt. You can see her answers on the card.*

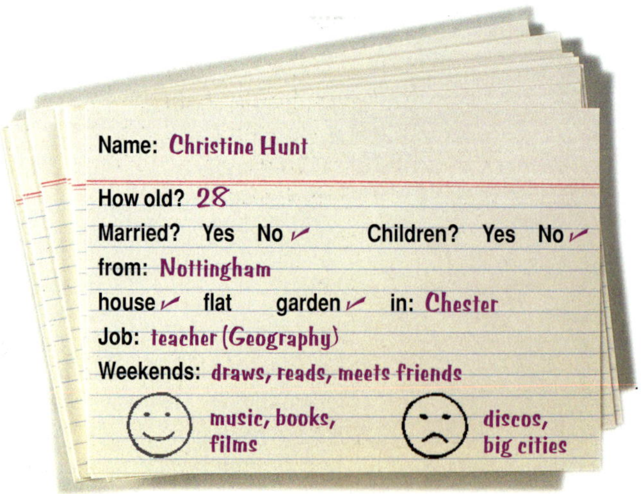
Name: Christine Hunt
How old? 28
Married? Yes No ✓ Children? Yes No ✓
from: Nottingham
house ✓ flat garden ✓ in: Chester
Job: teacher (Geography)
Weekends: draws, reads, meets friends
☺ music, books, films ☹ discos, big cities

Use the information and write a text about Miss Hunt. The following words can help you.

Christine Hunt is 28. She isn't ..., and she hasn't got ... . She's from ... .
She has got a house and ... in Chester now. She's a ... teacher.
At weekends she ... and ... .
She likes ..., but she ... discos or ... .

b *Bring a photo of a person from a magazine. Fill in a card like this for the person. Now write a text about him/her.*

17 LISTENING Drama group

a *The drama group is meeting. Look at the pictures before you listen. What's the group's new play about? Can you guess?*

b *Now look at the following faces. Who's who in the five scenes? Write* king, prince *or* dancing girl *for a), b) and c).*

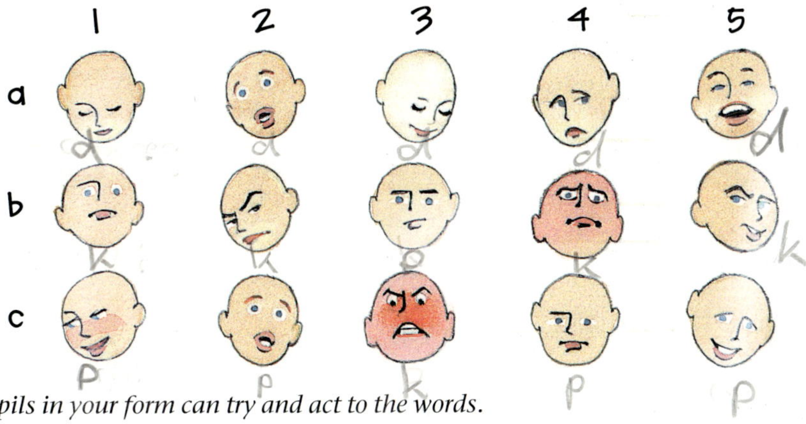

❖ **c** *Listen again. Three pupils in your form can try and act to the words.*

WORD WATCH

18 ▶ A letter from Katrin

a *Complete Katrin's letter to her cousin Ben. Use* about, after, at, before, for, from, in, of *and* to.

16th May

Dear Ben,

Thanks <u>for</u> your letter. Of course I can tell you ... my school.
... our school we start lessons ... 8 o'clock, and we go ... school every day ... Monday ... Friday. But we haven't got lessons ... the afternoons.
We haven't got activities ... my school, so I'm not ... a club. ... lessons I go ... a friend's house. I do my homework ... home ... the mornings ... school.
Here's a picture ... my school. Boring!
Is Susan still ... America?

Love,
Katrin

b *Write a letter like Katrin's about your school day. (You can put your letter in your scrapbook.)*

19 ▶ Big words, little words

Make new words from the letters in the following words:

1 Assembly
→ *a, May, yes, ...*
2 grandmother
3 tree house
4 restaurant
5 supermarket

20 ▶ Odd word out

1 uniform, black, green, grey
2 canteen, gym, living-room, classroom
3 breakfast, break, dinner, lunch
4 usually, sometimes, often, never
5 Maths, England, Music, English

21 ▶ The fourth word

1 parent – child teacher – ?	4 start – finish love – ?
2 big – little same – ?	5 play – chess ? – homework
3 over – under before – ?	6 draw – picture ? – photo

22 ▶ A school network

Copy and complete the network about schools. Try and find lots of words.

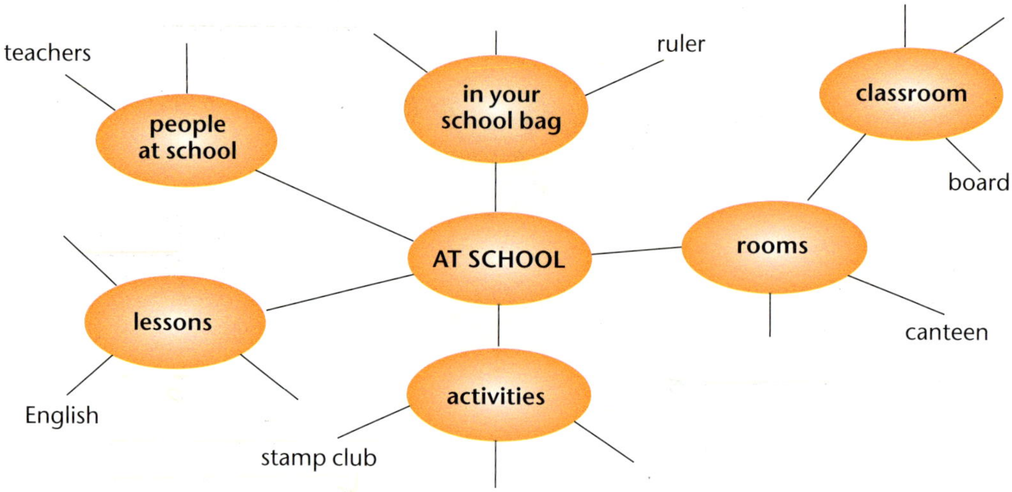

REVISION

23 ▶ Don't stand on your chair

Make sentences.

Please	—	stand on your chair.
	don't	do your homework at home.
		tidy up the classroom after the lesson.
		draw on your desk.
		sleep in the lesson.
		open your books at page 82.
		speak German in the English lesson.
		sing with me.
		write in your book.
		look at the pictures on page 70.

24 ▶ Sanjay's favourite sport

Fill in the correct personal pronoun.

I like football. But *it* (he/it/they) isn't my favourite sport. My favourite sport is judo. My sister always comes with … (her/I/me) to the matches. …'s (You/Her/She) a big fan. Her friends sometimes come with … (her/them/our). …'re (You/She/They) big fans, too. …'ve (We/Me/You) got lots of fans. … (We/They/I) come to all our matches – … (they/us/we) can hear … (us/they/them). That's very good for … (them/us/we): …'re (you/we/they) Chester champions! Mr Martin is our trainer. …'s (He/She/It) really good. … (My/Me/I) think … (my/me/I) can learn a lot from … (him/her/them).

The Saturday match

Before you read the story tell your partner what you usually do on Saturday mornings. Then look at the pictures of Debbie, Nick and Jenny. Can you guess what they usually do on Saturday mornings? Now read the story.

It's Saturday – it's the weekend. Great!

On Saturday mornings Debbie and Nick usually help their mother and father in the house. They make the beds and wash the dishes. It's very boring, but they can listen to the radio.

Nick is lucky. He's in the Kingsway under-14 football team, so he sometimes plays football on Saturday mornings. Ben is in the Kingsway team, too. So C1B1 is often lonely on Saturday mornings.

Jenny always sleeps late on Saturday mornings ... very late!

But this Saturday is different. Jenny isn't sleeping late. She and Debbie and lots of Kingsway kids are at school today. Why? Because today's football match is special. Kingsway and Blacon High School – Kingsway's big rivals – are playing.

Jenny is playing a sports reporter on the radio: 'Baker is running ... and ... yes, Baker has got the ball! Baker to Smith, Smith to Scott ... Oh! No, it's OK, and ... Scott to Baker, Baker has got the ball and ... yes! It's a goal! It's a goal! One nil to Kingsway!'

It's half-time. At half-time the teams always eat oranges. Nick usually eats oranges with the team, but not today. Today Nick is talking to Debbie. What are the twins talking about?

NICK Mr Martin always sits down on the bench and takes off one shoe at half-time. Watch ... Well, I've got an idea ...

Mr Martin is sitting on the bench ... and here's Miss Hunt.

MR MARTIN Good morning, Christine.

MISS HUNT Hello, Jeff. My boys are really good!

MR MARTIN Er, yes. Yes, they are. Er, Christine ...

MISS HUNT Yes, Jeff?

MR MARTIN What about dinner ... this evening?

MISS HUNT Well, ...

DEBBIE Hello, Miss Hunt. Hello, Mr Martin.

MR MARTIN Oh. Debbie.

MISS HUNT Hello, Debbie.

DEBBIE It's a good match today!

MISS HUNT Yes, it is. Nick is very good this morning. Where *is* ...

DEBBIE Can I fetch you an orange, Miss Hunt?

MISS HUNT No, thank you, Debbie.

DEBBIE What about you, Mr Martin?

MR MARTIN No, thank you, Debbie.

DEBBIE Oh well. Bye then.

MR MARTIN Goodbye, Debbie.

NICK Bye, Mr Martin.

MISS HUNT Oh, Nick! You're here, too?

MR MARTIN Goodbye, Nick. Well now, what about dinner, Christine?

It's time for the second half of the match. All the boys are back. They're waiting for the whistle. But where's Mr Martin?

There he is!

WORKING WITH THE TEXT

1 ▶ Saturday morning

Complete the sentences.

On Saturday mornings, Debbie and Nick usually ... in the house. And Jenny ... . Today is different. Jenny, Debbie and lots of Kingsway kids ... . Ben and Nick are in ... . Kingsway and Blacon High School ... today. At half-time the teams ... oranges. Mr Martin always ... at half-time. The boys can't start the second half because Mr Martin ... his shoe. ... has got it.

2 ▶ Who thinks ...?

1 'Saturday mornings at home are terrible.' – *Debbie.*
2 'I'm so lonely.'
3 'Jenny is really funny.'
4 'Well, he's a nice man.'
5 'Go away, you terrible girl.'
6 'Oh, good. They can't see me.'

This is a project about our town – Chester. Here's a street map[1] of the old city and pictures of five places[2] in Chester.

7CH

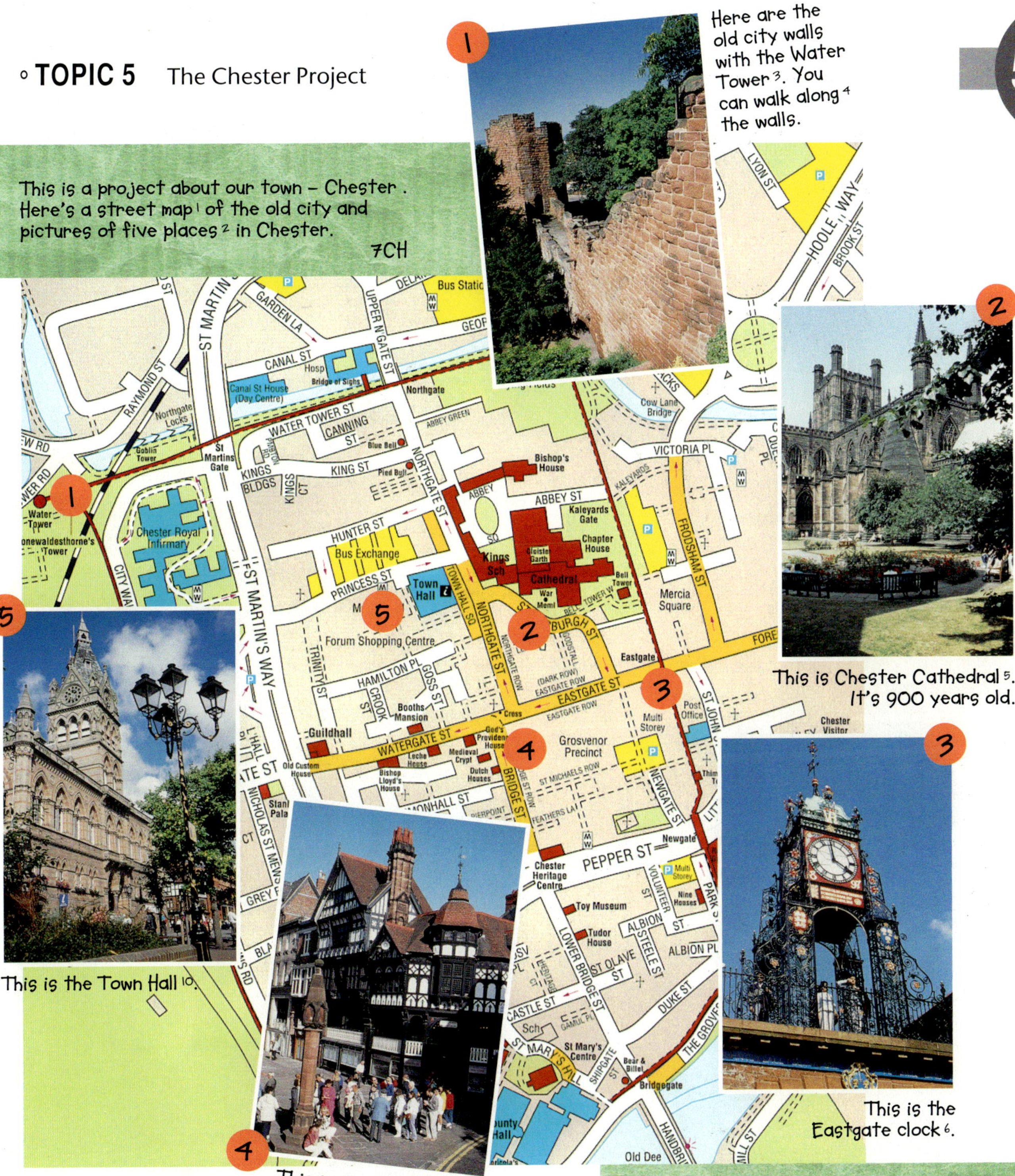

Here are the old city walls with the Water Tower[3]. You can walk along[4] the walls.

This is Chester Cathedral[5]. It's 900 years old.

This is the Eastgate clock[6].

This is the High Cross[7]. From here you can see 'the Rows'– rows of shops[8] on the first floor[9] of the old houses.

This is the Town Hall[10].

A nice day for parents – nice, but boring! Now look at the next page: Chester for kids. →

[1] street map ['stri:t mæp] *Straßenkarte* [2] place [pleɪs] *Ort, Stelle* [3] water tower ['wɔ:tə ˌtaʊə] *Wasserturm* [4] (to) walk along ['wɔ:k‿ə'lɒŋ] *entlangspazieren* [5] cathedral [kə'θi:drəl] *Kathedrale, Dom* [6] clock *Uhr* [7] High Cross [ˌhaɪ 'krɒs] *„Hochkreuz" (Art Obelisk im Stadtzentrum von Chester)* [8] rows of shops [ˌrəʊz‿əv 'ʃɒps] *Einkaufsarkaden* [9] floor [flɔ:] *Stock(werk)* [10] town hall [ˌtaʊn 'hɔ:l] *Rathaus*

Chester for kids

Lots of kids go to Northgate Arena[1].
You can swim[2] there.
A ticket[3] is £1
for children under 12.

SWIMMING

LEISURE POOL

Public Swimming	Mon - Fri	12.00 - 9.30pm
	Sat - Sun	10.00 - 5.00pm
Bank Holiday		
School Holidays	Weekdays	10.00 - 9.30pm
Adults Only	Monday	7.30 - 9.30pm
Families Only	Friday	6.00 - 7.30pm
Early Morning Dip	Mon - Fri	7.15 - 8.30am
	Sat	8.30 - 9.45am

TRAINING POOL

Lunchtime Swim	Mon - Fri	12.30 - 2.00pm
Late Night Swim		
Mixed Adults	Mon & Wed	9.30 - 10.30pm
Ladies Only	Tues	9.30 - 10.30pm

Children & Adult Swimming Lessons
Various times, contact
Mr Peacock 01244 377086

Boat rides[4] on the River[5] Dee are great.

The boats go under the old suspension bridge[6].

Nick is a terrible photographer[7].

There are lots of shops[8] in Chester.

But shopping is boring.

[1] arena [ə'ri:nə] *hier: Sporthalle, Fitnesszentrum* [2] (to) swim [swɪm] *schwimmen* [3] ticket ['tɪkɪt] *Eintrittskarte* [4] boat ride ['bəʊt raɪd] *Bootsfahrt* [5] river ['rɪvə] *Fluss* [6] suspension bridge [sə'spenʃn brɪdʒ] *Hängebrücke* [7] photographer [fə'tɒgrəfə] *Fotograf/in* [8] shop [ʃɒp] *Geschäft, Laden*

Chester Zoo

Chester Zoo[1] is over 65 years old. There are lots of animals[2] there and you can buy a ticket for the overhead railway[3] and go on a 'Zoofari'.

Chester has got a toy museum[4]. It's in an old house. You can see old dolls[5] there, and lots of very small model[6] cars.

And at the Chester Candle Shop you can make candles.

PROJECT

What can kids do in your town or village? Work in groups. Find or take photos of interesting[7] places – or draw them. Write two or three sentences about the places. The following questions can help you:
– Where are they?
– What can you do/see/listen to/… there?
– Must you buy a ticket? How much are tickets?
Make a poster with your group.

[1] zoo [zuː] *Zoo* [2] animal ['ænɪml] *Tier* [3] overhead railway [ˌəʊvəhed 'reɪlweɪ] *Hochbahn* [4] toy museum ['tɔɪ mjuːˌzɪəm] *Spielzeugmuseum* [5] doll [dɒl] *Puppe* [6] model ['mɒdl] *Modell-* [7] interesting ['ɪntrəstɪŋ] *interessant*

6 UNIT 6 Out shopping

Debbie and Jenny read the kids' magazine *Tops* every week.

CLOTHES

Fashion for the beach

Girls' swimsuits must be bright, bright, bright! Swimsuits by *Fun Fashions*, £39.

Don't put your old jeans or shorts in the bin! Wear them at the beach. The white T-shirt is in again.

Swimming-trunks are bright, too. Trunks by *Fun Fashions*, £22.

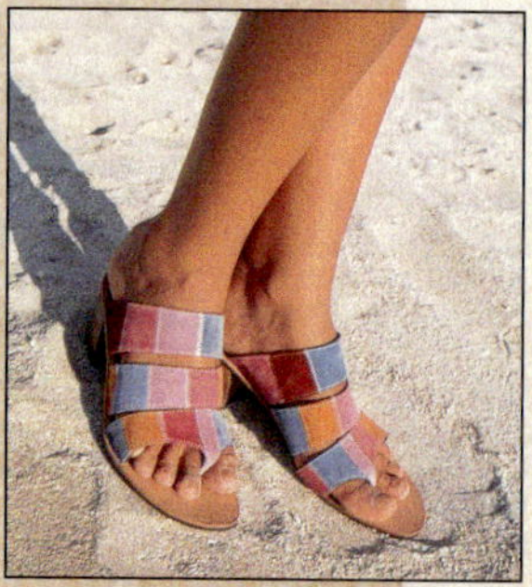

Don't wear shoes at the beach – wear sandals. Sandals by *Fun Fashions*, £30.

Boys' shirts are great for girls this year. Shirt by *Marco*, £18.

TOPS

And after the beach, the tartan trend

A jacket with a tartan skirt – great! Jacket and skirt by *Marco*, £55.90.

A tartan dress shows how pretty you are. Dress by *Fun Fashions*, £24.99. Blouse by *Marco*, £21.99.

A red pullover always looks great with tartan. Pullover and trousers by *Fun Fashions*, £37.99.

MEGA IN

- bright swimsuits
- tartan
- all clothes by *Marco & Fun Fashions*

YEAH!

MEGA OUT

- bikinis
- shoes at the beach
- white socks

YUCK!

TOPS

▶▶▶ NOW YOU

a *Say what you like about the* Tops *fashion pages. Is there a magazine like* Tops *in Germany? Is it interesting? Why/why not?*

b *Make a list: what's mega in at your school this year? What's mega out?* → P 15

1

JENNY	Isn't this blouse pretty?
DEBBIE	Yes, it is. And what about these shoes? Aren't they nice?
SITA	Red shoes? Yuck!
JENNY	But these sandals here are great.

2

DEBBIE	And what about that skirt on the right? I need a new skirt.
JENNY	I think it's too long. But those T-shirts there are super.
DEBBIE	Oh, look at that dress! Isn't it great?
JENNY	Yes, it is!

3

SITA	Let's go, you two.
DEBBIE	Why, Sita?
SITA	I think fashion is boring. And look at those prices! That dress is £49!
DEBBIE	Yes, but it's by Marco.
SITA	They put the name 'Marco' on the clothes and the price goes up. It isn't right.
JENNY	Maybe you're right …
DEBBIE	Yes, but I still want that dress.
SITA	Oh Debbie!

Looking at language

Find expressions with *this, these, that, those*.

this blouse … *that* … …

these … … *those* …

→ S 6: 1 (p. 139)
→ P 1, 2, 19

ACTIVITY

a *Here are four silly adverts. Match the slogans to the pictures.*

1 Have fun with 'Joey' jeans.
2 Pretty pullovers by 'Pam'.
3 Be a man in a 'Marco' jacket.
4 It's bright! It's right! It's 'Fun Fashions'!

a

b

c

d

b *Draw and write a silly advert. You can put it in your scrapbook.*

→ P 14

▶ **4**

It's Saturday afternoon. Every Saturday Mrs Baker goes to her drama class. Mr Baker and the children are at home.

MR BAKER OK, kids. Let's go. Mum has got some old clothes and toys for Oxfam – I must take them to the shop.
DEBBIE Bye, Dad. Have fun at Oxfam.
MR BAKER Very funny, Debbie. Please come and help me.
NICK Have fun, Debbie.
MR BAKER You, too, Nick.
NICK Oh, Dad. The Oxfam shop is –
DEBBIE – boring!
MR BAKER Maybe, but it needs these clothes and toys. Let's go, you two.

→ P 3

▶ **5**

ASSISTANT May I help you?
MR BAKER Yes, we've got some old clothes and toys for Oxfam.
ASSISTANT Oh, thank you. Please put them there.
MR BAKER Maybe you can tell me … Do you take pictures, too?
ASSISTANT Yes, we do.
MR BAKER And do you take sofas?
ASSISTANT No, sorry, we don't.

▶▶▶ **NOW YOU** and your partner

You're at the Oxfam shop. One of you has got things for Oxfam, one of you is the assistant.

A	Do you take *books*?	B	*Yes, we do.*
A	Do you take *beds*?	B	*No, we don't.*
A	Do you take …?	B	…

→ S 6: 2a (p. 140)
→ P 4, 5

▶ 6

Now Debbie and Nick are trying on clothes at the Oxfam shop – and it's fun. But not for Mr Baker.

MR BAKER Debbie, Nick. We can go now.
DEBBIE Oh, Dad. *Must* we?
MR BAKER But Oxfam is boring, right?
NICK No, it isn't. It's fun.

▶ 7

DEBBIE Nick, do you like this dress?
NICK No, I don't. I don't wear dresses.
DEBBIE It's for me, silly.
NICK Oh. Well, then it's OK. – Hey, Debbie. Does this shirt look good on me?
DEBBIE No, it doesn't. It looks really stupid.
NICK Thank you, Debbie. And what about this jacket? Does it look good?
DEBBIE Well, yes, it does. It looks great on *you* – a stupid jacket and a stupid shirt for a stupid boy. – But look! This dress looks like the dress in the boutique. And it's only £9.99!

▶ 8

Debbie is at Jenny's house now – with the dress from Oxfam.

JENNY Hey, that's the dress from the boutique!
DEBBIE No, it isn't. It's from Oxfam.
JENNY Really? How much?
DEBBIE £9.99. Does it look good?
JENNY Yes, it does. It's great. Can I try it on?
DEBBIE OK.

JENNY Well, does it look good on me, too?
DEBBIE Well, Jenny ... No, it doesn't. It's the wrong way round.

▶ **Looking at language**

Collect simple present questions and short answers from pages 91 and 92.

Do you take pictures?
– Yes, we ... .
...
Does this shirt ...?
– No, it ... .

▶▶▶ **NOW YOU** and your partner

Talk to your partner.

Does your	mother father sister dog ...	wear	jeans shirts bright colours tartan ...	?

A *Does your mother wear jeans?*
B *No, she doesn't.*
B *Does your dog wear tartan?*
A *Yes, she does.*

→ S 6: 2a (p. 140)
→ P 6, 7, 8, 9, 17, 20

▶ **9**

Ben is lonely. His mum and dad are out shopping. And his grandma is at her judo class.
First Ben phones Sita. But Mr Gupta says, 'Sorry, she's out shopping.'
Then he phones Debbie and Nick. But Mrs Baker says, 'Sorry, they're out shopping.'
'I hate shopping,' Ben says, and then he goes to his computer. 'Good old C1B1 – *he* doesn't go shopping.'

→ S 6: 2c (p. 141)

▶ **10**

C1B1 Hi, Ben. You don't look happy.
BEN I'm not happy – all my friends are out shopping!
C1B1 Out shopping? What's that?
BEN Shopping is … well, you go out and buy things.
C1B1 What do you buy?
BEN Lots of different things.
C1B1 And why do you buy things?
BEN Because we sometimes need food or clothes or …
C1B1 … computers or computer games?
BEN Yes, that's right. And we pay for them with money. That's shopping.

▶ **11**

C1B1 Where do you buy food, Ben?
BEN At the supermarket.
C1B1 And where do you buy clothes?
BEN Sometimes at a special shop for men's clothes. And sometimes at a department store. You can buy everything at a department store.
C1B1 Everything?! Then I must go now. Goodbye.

→ S 6: 2b (p. 140)
→ P 10, 11, 12, 13, 16

RAP I hate shopping

Let's go shopping.
Oh, no, not that!
Do you want a T-shirt,
or a nice new hat[1]?
No, I don't want a T-shirt
and I don't want a hat.
I HATE SHOPPING –
and that's that[2]!

[1] hat [hæt] *Hut* [2] that's that *damit basta*

x lesen üben

1 ▶ I like this shirt

a *Use* this *or* these *and the correct pronouns.*

1 I like *this* shirt here. Can I buy *it*?
2 What about *these* shoes? *They*'re nice, too.
3 … pullover is really pretty. How much is …?
4 … swimsuit is very bright. I like … .
5 … sandals are cheap. Let's buy … .
6 I like … shorts. Are … expensive?

b *Use* that *or* those *and the correct pronouns.*

1 *That* jacket there is nice. And *it*'s cheap!
2 *Those* trousers in the window are by Marco. *They* must be expensive.
3 … swimming-trunks are really bright. …'re great.
4 I don't like … bikini. …'s very small.
5 I hate … shoes. …'re red!
6 … dress in the magazine is really pretty. Is … expensive?

◆◆ 2 ▶ Are those your books?

Work with a partner and make short dialogues with this/that, these/those.
Use these words: basket • books • cage • clothes • games • school bag

1 2 3

4 5 6

1 A Are *those* your books? B No, they aren't. *These* are my books.

3 ▶ Oxfam – what's that?

a *Look at the Oxfam advert on page 91 – the photos and the words. You don't know all the words, but that's OK. Now look at sentences 1–8. What sentences are right? What sentences are wrong?*

b *Can you correct the wrong sentences?*

1 People at Oxfam don't like their work.
2 Oxfam helps poor people.
3 Only young[1] people work at Oxfam.
4 Oxfam's motto is 'Working for fairer people'.
5 Oxfam's work is good for people.
6 People at Oxfam are lonely.
7 Only women help Oxfam.
8 Oxfam says, 'Come and work for our team.'

[1] young [jʌŋ] *jung*

◆◆ 4 ▶ Do you ...?

Work with your partner. You need two dice. You can make them at home out of cardboard:

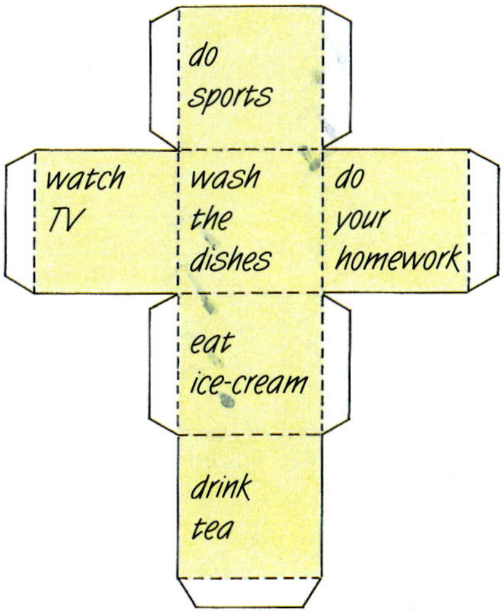

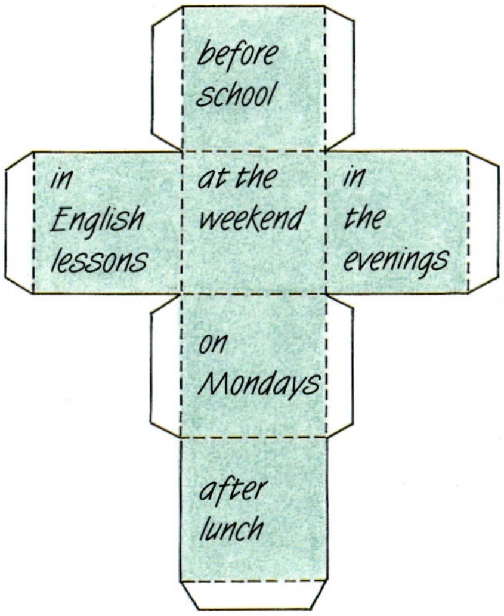

Throw the dice and ask questions. Swap the dice after every dialogue.

A *Do you wash the dishes at the weekend?* **B** *Yes, sometimes.*
B *Do you drink tea in English lessons?* **A** *No, of course I don't.*

These words can help you with your answers:
Yes, I do.
Yes, of course.
Yes, sometimes.
No, I don't.
No, never/only on Fridays/...

◆◆ 5 ▶ Do you know your partner?

a *Make a chart like this in your exercise book. Then read the sentences on the right. Do you think the sentence is true for you or your partner? Then write* yes *in your chart. Do you think it isn't true for you or your partner? Then write* no.

	Me	My partner	Points
1	no	yes	?
2	?	?	?
...	?	?	?

1 You like black clothes.
2 Your parents give you money for your clothes.
3 You always buy your clothes at the same shop.
4 You go shopping with your mother.
5 You go shopping alone.
6 You like jeans.
7 Your parents usually like your clothes.
8 You and your friends wear the same clothes.

b *Now ask your partner and find out his/her answers:*
Do you like black clothes?
– Yes, I do./No, I don't.

c *Are you right? One point for every correct answer!*

Points	
7–8 points	You must be very good friends.
5–6 points	You know a lot about your partner.
3–4 points	You don't know a lot about your partner.
0–2 points	Is your partner new in your form?

◆◆ 6 ▶ Ben and Grandma Scott

Work with your partner. Ask and answer questions about Ben and his grandma.

Partner A

	Grandma Scott	Ben
do judo	✔	
like C1B1	✔	
play computer games	✔	
make dinner	✔	
wear funny clothes		✗
hate fashion		✔
drink tea		✗
read a lot		✔

A Does Ben do judo?
B No, he doesn't.
A … Ben like C1B1?
B Yes, … .
…

B … Grandma Scott … judo?
A Yes, … .
…

Partner B

	Grandma Scott	Ben
do judo		✗
like C1B1		✔
play computer games		✔
make dinner		✗
wear funny clothes	✗	
hate fashion	✔	
drink tea	✔	
read a lot	✔	

7 ▶ Pat's room

Pat is Debbie's friend. You don't know her, but her room tells you a lot about her and what she does.

Look at the picture for two minutes. Now work with a partner. Your partner must close his/her book and you must ask questions:

You Does Pat draw pictures? < **Your partner** Yes, she does. – **You** Yes, that's right.
Your partner No, she doesn't. – **You** That's wrong.

Swap after five questions.

8 ▶ Do they or don't they?

Complete the sentences. Use do, don't, does *or* doesn't.

1 *Do* you often buy new clothes, Jenny? – No, I *don't*.
2 … Oxfam fetch clothes from people's houses? – No, it … .
3 … Nick and Debbie make breakfast on Sundays? – No, they … .
4 … Mrs Baker go to a drama class on Saturday afternoons? – Yes, she … .
5 … you like fashion, Sita? – No, I … .
6 … you help in your parents' restaurant, Sita and Sanjay? – Yes, we … .
7 … Debbie want a new dress? – Yes, she … .
8 … Marmalade like music? – No, she … .

9 ▶ Does Sita play chess?

Make short dialogues.

1 Sita / play / chess? – Yes, … .
Does Sita play chess?
– *Yes, she does.*
2 you / like / Maths?
– No, … . But / Geography
… you like Maths?
– *No, I … . But I like Geography.*
3 Susan Scott / work / in Germany?
– No, … … in the USA.
4 Debbie and Jenny / act / in plays?
– Yes, … .
5 Debbie / like / fashion?
– Yes, … .
6 Mr Scott / come / from Germany?
– No, … … from England.
7 the Snows / eat / breakfast together on Saturdays?
– No, … . But / on Sundays.

10 LISTENING Where's Sarah?

Sarah Ball isn't at home, and she isn't at school. Now the police are looking for her. One of these four girls is Sarah. But who is it?

a *Before you listen to the cassette/CD, look at the pictures and say what the girls are wearing.*

b *Listen to the cassette/CD and say who Sarah is. Say why it can't be one of the other three.*
Number 1 is wearing a yellow jacket. Sarah's jacket is red and blue. …

11 SOUNDS The letter 'o'

a *The letter 'o' – together with other letters – has got lots of different sounds. Say these words. Then listen to the cassette/CD and put the words in the right group:*

afternoon • before • cousin
divorced • do • does • door • floor
goes • group • lonely • lots • mother
move • often • problem • radio
shoe • show • sometimes • sorry

[əʊ]	[ɒ]	[ɔː]	[uː]	[ʌ]
clothes	dog	board	too	love
…	…	…	…	…

b *Listen to the cassette/CD. Then try and say this little poem:*
Does doesn't go with *goes*, and *shoes* doesn't go with *shows*.
But why doesn't *does* go with *goes* or *shoes* with *shows*?
That's easy, my friend: they've all got different 'o's!

12 ▶ Ben and C1B1 are talking

Ask C1B1's questions and find Ben's answers.

C1B1

1 Why … you talk to me every day?
2 What … your sister do in the USA?
3 Why … your mum speak German?
4 Why … people take things to the Oxfam shop?
5 What … people buy at Oxfam?
6 Where … your grandma go on Saturdays?
7 Where … your friends meet at weekends?

BEN

a Because she's from Germany.
b Because they've got lots of things, and they don't need them.
c She's an au pair.
d She goes to her judo class.
e Because I'm often lonely.
f They sometimes go to the swimming-pool.
g They buy old clothes and other things.

◆◆ 13 ▶ School around the world

Partner A

Name	Where … come from?	When … go to school?	What … like at school?
Debbie + Nick	Chester	8.30	?
Esra	?	?	Maths
Wencke	Oslo	?	?
Lei Wang + Sung Ta	?	7.10	English, Maths
Jens + Maike	?	7.15	?
Andy	New York	?	Music, Geography

Partner B

Name	Where … come from?	When … go to school?	What … like at school?
Debbie + Nick	?	?	English, French
Esra	Istanbul	7.30	?
Wencke	?	7.40	Music, French
Lei Wang + Sung Ta	Hong Kong	?	?
Jens + Maike	Leipzig	?	Maths, German
Andy	?	7.45	?

a *Ask your partner questions and write the missing information in your exercise book.*

b *Write texts like this about the people:*
Debbie and Nick come from Chester. They go to school at 8.30. They like English and French.

14 ▶ Two texts about shopping

Finish Sita and Debbie's texts about shopping. Use and, but, or, so.

*I think fashion is boring, and I don't really like shopping. I'm lucky: we wear uniforms at school, … I don't need lots of clothes.
I like nice clothes, … I must sometimes go shopping. I usually go alone … with my mother, … it isn't so boring with friends.*

Sita Gupta

Sita is a good friend, … we've got very different ideas about shopping. I love it, … I try and go to the shops every week. I look at lots of different clothes – blouses, skirts, dresses, T-shirts – … I sometimes buy them.
I like shopping with friends … with my mum, … I never go to the shops alone. That's boring!

Debbie Baker

WORD WATCH

◆◆ 15 ▶ Clothes

Look at the picture. Some clothes are only for boys. Some are only for girls. And some are for boys and girls. Make three lists and compare them with your partner's lists.

16 ▶ Word partners

Find the partners and put them in the sentences.

get • listen
look • look • pay
sit • tidy • try

at • down
for • for • on
to • up • up

1 When do you … in the mornings?
2 Here's a chair. Why don't you …?
3 I only … the radio in the car.
4 Please … your room. It isn't very tidy.
5 Can you … my ruler? I can't find it.
6 My money is at home. Who can … my sandwiches?
7 I collect stamps. Let's … them.
8 Please … this dress. It's a good colour for you.

17 ▶ Word link

Match the adjectives from the list to the groups of nouns.

big • boring • good • pretty
small • wrong

small	box, car, cat, dog, room, town, village
…	box, brother, car, city, difference, dinner, house, room, school, sister, star
…	answer, telephone number, time, way round
…	afternoon, book, friend, idea, match, morning, music, restaurant
…	activity, afternoon, book, film, lesson, match, party, video
…	clothes, dress, girl, name, woman

18 ▶ Find the word

First read Why, Gillian, why? *(p. 101–103). Then complete the sentences. Write down the letters and put them in the right order. What's the new word?*

1 Sita says Gillian has got a … jacket. (4th letter) → pretty → T
2 The scarf is from the new … in Eastgate Street. (2nd letter)
3 The assistant asks, 'May I … you?' (4)
4 Gillian looks at a … . (6)
5 She wants the blouse in … 10. (1)
6 The assistant thinks the two … are thieves. (4)
7 Mr Gupta comes to the boutique after … minutes. (3)
8 Mr Gupta knows Sita isn't a … . (2)
9 Mr Gupta doesn't believe the assistant. He wants … . (5)
10 Gillian must wait for her parents, or the assistant can phone the … . (4)

REVISION

19 ▶ In the shop

a *Make a list of the things in the shop:*

six little children
lots of tortoises
...

◆◆ **b** *Now play a game with your partner.*

A I can see six little children.
B I can see six little children and five mice.
A I can see six little children, five mice and ...

20 ▶ Can you tell me ...?

Fill in the correct word: can, can't *or* must.

1 ... you tell me how much these trousers are, please?
2 Where ... I try on these shorts, please?
3 I ... wear these shoes. They're too small.
4 I ... buy that dress! It's really pretty.
5 We ... wear bikinis this year. They're mega out!
6 *Tops* says: swimsuits ... be bright this year.
7 I ... buy a new jacket. I haven't got the money.
8 You ... buy clothes at the Oxfam shop. You don't need lots of money.

Before you read the story about Sita and Gillian, answer these questions:
- What can you buy in a boutique? Make a list.
- Do you go and buy your clothes with your parents, with a friend or alone?
- Where do you buy your clothes?
- Do you or your parents pay for your clothes?

Why, Gillian, why?

Excuse me. Have you got this blouse in size 10? My friend …
8
Hey! What are you doing?
Run, Sita!
What …
9
Stop that girl, Sarah!
What's happening?
10
What have you got in your bag?
Nothing.
Open your bag and put everything on the table here.
11
Gillian! That's the T-shirt from …
Shut up, Sita.
12
Now, you two. Have you got the money for this? – No? Then give me your parents' phone numbers.
13
I'm very sorry. I can't com now.
14
But Gillian's parents aren't at home …

WORKING WITH THE TEXT

1 ▶ Right or wrong?

Correct the wrong sentences.

1 Gillian has got a pretty jacket.
2 Sita and Gillian meet at Sita's flat.
3 The two girls try on sandals and swimsuits in the boutique.
4 Gillian puts a T-shirt in her bag.
5 The assistant finds a new blouse in Gillian's bag.
6 Mrs Gupta says Sita is *not* a shoplifter.
7 Gillian can't go home now. Her parents or the police must come first.

◆◆ **2 ▶ What do you think …?**

Talk about the story with your partner.

1 Gillian is a shoplifter. When do you first know it?
PARTNER A *In the second picture. Gillian says …*
PARTNER B *Well, in the fifth picture she says …*
2 What do you think? Is Gillian bad, clever, stupid, a good friend, …?
PARTNER A *I think she's bad. She's a shoplifter.*
PARTNER B *I think she's a good friend. She wants the T-shirt for Sita.*
3 And what about Sita?

→ P 18

TOPIC 6 Poems[1], poems, poems

MICE

I think mice
are rather[2] nice.

Their tails[8] are long,
their faces[9] small,
they haven't any
chins at all.[3]
Their ears[10] are pink,
their teeth[11] are white,
they run about
the house[4] at night.
They nibble[6] things
they shouldn't touch[7]
and no one seems
to like them much.[5]

*But **I** think mice*
are nice.

(Rose Fyleman)

There is a bee,[16] sits on a wall,
It says 'Buzz, buzz.'
And that is all.

1 What kind of[12] text is this?
2 What's the title[13]?
3 What are the first two lines[14]?
4 What comes next[15]?

Now read the next four poems.

[1] poem ['pəʊɪm] *Gedicht* [2] rather ['rɑːðə] *ziemlich* [3] they haven't any chins at all [eni ˌtʃɪnz_ət_'ɔːl] *sie haben überhaupt kein Kinn* [4] about the house *hier: im Haus umher* [5] no one seems to like them much [siːmz] *niemand scheint sie sehr zu mögen* [6] (to) nibble ['nɪbl] *anknabbern, nagen an* [7] things they shouldn't touch [ˌʃʊdnt 'tʌtʃ] *Dinge, die sie nicht anrühren sollten* [8] tail [teɪl] *Schwanz* [9] face [feɪs] *Gesicht* [10] ear [ɪə] *Ohr* [11] teeth [tiːθ] *Zähne* [12] kind of [kaɪnd] *Art* [13] title ['taɪtl] *Titel* [14] line [laɪn] *Zeile* [15] next [nekst] *als Nächstes* [16] bee [biː] *Biene*

LAZY[1] JANE

Lazy
lazy
lazy
lazy
lazy
lazy
Jane,
she
wants
a
drink
of
water[2]
so
she
waits
and
waits
and
waits
and
waits
and
waits
for
it
to
rain.[3]

(SHEL SILVERSTEIN)

I scream[4]
You scream
We all scream
for ICE-CREAM!

THE RAIN[5]

RAIN ON THE GREEN GRASS[6]
AND RAIN ON THE TREE.
RAIN ON THE ROOF[7],
BUT NOT ON ME!

▶▶▶ **NOW YOU** for your scrapbook

Write a poem.
Here are some examples[8]:

Red	Brown[10]
Exercise book	Ice-cream
Lots of homework	It is chocolate
I can't do it	But I hate chocolate
– Help[9]!	– Yuck!

Here's some help:

1st line – a colour; for example 'blue' (one word)
2nd line – a thing (two words)
3rd line – about the thing (three words)
4th line – about me (four words)
5th line – a last[11] word (one word)

[1] lazy ['leɪzi] *faul, träge* [2] a drink of water ['wɔːtə] *ein Schluck Wasser* [3] she waits for it to rain *sie wartet darauf, dass es anfängt zu regnen* [4] (to) scream (for) [skriːm] *schreien (nach)* [5] rain [reɪn] *Regen* [6] grass [grɑːs] *Gras; Rasen* [7] roof [ruːf] *Dach* [8] (for) example [ɪg'zɑːmpl] *(zum) Beispiel* [9] help *Hilfe* [10] brown [braʊn] *braun* [11] last [lɑːst] *letzte(r, s)*

7 UNIT 7 A trip to the zoo

Adopt an animal at Chester Zoo!

Do you like elephants? Tigers? Tortoises? They're all great animals ... and they're all in danger.

Here at Chester Zoo we try and save animals in danger. Please help us. We must feed these animals and need lots of money. *Your* money can help us with our work.

Elephants

Monkeys

Tigers

Giraffe

Adopt an animal now! For £15 you can adopt a small bird, for £30 a tortoise, for £600 a lion, for £1000 a tiger. You can't take the animal home. But you can come and see it – often.

Tortoise

Zebras

Lion

Our shopping list for one week

80 kilos of bread
538 kilos of meat
192 kilos of fish
154 kilos of tomatoes
210 litres of milk
1000 oranges

Penguin

Sea lions

PROJECT 'Our zoo' (Part 1)
What's your favourite animal? Draw or find a picture of it. Now start a poster. Stick the picture onto a big piece of paper and write the name of the animal under it. What does your animal eat? Write or draw.

Lions
My favourite animals are lions. They eat lots of meat every day.

▶ 1

It's 8 o'clock on Thursday morning. Mr and Mrs Scott are late. 'Let's go, Ben!' But what about Ben's sandwiches? Ben usually eats lunch in the school canteen. But he hasn't got lessons today – there's a trip for 7CH! So Ben must take his lunch with him.

'Quick, Ben, come to the kitchen with me!' Grandma Scott says. 'Now, Ben, is white bread OK?'
'Yes, Grandma.'
'Ham or cheese?'
'Cheese, please.'
'An apple or a banana?'
'An apple *and* a banana, please, Grandma.'

→ P 15

▶ 2

It's 9 o'clock. The children and their teachers are waiting in front of the school.

BEN I don't like zoos.
DEBBIE Why not?
BEN Because I don't like animals – they're dirty.
DEBBIE Well, I love zoos because I love animals.
JENNY And I *hate* zoos because I love animals.
DEBBIE What?!
JENNY Zoos are terrible for the animals. They're in cages and they can't run around or …
NICK Look, there's the bus.
BEN Let's go! I always try and sit at the front when I'm on a bus.

▶▶▶ NOW YOU and a partner
Talk about zoos. Is there a zoo in/near your town? Do you like it? Do you know other zoos? Do you like zoos? Why/Why not?

▶ 3

Now the children are on the bus. They often sing when they're on a trip. At the moment they're singing a song about the zoo.

SONG In Chester town there is a zoo *(Sing it to the tune of* Old MacDonald.*)* Words by J Blombach

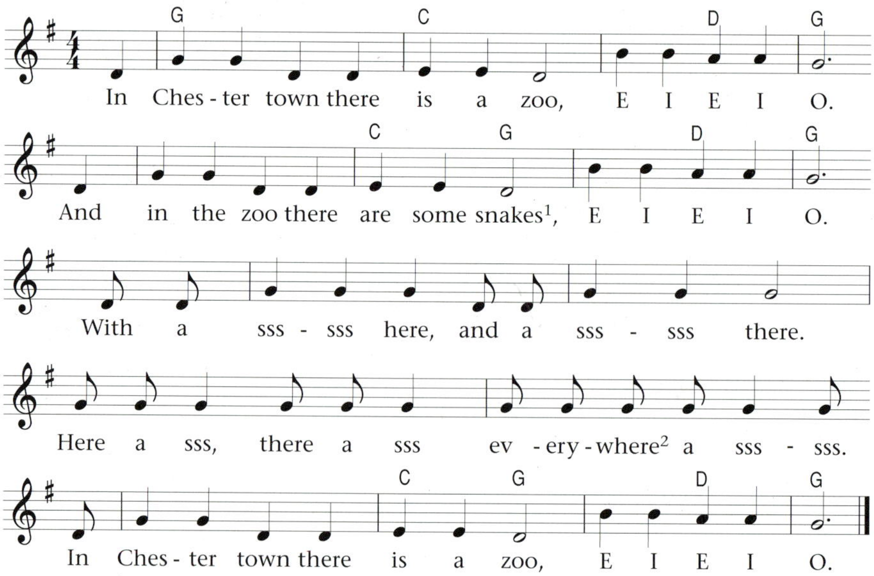

… And in that zoo there are some monkeys
… With a hee-hee here and …

… And in that zoo there are some lions
… With a grr-grr here and …

→ S 7: 1a (p. 141)
→ P 1, 2

[1] snake [sneɪk] *Schlange* [2] everywhere ['evriweə] *überall*

4 ▶ Animal feeding times

They feed the sea lions at 10.30 every day.
They … the monkeys at … .
They … the lions at … .
They … the penguins at … .

Look, it's *2.15*. 

They're *feeding* the … now.

Look, it's  .

They're …

Look, …  … .

Look, …  … .

→ S 7: 2, 3 (p. 142/143)
→ P 3, 4, 5, 6

▶ 5

The pupils have all got a questionnaire with the name of an animal.

MISS HUNT OK then, go and find your animals. See what they're doing. Are they sleeping? Or eating? Or playing? Where and when do they usually sleep, play and eat? For example, monkeys sleep in trees at night. Find out all about your animals. Then meet me here at 1 o'clock.

PROJECT 'Our zoo' (Part 2)

Find more information about your favourite animal. Look at the questionnaire and answer the questions about your animal. You can use animal books or you can ask your biology teacher or your parents for help. Write and draw the new information on your poster.

LIONS

Lions are my favourite animals. They are from Africa. They are dangerous animals. They have got long, sharp teeth. They sleep at night and sometimes during the day. Lions are very fast. They eat five to seven kilos of meat every day. Lions are not in danger.

QUESTIONNAIRE

Your animal: elephant

1. Where is your animal from? ____________
2. Where does it sleep? ____________
3. When does it sleep? ____________
4. What does it eat? ____________
5. Is your animal in danger? ____________
6. Why is it special? ____________

→ S 7: 1b (p. 142)
→ P 7, 8

▶ 6

At the zoo there's a farm with cows and sheep and pigs. Ben and Jenny are there now. Ben is on the farm because his animal is a pig. Jenny is there because she likes farms.
'You're lucky, Ben,' Jenny says.
'Why?' Ben asks.
'You live in the country with all these animals around you, and green fields, and trees.'
'Yuck! The fields and the trees are boring and the animals are all dirty and stupid, like this pig! I hate the country! In towns there are computer shops and hamburger restaurants and ...'

→ P 16

▶▶▶ **NOW YOU** and a partner
What do you like – the town or the country? Say why.

▶ 7

Miss Hunt and Mr Martin are sitting on a bench.
'Christine,' he says, 'What about ...? Oh, no! The "terrible twins" are here!'
'Hello, Miss Hunt. Hello, Mr Martin,' Nick says.

'Are your questionnaires finished, you two?' Miss Hunt asks.
'Er ... no,' Debbie says.
'Well, go and finish them – now!'
'Those "terrible twins",' Mr Martin says.
'But I've got an idea ... –
Now, Christine, what about dinner this evening?'

→ P 17

▶ 8

It's 1 o'clock and time for lunch. Mr Martin is talking to the 'terrible twins'.

MR MARTIN Debbie, Nick, come here a minute, please. Before you eat your lunch, can you go to the Tropical House and try and find a snark, please?

DEBBIE A snark?

MR MARTIN Yes. It's my favourite animal. It has got big ears, yellow eyes and a long tail. Please wait there – and when you see it, come and tell me, OK?

NICK OK.

→ P 9

▶ 9

It's 1.30 now. The children are eating their sandwiches.

JENNY Your sandwich looks nice, Sita.
SITA It *is* nice. It's cheese and tomato.
JENNY Mmmmm, you're lucky. My mum usually gives me ham sandwiches.
BEN My favourite sandwich is a BLT.
SITA What's a BLT?
BEN Bacon, lettuce and tomato.
SITA Oh, I never eat bacon. I'm a vegetarian.
JENNY Hey, Sita, Ben! Where are Debbie and Nick?

→ P 10, 11, 12, 13, 14

▶ 10

It's 2 o'clock. The children are back at the school bus.
'Please, Miss Hunt,' Jenny says. 'Nick and Debbie aren't here.'
'No, of course they aren't,' Mr Martin says. He's laughing. 'Ben, can you fetch them, please ?'
'But where are they?' Ben asks.
'They're in the Tropical House. They're looking for a snark. It's my favourite animal.'
'But a snark isn't a real animal,' Ben says.
'That's right, Ben,' Mr Martin says. 'But it's still my favourite animal because it keeps "terrible twins" quiet!'

ACTIVITY

Make a chocolate tortoise.

You need:
- half an apple
- 100 grammes of chocolate
- 5 green grapes
- cocktail sticks

Now:
Put the chocolate in a bowl.
Put the bowl over a saucepan of hot water.
Melt the chocolate.
Coat the apple with the chocolate.
Choose four small grapes for the feet and one big grape for the head.
Put the cocktail sticks into the grapes and then into the apple.

1 ▶ Because ...

Match the two parts and make sentences with because. *Be careful with the word order.*

1 People can adopt animals at Chester Zoo ... (money / the zoo / needs).
People can adopt animals at Chester Zoo *because the zoo needs money.*
2 Chester Zoo helps animals ... (they / lessons / haven't got).
3 Ben isn't at school today ... (time / his parents / haven't got).
4 Grandma Scott is making sandwiches for Ben ... (are / they / in danger).
5 The children and their teachers are in front of the school ... (dirty / are / they).
6 Debbie loves the zoo ... (they / are waiting / for the bus).
7 Ben doesn't like animals ... (there / a trip / is).
8 The children are singing ... (animals / she / loves).

2 ▶ Animal fun

Put the words in the right order.
Then you can understand these animal jokes.

1 What time is it when an elephant (sits / your / on / car)?
– Time for a new car!

3 Excuse me.
Have you got pigs' feet[3]?
– Yes, I have.
Well, don't worry. People can't see them when you (wearing / shoes / are).

4 Why is that cow[4] jumping[5] up and down?
– Because her children (a / milkshake / want).

2 Hey you!
You can't catch[1] fish here!
– I'm not catching fish.
Look! I'm just (pet worm[2] / my / washing).

[1] (to) catch [kætʃ] *fangen* [2] worm [wɜːm] *Wurm* [3] pigs' feet [ˌpɪgz ˈfiːt] *Schweinefüße* [4] cow [kaʊ] *Kuh* [5] (to) jump [dʒʌmp] *springen*

3 ▶ usually – now

Complete the sentences with the right form of the verb.

1 (read) Debbie usually *reads* fashion magazines.
But now *she's reading* a TV magazine.
2 (watch) Nick usually ... football on TV. But now ... a cowboy film.
3 (play) Ben usually ... chess with C1B1. But now ... chess with his grandma.
4 (draw) Sita usually ... little pictures. But now ... a big poster.
5 (listen) Sanjay usually ... to CDs. But now ... to the radio.
6 (write) Trundle usually ... with a pencil. But now ... with a pen.

4 ▶ At the zoo or at school?

a *Here's a text by Jenny before the trip to the zoo. Put in the right forms of the verbs.*

When I (go) to the zoo, I often (look) at the monkeys first. They always (climb) around their cage and they (be) very funny. I (not like) the big cats. The lions usually (sleep) behind the trees, and the tigers never (move). But I (love) the elephants because they (like) people. They (look) at people and then they (make) their elephant sound. My friend (not like) the monkeys or the elephants. He always (go) and (watch) the sea lions.

b *And here's a text by Ben's cousin Julia in Berlin. Put in the right forms of the verbs.*

At the moment, on Tuesday, July 2nd, at 11.38, I (sit) in the classroom of Form 5c. We (do) a boring English exercise. I (write) in green with a felt-tip, but my partner (use) a blue biro.
Our teacher (not work). He (look) at the posters in our classroom. Two boys behind me (not do) English. They (read) a book for our Geography lesson.
Oh, we (finish) the lesson now. Herr Benn (talk).

c *What's happening now where you are? Look around you, use your imagination – and write a text. (You can put it in your scrapbook.)*

5 ▶ Robby, the house robot

a *Robby, the house robot, works for the Greens. He does lots of jobs for them. But today he has got a computer virus, and he's doing lots of silly things.*

1 (wash / wash) Robby *usually/always washes* the Greens' clothes, but *now/today he's washing* their shoes.
2 (wash / wash) Robby … the dishes, but … the children's toys.
3 (clean / make) Robby … the rooms, but … them dirty.
4 (bring / bring) Robby … the Greens their breakfast, but … them old shoes.
5 (give / give) Robby … the children their breakfast, but … them fish.
6 (take / take) Robby … the children to school, but … them to the zoo.
7 (wash / draw) Robby … the Greens' car, but … on it.
8 (make / make) Robby … hamburgers and chips for dinner, but … football and chips.

b *Can you find more funny things? Draw a picture and write a sentence.*

◆◆ 6 ▶ Spot the differences

Partner A has got Miss Hunt's seating plan[1]. That's where the children usually sit.

Partner B's plan shows where the children are sitting today. Can you spot the differences?

Partner A Usually …

	1	2	3	4	5
3rd row	Peter	Debbie	Sandra	Dave	Sita
2nd row	Alan	Ben	Asif	Nick	Ann
1st row	Jenny	Tom	Mark	Sue	Bina
		Teacher			

Partner B Today …

	1	2	3	4	5
3rd row	Ben	Sandra	Nick	Alan	Asif
2nd row	Debbie	Jenny	Sita	Peter	Mark
1st row	Ann	Bina	Dave	Tom	Sue
			Teacher		

A Debbie usually sits in the second seat[2] in the third row[3].
B Well, today she's sitting in the first seat in the second row.

[1] seating plan ['si:tɪŋ plæn] *Sitzplan* [2] seat *Platz* [3] row [rəʊ] *Reihe*

7 ▶ Who? What? Where? When? *Help Trundle and make the sentences.*

8 GAME Guess who

a *Write your name on a small card. Now write: What? Where? When? Then write your answers. – Example:*

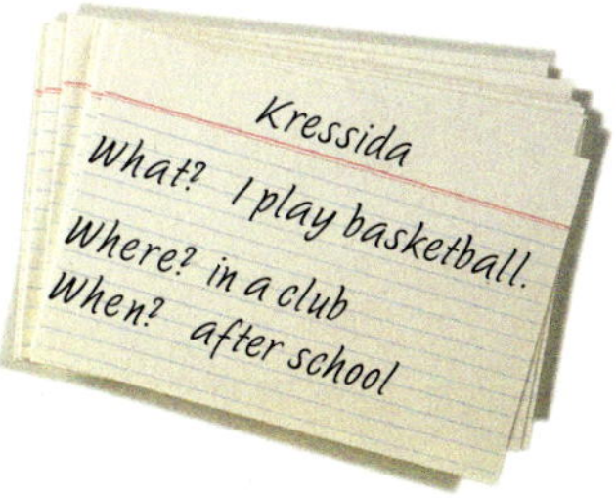

b *Now put all the cards in a box. One pupil must take a card. He or she reads out the information but doesn't say the name. The other pupils must guess who it is!*
This pupil plays basketball in a club after school. Guess who!
– Oh, I know. That's Kressida.

9 LISTENING What's where in the zoo?

1 *You know a lot of different animals in English now. Make a list.*
2 *It's Lynn's first trip to the zoo, so she asks the zoo keeper some questions. Can you see Lynn and the keeper on the plan? – Now listen to the text and look at the plan.*
3 *Copy the plan into your exercise book. Listen again and write the names of the animals in the right cages on your plan. – Where's the pool?*

◆◆ 4 *Imagine: the animals are in different cages now. Make a new plan. Where are your animals? Tell your partner.*

10 SOUNDS The letter 'r'

a *All the words in the box have got the letter 'r' – but you can't always hear it. Listen to the cassette/CD and put the words in two groups.*

Group A you *can't* hear the 'r'	**Group B** you *can* hear the 'r'
board	boring
careful	…
…	

board • boring • careful • dirty
four • garden • German • hear
hearing • here • learn • married
nurse • parents • partner • scarf
story • their • wear • wearing
we're • word • worry

b *Listen to these sentences. Then say them.*
Draw a picture‿and colour‿it.
She's wearing a red pullover‿and a blue skirt.
His sister‿is an au pair‿in the USA.
Our‿aunt lives in Chester.

c *Say these sentences. Be careful with the 'r'. Then listen and check.*
There are four English books on the table.
My mother and father are from Turkey.
I've got a brother and four sisters.

REVISION

11 ▶ Ben doesn't usually take sandwiches to school
Use don't *or* doesn't.

1 Ben … usually take sandwiches to school.
2 The children … usually meet their teachers in front of the school.
3 Ben … like animals.
4 Jenny … like towns.
5 Debbie and Nick … know what a snark is.
6 Sita … know what a BLT is.

12 ▶ Elephants don't use the phone!

Ten things are wrong here. Can you say what they are?

Elephants don't usually use the phone. A giraffe doesn't usually ...

13 ▶ Does Sita eat meat?

Ask questions and complete the answers. Work with a partner.

1 Sita / eat / meat? – No, she ... . She's a vegetarian.
Does Sita eat meat? – No, she *doesn't.* She's a vegetarian.
2 on Saturdays / go to judo class / Grandma Scott? – Yes, she ... . She's very good, too.
3 Trundle / in Jenny's room / sleep? – No, ... He's got a very nice cage in the garden.
4 take / Mr and Mrs Scott / Ben to school? – Yes, ... Then they go to work.
5 the country / Ben / like? – No, ... He thinks it's boring.
6 the twins / to Blacon High School / go? – No, ... They go to Kingsway High School.
7 Miss Hunt / ride / her bike to school? – Yes, ... She rides it at weekends, too.
8 Mr Martin / Miss Hunt / like? – Yes, ... And she likes him, too.

❖ 14 ▶ Be an animal

What animal are you? Can the pupils in your form guess? They can ask 20 'yes/no' questions.

WORD WATCH

◆◆ 15 ▶ Breakfast, lunch, dinner

Look at the picture. Tell your partner: what do you like for breakfast? For lunch? For dinner? What don't you like?

For breakfast I like … . I don't like … .
For lunch I like … .

16 ▶ Town and country

a *Make one list for 'town' and one for 'country'. Some words can be in both lists.*

◆◆ **b** *Talk about your lists with your partner. Are there differences?*

school, cars, police, climb, play, shopping, restaurant, dirty, trees, supermarket, grey, swimming-pool, blue, bright, green, farm, computer shops, quiet, great, boutique, friends, fashion, money, tree house, time, garden, stupid, animals

17 ▶ At, in, on

Find words for these prepositions.

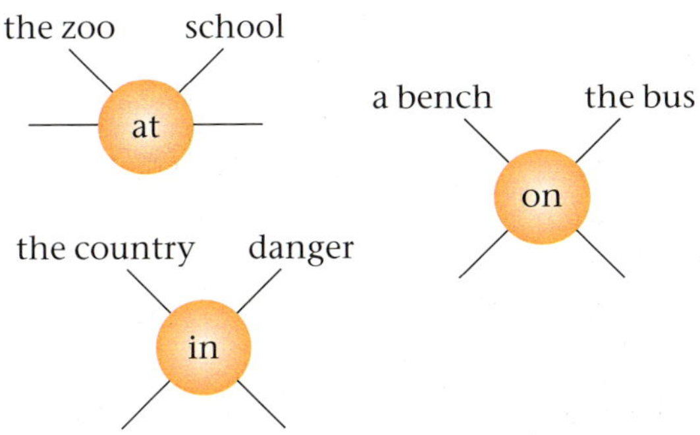

Have you got lots of words?

	Words
1–8	You must learn more words!
9–16	Good. Your English vocabulary is OK.
17+	Great! You must really like English.

7 T The end-of-term party

Look at the children and their costumes. Who's the black cat? The tiger? The tortoise? The monkey? And the rabbit? Who has got the best costume?

It's Friday night at Kingsway High School – a very special Friday night. It's the end-of-term party. Tickets are £1.50. The money is for the animals at the zoo. It's a fancy-dress party, so all the kids are wearing costumes – animal costumes. And there's a prize for the best costume.

The music is playing. Some kids are dancing, some kids are eating and drinking and talking.

SANJAY Hi! You've got a great costume!
SALLY Thank you, Sanjay.
SANJAY Oh, so you know me. But I don't know you.
SALLY Then guess! Who am I?
SANJAY Are you Rebecca Williams?
SALLY No, I'm not! Rebecca is only 11!
SANJAY Ooops, sorry! I know – you're Sally Snow, right?
SALLY Miaow.
SANJAY Let's dance.

NICK Look, Debbie. There's Sanjay. He's dancing with Sally. They look great together.

DEBBIE Thank you, Nick. Why don't you go away – go and annoy Mr Martin.

NICK Good idea.

NICK Hello, Mr Martin.

MR MARTIN Hello, Nick.

NICK Listen, they're playing a slow song ... and Miss Hunt isn't dancing, Mr Martin.

MR MARTIN Well, Nick, why don't you go and ask her? Christine ...

Ben is standing around all alone. Sita is alone, too.

SITA Hi, Ben.

BEN Hello. Er ... who are you?

SITA It's me – Sita.

BEN Oh, Sita! Hello.

SITA What do you think of Nick's costume? Isn't it great?

BEN Yes, it is, but what animal is he?

SITA I don't know!

It's five minutes to nine. The disco must finish at nine o'clock. In front of the school, lots of parents are waiting for their children.

Now Mr Martin is at the microphone. It's time for the prize for the best costume. 'We all think Nick Baker is wearing the best costume,' he says.

All the kids in 7CH cheer.

'Very good, Nick,' Mr Martin says. 'But tell us, please, what animal are you?'

'I'm your favourite animal, Mr Martin. I'm a snark!'

WORKING WITH THE TEXT

1 ▶ Answer the questions

1. What's happening at Kingsway High School tonight?
2. Why are all the kids wearing costumes?
3. What are the children doing?
4. What does Sita think of Nick's costume?
5. Why's Mr Martin at the microphone at five minutes to nine?
6. Who's wearing the best costume?

2 ▶ For the school magazine

These four pictures are for the Kingsway High School magazine. Write about them.

TOPIC 7 Merlin's return[1] A play for the classroom

STORYTELLER This is a play about four children – Rachel, Nazma, Mike and Joe – and about an old, old wizard[2]. Here are the children now. They're playing the game 'What's the time, Mr Wolf?' Mike is Mr Wolf.

CHILDREN What's the time, Mr Wolf?

MIKE It's four o'clock. *(The children take four steps forward[3].)*

CHILDREN What's the time, Mr Wolf?

MIKE It's two o'clock. *(They take two steps forward.)*

CHILDREN What's the time, Mr Wolf?

MIKE It's dinner time! *(Mike turns to catch[4] the other children. He catches Nazma.)* Now you're Mr Wolf, Nazma.

STORYTELLER But then the children hear a funny noise[5].

MERLIN Aaaagh!

RACHEL What's that?

JOE I don't know.

NAZMA It's coming from behind that bench[6]. Let's go and look.

MIKE Be careful!

STORYTELLER There's an old man here behind the bench. He's wearing very funny clothes – a long, long coat[7] and a big pointed hat[8].

MERLIN Aaaaagh!

JOE Hello! Who are you?

RACHEL Are you all right[9]?

NAZMA Can we help you?

MERLIN My name is Merlin. I'm not all right – you can see that! And yes, of course you can help me. I can't get up, I'm hungry[10] and … I think I'm in the wrong time.

JOE The wrong time? What are you talking about?

MERLIN Is this the year 500?

MIKE No, it isn't. It's 1998.

MERLIN You see! I'm in the wrong time! Now, help me up, please.

STORYTELLER The children help Merlin.

RACHEL Here, Mr Merlin, sit on this bench.

MERLIN Not *Mr* Merlin, just Merlin, please. Thank you my dear.

MIKE What about a biscuit[11] … or a piece of cake … Merlin?

MERLIN Oh, very nice! A piece of cake please and ... what are these?

MIKE They're chocolate biscuits.

MERLIN Chocolate biscuits? Mmmm. Very good!

STORYTELLER Merlin eats *three* pieces of cake and *four* chocolate biscuits.

MERLIN Mmm, very, very good. Now, tell me about your time. What do you do?

RACHEL We go to school.

[1] return [rɪ'tɜːn] *Wiederkehr* [2] wizard ['wɪzəd] *Zauberer* [3] (to) take a step forward [step], ['fɔːwəd] *einen Schritt vorwärts machen* [4] (to) turn to catch [tɜːn], [kætʃ] *sich umdrehen um zu fangen* [5] noise [nɔɪz] *Geräusch* [6] bench [bentʃ] *Bank* [7] coat [kəʊt] *Mantel* [8] pointed hat [ˌpɔɪntɪd 'hæt] *spitzer Hut* [9] Are you all right? [ɔːl 'raɪt] *Geht es Ihnen gut?* [10] hungry ['hʌŋgri] *hungrig* [11] biscuit ['bɪskɪt] *Keks*

MERLIN School? Is that where you learn things in 1998?

RACHEL Yes, of course it is.

MERLIN Of course? What do you mean[1] 'of course'? In my time there are no[2] schools.

JOE Great! Can we come with you?

MERLIN And what do you do when you aren't at school?

NAZMA We play computer games ...

JOE Or ride our bikes ...

RACHEL Or go to the swimming-pool ...

MIKE Or watch TV ...

MERLIN Stop! Stop! Computer games? Bikes? Swimming-pool? TV? What are you talking about?

NAZMA Haven't you got computers and bikes and swimming-pools and TVs in your time?

MERLIN No, we haven't! What are they?

NAZMA Well, a computer game ... you play a computer game with a computer.

MERLIN And who is A. Computer?

(The children laugh.)

NAZMA A computer isn't a person ...

MERLIN Hrmph! In my time children play games with children! And a bike?

JOE A bike has got two wheels[3] and you can ride it. Look.

(He acts riding a bike.)

RACHEL And a swimming-pool ... you can swim in a swimming-pool.

(She acts swimming.)

MIKE And a TV shows films. You can sit and watch it.

(He acts watching TV.)

MERLIN Well, well, well. And have you all got a bike and a swimming-pool and a TV?

NAZMA No. They cost[4] a lot of money ...

MERLIN Money? Ah, you mean gold?

JOE Gold? No, pounds and pence.

MERLIN Pounds and pence? Mmm. And where do these pounds and pence come from?

JOE From our parents.

MERLIN And where do they get[5] this 'money'?

MIKE They work for it.

MERLIN And what work do your parents do?

MIKE My dad works in a factory[6] – every day from 6 o'clock in the morning to 3.30 in the afternoon. And my mum works in a supermarket every morning.

MERLIN And do they like their work?

MIKE No, they don't .

MERLIN 1998 you say? Dear, oh dear![7] What a very funny time! Schools, money, work ... I like 500 better[8]! You must come and visit[9] me! Goodbye.

STORYTELLER And with a 'whoosh', Merlin disappears[10].

RACHEL Merlin! Merlin? Oh!

MIKE Well, let's go and visit him.

RACHEL Of course, Mike. No problem! 'Four tickets to the year 500, please.' Oh ...!

(The four children disappear.)

MIKE'S MUM Tea's ready[11], kids! Mike! Mike! Where are you all?

[1] (to) mean [mi:n] *meinen* [2] no *kein, keine* [3] wheel [wi:l] *Rad* [4] (to) cost [kɒst] *kosten* [5] (to) get [get] *bekommen* [6] factory ['fæktəri] *Fabrik* [7] Dear, oh dear! ['dɪər‿əʊ dɪə] *Ach je!, Du liebe Zeit!* [8] (to) like sth. better *etwas lieber mögen* [9] (to) visit ['vɪzɪt] *besuchen* [10] (to) disappear [ˌdɪsə'pɪə] *verschwinden* [11] ready ['redi] *fertig*

○ TOPIC Merry Christmas[1]*

15th December

Dear Santa Claus, 7
Please put a cat book and a box for cassettes in my stocking. And a game, please.
There's tea for you on my chair.
Thank you.
Love, 8
Pam

This is Santa Claus[2].

It's late on 24th December. He's going to all the houses and flats and putting presents[3] in the children's stockings[4].

A lot of children write to[5] Santa at Christmas. Here's one letter from[6] a little girl in London.

▶▶▶ NOW YOU

Write a letter to Santa Claus.

It's 25th December, Christmas Day[9]. It's 2 o'clock in the afternoon – time for Christmas dinner.

ACTIVITY

In Great Britain people write a lot of Christmas cards. Make a Christmas card. Draw and colour[13] the front[14]. Write 'Merry Christmas and a happy New Year' in the card.

[1] Merry Christmas [ˌmeri ˈkrɪsməs] *Frohe Weihnachten* [2] Santa Claus [ˈsæntə klɔːz] *der Weihnachtsmann* [3] present [ˈpreznt] *Geschenk* [4] stocking [ˈstɒkɪŋ] *Strumpf* [5] (they) write to *(sie) schreiben an* [6] a letter from *ein Brief von* [7] Dear ..., [dɪə] *Liebe/r ..., (Briefanrede)* [8] Love, ... [lʌv] *Alles Liebe ... (am Briefende)* [9] Christmas Day [ˌkrɪsməs ˈdeɪ] *der erste Weihnachtsfeiertag* [10] Christmas pudding [ˌkrɪsməs ˈpʊdɪŋ] *Plumpudding* [11] turkey [ˈtɜːki] *Truthahn, Puter* [12] cracker [ˈkrækə] *Knallbonbon* [13] (to) colour *bemalen* [14] front [frʌnt] *Vorderseite*

* *Merry Christmas* ist nach Topic 3 einsetzbar.

CHRISTMAS CAROL[1] We wish[2] you a merry Christmas

ACTIVITY

Make a Christmas cracker with:

1 In every[3] cracker there's a hat[4].

2 In every cracker there's a small present.

3 In every cracker there's a riddle[5].

Q: What's a tortoise after[6] he's five?
A: Six.

Q: What's big and black and eats[7] beds?
A: A big, black bed-eater[8].

4 Now cut out[9].

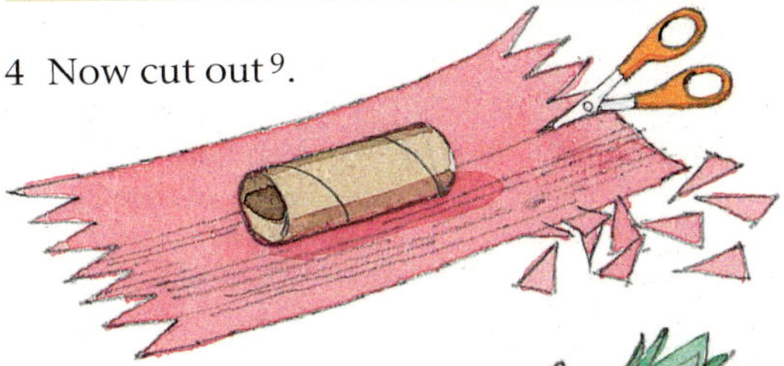

5 Put the hat, the riddle and the present in the middle[10].

6 Roll up[11] and tie[12].

[1] Christmas carol [ˌkrɪsməs ˈkærəl] *Weihnachtslied* [2] we wish [wɪʃ] *wir wünschen* [3] every [ˈevri] *jede(r, s)* [4] hat [hæt] *Hut* [5] riddle [ˈrɪdl] *Rätsel*
[6] after [ˈɑːftə] *nachdem* [7] (it) eats [iːts] *(es) isst* [8] bed-eater [ˈbedˌiːtə] *Betten(fr)esser/in* [9] (to) cut out [kʌt] *ausschneiden* [10] middle [ˈmɪdl] *Mitte*
[11] (to) roll up [ˌrəʊl‿ˈʌp] *aufrollen* [12] (to) tie [taɪ] *zusammenbinden*

LANGUAGE SUMMARY

So wie jedes Spiel bestimmten Spielregeln folgt, so hat auch jede Sprache bestimmte Regeln. Diese Regeln nennt man *Grammatik*. Bei einem Spiel sind zwar die Regeln nicht das Wichtigste, aber das Spiel funktioniert nur richtig, wenn man die Regeln kennt. Das ist bei Sprachen nicht anders.

Auf den folgenden *LANGUAGE SUMMARY*-Seiten findest du die „Spielregeln" der englischen Sprache. Hier kannst du nachschlagen,

- wenn du Hausaufgaben machst,
- wenn du etwas vergessen hast,
- wenn du etwas wiederholen willst,
- wenn du dich auf einen Test oder eine Klassenarbeit vorbereitest,
- wenn du selbstständig etwas lernen musst, weil du in der Schule gefehlt hast.

Wie finde ich mich im *LANGUAGE SUMMARY* zurecht?

Die *LANGUAGE SUMMARY*-Abschnitte fassen zusammen, was du in den sieben Units – den Kapiteln deines Englischbuchs – über die englische Sprache gelernt hast. Die kleinen Hinweise in den Units sagen dir, welcher Abschnitt des *LANGUAGE SUMMARY* zu welchem Unit-Teil gehört.
Ein Beispiel:
In Unit 1 auf Seite 15 unten findest du den Hinweis → **S1: 2a, b (p. 127)**. Das heißt, zu Seite 15 gehören die *LANGUAGE SUMMARY*-Abschnitte Unit 1: 2a und 2b auf Seite 127.

Wie ist das *LANGUAGE SUMMARY* aufgebaut?

Links stehen immer die Regeln sowie nützliche Hinweise, Merkkästen und Lerntipps – auf Deutsch.

Rechts stehen Beispiele und Übersichten.

Alexander und Dilek und die Zirkusartisten helfen dir, alles besser zu behalten.

Die Warndreiecke (⚠) weisen dich auf Fehlerquellen und auf unbedingt zu beachtende Regeln hin – ähnlich wie Achtungsschilder im Straßenverkehr.

Der Hinweis → **P 1, 2, 3 (p. 18)** bedeutet, dass zu diesem Abschnitt die Übungen 1, 2 und 3 von Seite 18 gehören. (Das *P* kommt von *Practice*, und das heißt *Übung*.)

Zum Abschluss einer jeden Unit gibt es dann noch eine Übersicht über all das, was du nun schon auf Englisch ausdrücken kannst („In dieser Unit hast du gelernt ...").

Was ist, wenn ich etwas nicht verstehe?

Am besten ist es natürlich, du fragst deine Lehrerin oder deinen Lehrer. Aber vielleicht liegt es ja nur daran, dass du einen bestimmten Ausdruck nicht verstanden hast? Dann kannst du dir selbst helfen: Schlag auf der nächsten Seite in der Liste der **grammatischen Fachbegriffe** *(Grammatical terms)* nach.

GRAMMATICAL TERMS (Grammatische Fachbegriffe)

Summary-Abschnitt			
	adjective ['ædʒɪktɪv]	Adjektiv (Eigenschaftswort)	*good, new, red, funny, boring*
	adverb ['ædvɜ:b]	Adverb (Umstandswort)	*always, here, really, today*
U5/2	**adverb of frequency** ['fri:kwənsi]	Häufigkeitsadverb	*always, usually, often, sometimes, never*
U2/3	**article** ['ɑ:tɪkl]	Artikel (Begleiter)	*the, a/an*
	auxiliary [ɔ:g'zɪliəri]	Hilfsverb	
U2/3	**definite article** [ˌdefɪnət_'ɑ:tɪkl]	bestimmter Artikel	*the*
U3/2	**imperative** [ɪm'perətɪv]	Imperativ (Befehlsform)	***Open** your books. **Don't move.***
U2/3	**indefinite article** [ɪnˌdefɪnət_'ɑ:tɪkl]	unbestimmter Artikel	*a/an*
U3/1	**infinitive** [ɪn'fɪnətɪv]	Infinitiv (Grundform)	*(to) open, (to) see, (to) hear*
U4/2b	**irregular plural** [ɪˌregjələ 'plʊərəl]	unregelmäßiger Plural	*man – **men**; woman – **women**; child – **children**; mouse – **mice***
U1/2b	**long form** ['lɒŋ fɔ:m]	Langform	*I am; we have got; what is*
U4/1	**modal auxiliary** [ˌməʊdl_ɔ:g'zɪliəri]	modales Hilfsverb, Modalverb	*can, may, must*
	negative statement [ˌnegətɪv 'steɪtmənt]	verneinter Aussagesatz	*I'm not eleven. I haven't got a brother.*
U1/1 + U4/2	**noun** [naʊn]	Nomen (Substantiv, Hauptwort, Namenwort)	*Nick, Debbie, girl, brother, town, name, time, problem*
	object ['ɒbdʒɪkt]	Objekt	*Sita is cleaning **the kitchen**. Sanjay is helping **her**.*
U1/1a + U1/2a + U4/3	**personal pronoun** [ˌpɜ:snəl 'prəʊnaʊn]	Personalpronomen (persönliches Fürwort)	*I, you, he, she, it, we, they, me, him, her, us, them*
	plural ['plʊərəl]	Plural (Mehrzahl)	
	positive statement [ˌpɒzətɪv 'steɪtmənt]	bejahter Aussagesatz	*I'm eleven. I've got a brother.*
U2/1	**possessive determiner** [pəˌzesɪv dɪ'tɜ:mɪnə]	Possessivbegleiter (besitzanzeigender Begleiter)	*my, your, his, her, its, our, their*
	preposition [ˌprepə'zɪʃn]	Präposition (Verhältniswort)	*after, at, in, next to, on, to, under*
U3/3 + U7/2 + U7/3	**present progressive** [ˌpreznt prə'gresɪv]	Verlaufsform der Gegenwart	*Debbie **is reading** a book. Nick **isn't reading**. He's **playing**.*
	pronoun ['prəʊnaʊn]	Pronomen (Fürwort)	
	question word ['kwestʃən wɜ:d]	Fragewort	*who?, what?, when?, where?, why?, how?*
U2/4	**s-genitive** ['es ˌdʒenətɪv]	*s*-Genitiv	*Debbie**'s** brother; my teacher**'s** name*
	short answer [ʃɔ:t_'ɑ:nsə]	Kurzantwort	*Are you eleven? – **Yes, I am.** Have you got a pet? – **No, I haven't.***
U1/2b	**short form** ['ʃɔ:t fɔ:m]	Kurzform	*I'm; we've got; what's*
U5/1 + U6/2 + U7/2	**simple present** [ˌsɪmpl 'preznt]	einfache Form der Gegenwart	*I **start** school at 8.45 every day. Trundle **doesn't go** to school. **Do** you **like** school?*
	singular ['sɪŋgjələ]	Singular (Einzahl)	
	subject ['sʌbdʒɪkt]	Subjekt	***I**'m from Chester. Where are **you** from?*
U7/1a	**subordinate clause** [səˌbɔ:dɪnət 'klɔ:z]	Nebensatz	*Debbie likes zoos **because she likes animals**.*
	verb [vɜ:b]	Verb (Tätigkeitswort, Zeitwort)	*count, hear, open, rain, see*
U7/1	**word order** ['wɜ:d_ɔ:də]	Wortstellung	
	yes/no question	Entscheidungsfrage	*Are you eleven? Have you got a sister?*

Unit 1

1 Nomen

a Nomen und Personalpronomen

Wörter wie *Mädchen, Bruder, Lineal, Liebe* sind Nomen (Substantive). Mit Nomen werden Lebewesen, Dinge, Gefühle usw. benannt.
Nomen werden im Englischen immer klein geschrieben, nur Eigennamen (z.B. *Nick, Chester, Form 7CH*) werden groß geschrieben.

Nouns

Nouns and personal pronouns

Nick	Debbie	(the) biro (der) Kugelschreiber
		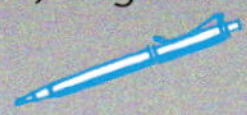
(the) brother (der) Bruder	(the) sister (die) Schwester	(the) cassette (die) Cassette 
(the) boy (der) Junge	(the) girl (das) Mädchen	(the) ruler (das) Lineal 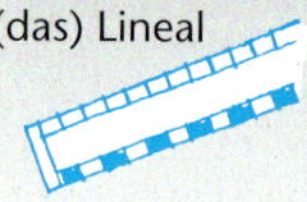

Wörter wie *ich, du, er, sie, es* usw. sind Personalpronomen. Sie werden auch **Für**wörter genannt, weil sie stellvertretend **für** Nomen stehen.
Die englischen Personalpronomen *he* und *she* stehen nur für Personen und Haustiere:

- männlich – *he (er)*
- weiblich – *she (sie).*

Das Pronomen *it* steht für alle anderen Lebewesen und für alle Dinge, Gefühle usw.

he	she	it
This is **Nick**. He's eleven.	This is **Debbie**. She's eleven, too.	This is my **biro**. It's blue. This is my **cassette**. It's in English. This is my **ruler**. It's blue.

→ P 1, 2, 3 (p. 18)

b Der Plural der Nomen

Der Plural (die Mehrzahl) wird gebildet, indem man ein *-s* an den Singular (die Einzahl) des Nomens anhängt:
Singular + -s = Plural

Bei der Aussprache der Pluralendung muss man aufpassen. Sie richtet sich nach dem letzten Laut des Singulars:

- [-s] nach stimmlosen (harten) Konsonanten, z.B. [-p, -t, -k].
- [-z] nach stimmhaften (weichen) Konsonanten, z.B. [-b, -d, -g, -l -n], und nach allen Vokalen.

Versuche, das „g" in „bag" stimmhaft auszusprechen (also wie das „g" in „girl"). Nach „g" und anderen stimmhaften Lauten wird das Plural-s wie der Summlaut der Biene gesprochen.

The plural of nouns

a felt-tip	[-p]	**Stimmlose Konsonanten**	two felt-tips	[-ps]
a cassette	[-t]		two cassettes	[-ts]
a book	[-k]		two books	[-ks]
a board	[-d]	**Stimmhafte Konsonanten, Vokale**	two boards	[-dz]
a bag	[-g]		two bags	[-gz]
a girl	[-l]		two girls	[-lz]
a boy	[-ɔɪ]		two boys	[-ɔɪz]

→ P 6 (p. 19)

2 Die Personalpronomen und das Verb *be*

a Bejahte Aussagesätze

Das Verb *be* entspricht dem deutschen Verb *sein*. Die Formen des Verbs *be* sind *am, are* und *is*.

Das englische *you are* entspricht dem deutschen *du bist, ihr seid, Sie sind*.

Personal pronouns and the verb *be*

Positive statements

Langformen		Kurzformen		
I **am**		I'**m**		ich bin
You **are**		You'**re**		du bist/Sie sind
He **is**		He'**s**		er ist
She **is**		She'**s**		sie ist
It **is**		It'**s**		er/sie/es ist
	eleven.		eleven.	
We **are**		We'**re**		wir sind
You **are**		You'**re**		ihr seid/Sie sind
They **are**		They'**re**		sie sind

b Kurz- und Langformen

Die Formen *am/are/is* werden meistens verkürzt, besonders beim Sprechen.
Bei den Kurzformen wird ein Buchstabe ausgelassen. Dafür bleibt ein Auslassungszeichen stehen, das Apostroph genannt wird (').

Du kannst dir neue Formen besser merken, wenn du sie aufschreibst und beim Lernen ständig vor Augen hast. Mach ein Poster oder ein Mobile mit den Formen. Hänge es in der Schule oder an deinem Arbeitsplatz zu Hause auf, bis du die Formen kannst.

Short and long forms

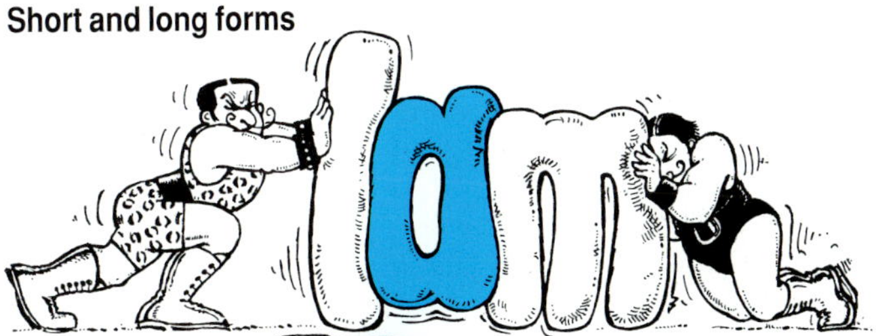

→ P 4, 5 (p. 19)

c Verneinte Aussagesätze

Wenn man Aussagen mit *am/are/is* verneinen möchte, fügt man das Wort *not* nach *am/are/is* in den Satz ein.

Negative statements

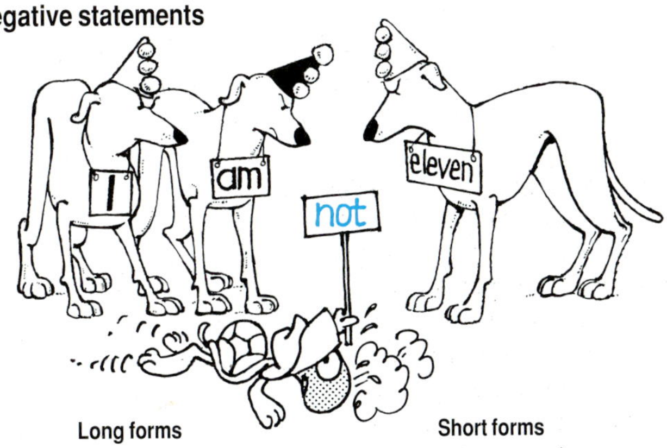

Auch bei der Verneinung gibt es Kurzformen.
Dabei fällt das *o* von *not* weg. Dafür steht ein Apostroph.

⚠ **Ausnahme:**
I am not → *I'm not*

Long forms		Short forms	
I **am not**		I'**m not**	
You **are not**		You **aren't**	
He/She/It **is not**		He/She/It **isn't**	
	eleven.		eleven.
We **are not**		We **aren't**	
You **are not**		You **aren't**	
They **are not**		They **aren't**	

→ P 7, 8 (p. 20)

d Entscheidungsfragen und Kurzantworten

Eine Frage, auf die die Antwort „Ja" oder „Nein" erwartet wird, nennt man Entscheidungsfrage.
In Entscheidungsfragen sind – wie im Deutschen – Subjekt *(subject)* und Verb *(verb)* einfach vertauscht:

Du bist elf.
Bist **du** elf?

Yes/No questions and short answers

Subject	Verb	
You	are	eleven.

Verb	Subject	
Are	you	eleven?

Auf Entscheidungsfragen antwortet man im Englischen meistens mit einer so genannten Kurzantwort, nicht nur mit „Yes" oder „No".

⚠ Bei den „Ja"-Antworten werden niemals Kurzformen verwendet.
Also **nicht**: ~~*Yes, I'm.*~~
sondern: *Yes, I am.*

Yes/No questions	Short answers
Am **I** clever?	Yes, **you** are.
	No, **you** aren't.
Are **you** from Berlin?	Yes, **I** am.
	No, **I'm** not.
Is **he/she/it** nice?	Yes, **he/she/it** is.
	No, **he/she/it** isn't.
Are **we** friends now?	Yes, **we** are.
	No, **we** aren't.
Are **you** in Form 7CH?	Yes, **we** are.
	No, **we** aren't.
Are **Susan and Paul** from Chester?	Yes, **they** are.
	No, **they** aren't.

→ P 9, 10 (p. 20/21)

e Fragen mit Fragewörtern

Auch in Fragen mit Fragewörtern sind Subjekt und Verb vertauscht (vgl. oben). Das Fragewort steht wie im Deutschen am Anfang.

In Verbindung mit den Fragewörtern wird *is* häufig verkürzt, z.B.:
What is → *What's*
Where is → *Where's*
How is → *How's*

Questions with question words

Question word	Verb	Subject	
Where	are	**you** from?	– **I'm** from Chester.
What	is	**your name?**	– **My name** is Debbie.
How	are	**you?**	– **I'm** fine.

In dieser Unit hast du gelernt …

– dich und andere vorzustellen.	▶ I'm Anke Schmidt. I'm eleven. I'm from Rostock. I'm German. And this is my friend Nicole.
– zu sagen, wie es dir geht, und andere zu fragen, wie es ihnen geht.	▶ I'm fine. How are you?
– Informationen über andere einzuholen.	▶ What's your name? How old are you? Where are you from?
– Gegenstände zu beschreiben.	▶ My pencil-case is green. What colour is your pencil-case?
– zu sagen, wie du etwas oder jemanden findest.	▶ My new school is great. My teacher is nice.

Unit 2

1 Die Possessivbegleiter

Wörter wie *mein, dein, euer* nennt man Possessivbegleiter (besitzanzeigende Begleiter).

⚠ **Vorsicht – Verwechslungsgefahr:**

your [jɔː] dein, euer, Ihr	**you're** [jʊə, jɔː] (*you are*) du bist, ihr seid, Sie sind
his [hɪz] sein	**he's** [hiːz] (*he is*) er ist
its [ɪts] sein, ihr	**it's** [ɪts] (*it is*) er/sie/es ist
their [ðeə] ihr *(pl)*	**they're** [ðeə] (*they are*) sie sind

Possessive determiners

I'm Debbie. This is	**my** brother Nick. mein
You're a good friend.	**Your** brother is my friend, too. dein/Ihr
He's eleven.	**His** sister is eleven, too. seine
She's a teacher. I'm in	**her** form. ihrer
It's a rabbit. Here's	**its** cage. sein
We're from Chester.	**Our** mum is from Chester, too. unsere
You're my friends. And	**your** friends are my friends. eure/Ihre
They're twins.	**Their** dog is my friend, too. ihr

→ P 1, 2 (p. 32)

2 Das Verb *have got*

a Bejahte Aussagesätze

Das Verb *have got* entspricht dem deutschen Verb *haben*.

Außer bei der dritten Person Singular (***has** got*) steht bei allen Personen die Form *have got*.

The verb *have got*
Positive statements

Long forms		Short forms
I **have** got		I've got
You **have** got		You've got
He **has** got		He's got*
She **has** got	a nice garden.	She 's got*
It **has** got		It's got*
We **have** got		We've got
You **have** got		You've got
They **have** got		They've got

Ich habe einen schönen Garten.
Du hast einen … usw.

→ P 3, 4 (p. 32/33)

* Die Kurzformen *he's got, she's got* und *it's got* werden in diesem Buch nicht verwendet, weil man sie leicht mit den Kurzformen *he's* (von *he is*), *she's* (von *she is*) und *it's* (von *it is*) verwechseln kann.

b **Verneinte Aussagesätze**

Wenn man Aussagen mit *have/has got* verneinen möchte, fügt man das Wort *not* zwischen *have/has* und *got* ein.

Jeder lernt anders. Probier mal verschiedene Wege aus, bis du einen entdeckst, mit dem du gute Lernerfolge hast. Frag ruhig auch mal deine Mitschülerinnen und Mitschüler. Wie lernen sie? Könnte ihr Weg auch für dich gut sein?

Negative statements

Long forms		Short forms
I **have not got**		I **haven't got**
You **have not got**		You **haven't got**
He **has not got**		He **hasn't got**
She **has not got**	a nice garden.	She **hasn't got**
It **has not got**		It **hasn't got**
We **have not got**		We **haven't got**
You **have not got**		You **haven't got**
They **have not got**		They **haven't got**

Ich habe keinen (*wörtlich:* nicht einen) schönen Garten.
Du hast keinen ... usw.

→ P 5 (p. 33)

c **Entscheidungsfragen und Kurzantworten**

In Entscheidungsfragen sind Subjekt und *have/has* vertauscht.

Yes/No questions and short answers

You have **got** a garden.

Have **you** **got** a garden? Hast du einen Garten?

Wie bei *be* (vgl. S. 128) antwortet man auch auf Entscheidungsfragen mit *have/has got* mit einer Kurzantwort. Dabei entfällt das *got*.

Auch hier gilt: bei den „Ja"-Antworten keine Kurzformen.
Also **nicht**: *Yes, ~~I've~~.*
sondern: *Yes, I have.*

Have **I got** a nice name?	Yes, **you** have. No, **you** haven't.
Have **you got** a dog?	Yes, **I** have. No, **I** haven't.
Has **he/she/it got** a garden?	Yes, **he/she/it** has. No, **he/she/it** hasn't.
Have **we got** time?	Yes, **you** have. No, **you** haven't.
Have **you got** your books?	Yes, **we** have. No, **we** haven't.
Have **your friends got** a pet?	Yes, **they** have. No, **they** haven't.

→ P 7, 8 (p. 34)

d Fragen mit Fragewörtern

Auch in Fragen mit Fragewörtern sind Subjekt und *have/has* vertauscht. Das Fragewort steht wie im Deutschen am Anfang.

Questions with question words

Question word	*have* / *has*	Subject	
What	**have**	**you got** in your bag?	– **I've got** a ruler in my bag.
Where	**has**	**Trundle got** his cage?	– **Trundle has got** his cage in the garden.

3 Der bestimmte und unbestimmte Artikel

Der **bestimmte Artikel** (deutsch: *der/die/das*) heißt im Englischen immer *the* und wird [ðə] oder [ði] gesprochen:

- [ðə], wenn das folgende Wort am Anfang mit einem Konsonanten (Mitlaut) gesprochen wird.
- [ði], wenn das folgende Wort am Anfang mit einem Vokal (Selbstlaut) gesprochen wird.

Der **unbestimmte Artikel** (deutsch: *ein/eine*) heißt im Englischen *a* oder *an*:

- *a*, wenn das folgende Wort am Anfang mit einem Konsonanten gesprochen wird.
- *an*, wenn das folgende Wort am Anfang mit einem Vokal gesprochen wird.

⚠ Es kommt auf die **Aussprache** des folgenden Wortes an, nicht auf die Schreibung:
Das *u* von *uncle* wird [ʌ] gesprochen, also als Vokal.
Das *u* von *unit* wird [ju:] gesprochen, also mit Konsonant am Anfang.

The definite and indefinite article

The definite article

[ðə]	**the** boy der Junge **the** school die Schule **the** girl das Mädchen	[ði]	**the** aunt **the** English girl **the** Indian boy **the** old school **the** uncle

The indefinite article

a	**a** boy ein Junge **a** school eine Schule **a** girl ein Mädchen	an	**an** aunt **an** English girl **an** Indian boy **an** old school **an** uncle

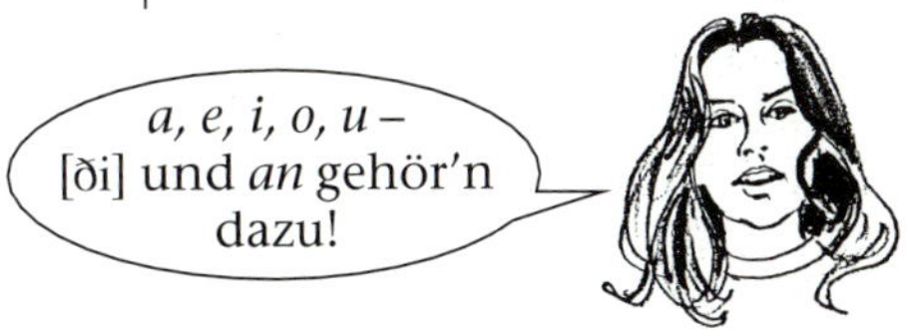

⚠ **the** uncle	[ði_'ʌŋkl]	aber:	**the** unit	[ðə 'ju:nɪt]
an uncle	[ən_'ʌŋkl]	aber:	**a** unit	[ə 'ju:nɪt]

→ P 9, 10 (p. 34)

4 Der *s*-Genitiv

Anders als im Deutschen wird das Genitiv-*s* im Englischen mit einem Apostroph angehängt. Vergleiche:
Englisch: *Ronny's brother*
Deutsch: Ronnys Bruder

Die Aussprache des Genitiv-*s* folgt den gleichen Regeln wie die Aussprache des Plural-*s* (vgl. S. 126).

The *s*-genitive

Debbie is eleven. **Debbie's** brother Nick is eleven, too.
Who is your **teacher**, Debbie?
– My **teacher's** name is Miss Hunt.

Debbie's friend	['debiz]
her mum's friend	[mʌmz]
Nick's friend	[nɪks]

Beim Plural auf *-s* wird nur ein Apostroph angehängt.
Beim Plural ohne *-s* wird der Genitiv gebildet wie beim Singular.

The girls' room is very nice. — Das Zimmer der Mädchen …
The Bakers' house is in Chester. — Das Haus der Bakers …
aber: the children's books — die Bücher der Kinder

Bei zwei Personen wird nur einmal *-'s* angehängt.

Jenny and Sally's mother is a nurse.
Jennys und Sallys Mutter …

→ P 11 (p. 34)

In dieser Unit hast du gelernt …

– über das zu sprechen, was jemandem oder zu jemandem gehört.

▶ Here's my school bag. It's blue. I've got a blue pencil-case, too.
My brother's name is Klaus.
My friends' house hasn't got a garden.

Unit 3

1 Der Infinitiv

Der Infinitiv (die Grundform) eines Verbs endet im Deutschen immer auf *-en* oder *-n: kommen, helfen, sein, … .*
Im Englischen hat der Infinitiv keine Endung.

The infinitive

come	help	clean
kommen	helfen	sauber machen

2 Der Imperativ

a Bejahte Imperative

Im Englischen hat der Imperativ (die Befehlsform) immer dieselbe Form wie der Infinitiv.
Nach Imperativsätzen steht meistens ein Punkt (kein Ausrufezeichen wie im Deutschen).
In Imperativsätzen wird fast immer *please* benutzt.

The imperative
Positive imperatives

Come here, please.
Komm/Kommt/Kommen Sie bitte her!
Help your sister, please.
Clean the bathroom, please.

→ P 1 (p. 46)

b Verneinte Imperative

Man bildet den verneinten Imperativ, indem man die Kurzform *don't* (von *do not* – wörtlich: *tu nicht*) vor den Infinitiv stellt.

Negative imperatives

Don't **come** now, please.
Komm/Kommt/Kommen Sie bitte nicht jetzt!
Don't **play** with Lulu, please.
Don't **clean** the living-room.

→ P 2 (p. 46)

3 Die Verlaufsform der Gegenwart

a Bejahte Aussagesätze

Mit dem *present progressive* (der Verlaufsform der Gegenwart) drückt man aus, dass jemand gerade etwas tut oder dass ein Vorgang noch im Gange ist (Englisch: *in progress*).
Das *present progressive* besteht aus einer Form von *be (am, are, is)* und der *-ing*-Form eines Verbs (z.B. *play* + *-ing* → *playing*).

I'm playing entspricht dem deutschen „Ich spiele (gerade)."
In manchen Gegenden sagt man auch „Ich bin am/beim Spielen."

The present progressive
Positive statements

Short forms		Long forms	
I'**m**	playing.	I **am**	playing.
You'**re**		You **are**	
He'**s**		He **is**	
She'**s**		She **is**	
It'**s**		It **is**	
We'**re**		We **are**	
You'**re**		You **are**	
They'**re**		They **are**	

Ich spiele gerade.
Du spielst/Sie spielen gerade.
Er spielt …

→ P 3 (p. 46)

b Besonderheiten der Schreibweise

Bei einigen Verben muss man auf die Schreibweise der *-ing*-Form achten:
- Endet der Infinitiv mit einem stummen *-e*, fällt das *-e* weg.
- Nach einem einzelnen, betonten Vokal wird ein einzelner Endkonsonant verdoppelt.

Ist a, e, i, o oder u
alleine und betont dazu
und wird das Verb mit „-ing" gekoppelt,
so wird der Konsonant verdoppelt.

Spelling problems

make **making**   come **coming**   write **writing**

swap **swapping**   sit **sitting**   run **running**

Aber:
clean **cleaning** (Vokallaut mit zwei Buchstaben geschrieben → keine Verdopplung)
open **opening** (Vokal unbetont → keine Verdopplung)

→ P 5 (p. 47)

c Verneinte Aussagesätze

Verneinte Aussagesätze im *present progressive* werden mit einer verneinten Form von *am/are/is* und der *-ing*-Form des Verbs gebildet.

Negative statements

Short forms		Long forms	
I'**m not**	playing.	I **am not**	playing.
You **aren't**		You **are not**	
He **isn't**		He **is not**	
She **isn't**		She **is not**	
It **isn't**		It **is not**	
We **aren't**		We **are not**	
You **aren't**		You **are not**	
They **aren't**		They **are not**	

→ P 4 (p. 46)

d **Entscheidungsfragen und Kurzantworten**

In Entscheidungsfragen sind Subjekt und *am/are/is* vertauscht.
Die Kurzantworten kennst du schon – sie sind genauso wie beim Verb *be* (vgl. S. 128).
Auch hier gilt: bei den „Ja"-Antworten keine Kurzformen.
Also **nicht:** *Yes, ~~I'm~~.*
sondern: *Yes, I am.*

Yes/No questions and short answers

You are wearing blue pullovers.
Are **you** wearing blue pullovers?

→ P 6 (p. 47)

e **Fragen mit Fragewörtern**

In Fragen mit Fragewörtern sind Subjekt und *am/are/is* vertauscht.
Das Fragewort steht wie im Deutschen am Anfang.

Questions with question words

What	am **I**	playing?
	are **you**	
	is **he**/is **she**/is **it**	
	are **we**	
	are **you**	
	are **they**	

→ P 7, 8, 9 (p. 47/48)

In dieser Unit hast du gelernt ...

- andere aufzufordern, etwas zu tun, oder anderen Befehle zu erteilen. ▶ Come and help me, please.
- andere aufzufordern, etwas zu unterlassen, oder anderen etwas zu verbieten. ▶ Don't open my school bag, please.
- zu sagen oder zu fragen, was jemand gerade tut. ▶ I'm cleaning my room. What are you doing?
- Vermutungen und Meinungen auszudrücken. ▶ I think this is the Scotts' house. I think 'C1B1' is a funny name.

Unit 4

1 **Die modalen Hilfsverben *can* und *must***

Can und *must* sind modale Hilfsverben. Sie lauten für alle Personen gleich.
Im Englischen steht der Infinitiv direkt hinter dem modalen Hilfsverb.

The modal auxiliaries *can* and *must*

Nick can **draw** the pictures for the invitation cards.
Nick kann die Bilder für die Einladungskarten **zeichnen**.
The children must **be** at school at 8.45.
Die Kinder müssen um 8.45 Uhr in der Schule **sein**.

⚠ Ben can **speak** a little German.
Ben kann ein bisschen Deutsch.

a *Can* (können, dürfen)

Mit *can* drückt man aus, dass jemand etwas tun kann (Fähigkeit) oder tun darf (Erlaubnis).

Can

Ben **can write** letters in German.
Jenny **can sing**.
| Fähigkeit („können")

Form 7CH **can go** now.
Can I **watch** TV, please?
| Erlaubnis („dürfen")

Die verneinte Form von *can* heißt für alle Personen *can't* (Langform: *cannot*).

Positive statements		Negative statements	
I / You / He/She/It / We / You / They	**can do** it.	I / You / He/She/It / We / You / They	**can't do** it.

In Fragen sind Subjekt und modales Hilfsverb vertauscht.

You **can** sing.
Can **you** sing?

Fragewörter stehen wie im Deutschen am Anfang.

What **can** we **play**?
Where **can** kids **go** in Chester?
How **can** you **read** this? It's in German!

b *Must* (müssen)

Mit *must* drückt man aus, dass jemand etwas tun muss.

Must

The children **must be** at school at 8.45.
I **must clean** the hamster's cage today.

Fragen mit *must* werden wie Fragen mit *can* gebildet.

Must we **go** now?
Must I **do** it today?
Must you **play** games in the classroom?

→ P 1, 2, 3 (p. 61)

2 Der Plural der Nomen (II)

The plural of nouns (II)

a Besonderheiten bei Aussprache und Schreibung

Problems of pronunciation and spelling

Du weißt bereits, dass der Plural normalerweise durch das Anfügen von *-s* gebildet wird. Du weißt auch schon, dass sich die Aussprache der Pluralendung nach dem letzten Laut des Singulars richtet (vgl. S. 126):

- *book* + *-s* → *books* [-s]
- *bag* + *-s* → *bags* [-z]

Es gibt aber auch einige Besonderheiten bei Aussprache und Schreibung.

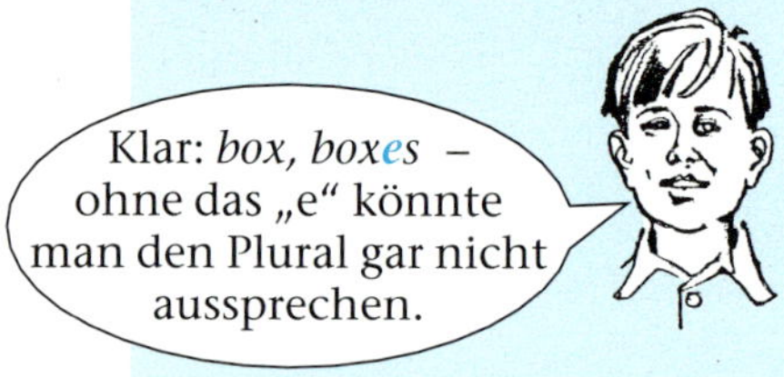

- Nach Zischlauten [-s, -z, -ʃ, -tʃ, -dʒ] wird *-es* angehängt (bzw. *-s*, falls der Singular auf ein stummes *-e* endet). Die Aussprache ist [-ɪz]:

box	[-s]	→	boxes	[-sɪz]
sandwich	[-dʒ]	→	sandwiches	[-dʒɪz]
watch	[-tʃ]	→	watches	[-tʃɪz]
cage	[-dʒ]	→	cages	[-dʒɪz]
nurse	[-s]	→	nurses	[-sɪz]
house	[-s]	→	⚠ houses	[-zɪz]

- *-y* nach Konsonanten wird zu *-ies*:

activity	→	activities	hobby	→	hobbies
city	→	cities	story	→	stories
family	→	families			

aber *-y* nach Vokal bleibt: boy → boys

- Nomen auf *-f* oder *-fe* bilden den Plural meist auf *-ves*:

bookshelf	[-f]	→	bookshelves	[-vz]
scarf		→	scarves	
wife		→	wives	

→ P 4 (p. 62)

b Unregelmäßige Pluralformen

Irregular plurals

Es gibt im Englischen einige wenige unregelmäßige Pluralformen. Die wichtigsten kennst du bereits.

man [mæn]	→	men [men]	mouse	→	mice
woman ['wʊmən]	→	women ['wɪmɪn]	(gold)fish	→	(gold)fish
child [tʃaɪld]	→	children ['tʃɪldrən]			

→ P 5 (p. 62)

3 Personalpronomen, Objektform

Personal pronouns, object form

Personalpronomen können Subjekt (z.B. *we*) oder Objekt (z.B. *us*) eines Satzes sein.
Beachte, dass auch nach Präpositionen die Objektform steht.

I don't know. Please tell **me**.
You're a good friend. So I can tell **you**.
Dave? **He** isn't here. I can't tell **him**.
Sandy? **She** isn't here. I can't tell **her**.
It's a big problem. Please help me with **it**.
We're building a treehouse. You can help **us**!
Are **you** two behind the tree? I can hear **you**.
They aren't here now. You can't play with **them**.

Um Grammatikformen zu lernen, kann es manchmal hilfreich sein, einen Text, der diese Formen enthält, auswendig zu lernen. Das Lied auf S. 59 zum Beispiel hilft dir, die Objektformen der Personalpronomen besser zu behalten.

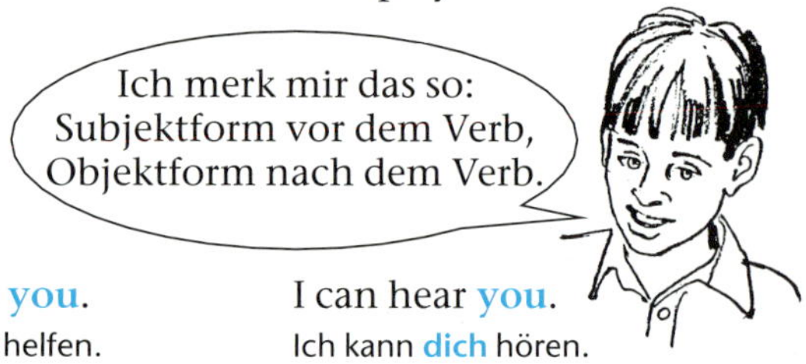

Im Englischen gibt es für jede Person nur eine Objektform.

I can help **you**. — Ich kann **dir** helfen.
I can hear **you**. — Ich kann **dich** hören.

Englisch: *me, you, …* – Deutsch: *mich/mir, dich/dir, …*

→ P 6, 7, 8 (p. 62/63)

In dieser Unit hast du gelernt ...

- zu sagen, was jemand tun oder nicht tun kann. ▶ I can sing, but my partner can't.
- zu fragen, ob jemand etwas tun darf. ▶ Can I use your ruler, please?
- zu sagen, was jemand tun muss. ▶ They must go at 4.30.
- zu sagen, dass es etwas gibt oder nicht gibt. ▶ There are three forms in the fifth year at my school. There isn't a good film today.

Unit 5

1 Die einfache Form der Gegenwart / The simple present
a Bejahte Aussagesätze / Positive statements

Mit dem *simple present* (der einfachen Form der Gegenwart) drückt man aus, dass etwas wiederholt (regelmäßig, immer, jeden Tag, oft, manchmal) oder nie geschieht.
Man benutzt diese Form auch, um allgemeine Aussagen zu machen:

- *I speak German.*
- *Cats eat mice.*

Wenn jemand etwas öfter macht, ist simple present angebracht.

I **start**	at 8.45 every day.
You **start**	
He/She/It **starts**	
We **start**	
You **start**	
They **start**	

Die einfache Form lässt sich wirklich einfach bilden: Sie entspricht dem Infinitiv – außer in der dritten Person Singular. In der dritten Person Singular wird ein *-s* an den Infinitiv angefügt.

He, she, it – das „s" muss mit!

→ P 1, 2, 3, 4, 5, 6 (p. 76/77)

b Die dritte Person Singular: Aussprache, Schreibweise

In der dritten Person Singular fügt man ein *-s* an den Infinitiv. Für die Aussprache und Schreibweise gelten die gleichen Regeln wie für den Plural der Nomen (vgl. S. 126, 136).

Bei drei Verben gibt es in der dritten Person Singular Besonderheiten, die man lernen muss.

The third person singular: pronunciation, spelling

Nick collect**s** stamps.
stimmloser Konsonant [-t] → stimmlose Endung [-ts]
Ben's mum tell**s** great stories.
stimmhafter Konsonant [-l] → stimmhafte Endung [-lz]
Sita play**s** chess.
Vokal [-eɪ] → stimmhafte Endung [-eɪz]

Nach Zischlauten [-s, -z, -ʃ, -tʃ, -dʒ] wird *-es* oder *-s* angehängt; die Aussprache ist [-ɪz]:
My dad wash**es** his car every Saturday.
Jenny danc**es** with the drama group.

-y nach Konsonanten wird zu *-ies*:
Debbie can't dance, but she tr**ies**.
try + *-s* → *tries* (aber *-y* nach Vokal bleibt: *play* + *-s* → *plays*)

Sally do**es** her homework in her room.
do [duː] + *-es* = *does* [dʌz]
Ben go**es** to Kingsway High School.
go [gəʊ] + *-es* = *goes* [gəʊz]
Sita say**s** she likes all her teachers.
say [seɪ] + *-s* = *says* [sez]

→ P 7, 8 (p. 78)

c Verneinte Aussagesätze

Verneinte Aussagesätze im *simple present* werden mit der verneinten Form des Hilfsverbs *do* + Infinitiv gebildet:
- *doesn't* ['dʌznt] (Langform: *does not*) in der dritten Person Singular
- *don't* [dəʊnt] (Langform: *do not*) in allen anderen Personen.

Negative statements

I **don't start**
You **don't start**
He/She/It **doesn't start**
We **don't start**
You **don't start**
They **don't start**
at 8 o'clock.

Nick and Ben	**play**	football.
Mr and Mrs Gupta	**don't play**	football.
Trundle	**likes**	music.
Marmalade	**doesn't like**	music.

→ P 9, 10, 11, 12, 13 (p. 78/79)

d Die dritte Person Singular – Zusammenfassung

Verben in der dritten Person Singular haben ein *s*.

The third person singular – summary

Nick **is** eleven.
He **hasn't** got a brother.
He **collects** stamps.
He **doesn't** go to the drama group with his sister.

Nur die modalen Hilfsverben (*can, must, may*) haben kein *s* in der dritten Person Singular.

Debbie **can** act.
But she **can't** dance.
She **must** help her parents on Saturday mornings.

2 **Häufigkeitsadverbien**
Da Sätze im *simple present* zum Ausdruck bringen können, dass etwas wiederholt geschieht, findet man in ihnen oft Häufigkeitsadverbien wie *always, usually, often, sometimes, never*.
Diese Adverbien stehen
- direkt vor dem Vollverb
- nach dem Hilfsverb
- nach *am, are, is*.

⚠ Häufigkeitsadverbien stehen niemals zwischen Vollverb und Objekt. Also **nicht**:
She ~~plays sometimes tennis.~~
Sie spielt manchmal Tennis.
sondern:
She sometimes plays tennis.

Adverbs of frequency

	Adverb of frequency
Susan	**always gets** up at 6.30.
Susan	steht immer um 6 Uhr 30 auf.
Brian and Carol	**never make** lunch.
Laurie **doesn't**	**often come** home before 4.30.
Lenny **can**	**usually play** with Susan after lunch.
Linda **has**	**sometimes got** lots of homework.
Susan **is**	**never** lonely.

→ P 14, 15 (p. 79/80)

In dieser Unit hast du gelernt ...

- über wiederholte Ereignisse zu sprechen.
  ▶ Assembly starts at 8.45 every day. Lessons finish at 3.30.
- allgemeine Aussagen zu machen.
  ▶ Cats eat mice.
- zu sagen, was jemand wiederholt (immer, jeden Tag, oft, manchmal) oder nie tut.
  ▶ Sita sometimes rides her bike to school. She never takes the bus.
- zu sagen, was für ein Hobby jemand hat.
  ▶ Nick collects stamps. He doesn't play tennis.

Unit 6

1 ***This, that – these, those***
Mit den Wörtern *this/that* (Singular) und *these/those* (Plural) weist man auf etwas hin. Wenn etwas näher beim Sprecher ist, verwendet man eher *this* bzw. *these*. Ist etwas weiter entfernt, verwendet man eher *that* bzw. *those*.

This, that – these, those

This room (here) is very small. Dieses Zimmer (hier) ...
That room (there) is nice and big. Das Zimmer (da) ...

This is my room. Dies (hier) ...
That's Debbie's room. Das (da) ...

These shoes (here) are very pretty. Diese Schuhe (hier) ...
Those shoes (there) are terrible. Die Schuhe (da) ...

These are by Fun Fashions. Diese (hier) ...
Those are by Marco. Die (da) ...

→ P 1, 2 (p. 94)

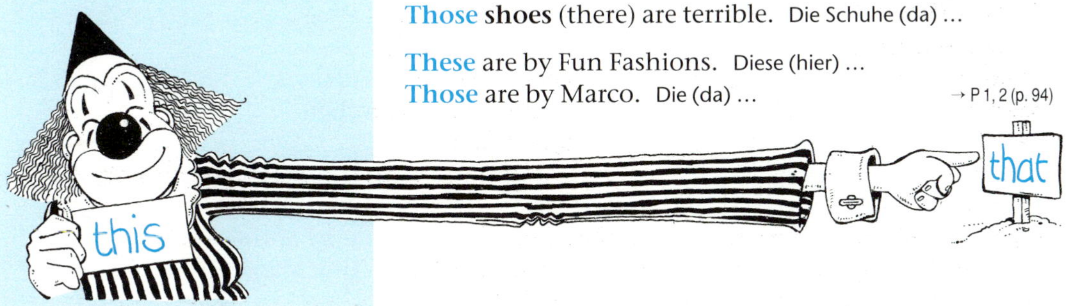

2 Die einfache Form der Gegenwart (II)

a Entscheidungsfragen und Kurzantworten

Bei Entscheidungsfragen und Kurzantworten im *simple present* stehen – wie bei der Verneinung (S. 138) – *do* oder *does:*

- *does* in der dritten Person Singular
- *do* in allen anderen Personen.

The simple present (II)

Yes/No questions and short answers

Do I **look** OK?	Yes, **you do**.
	No, **you don't**.
Do you **like** red shoes?	Yes, **I do**.
	No, **I don't**.
Does he/she/it **help** you?	Yes, **he/she/it does**.
	No, **he/she/it doesn't**.
Do we **look** OK?	Yes, **you do**.
	No, **you don't**.
Do you **do** judo?	Yes, **we do**.
	No, **we don't**.
Do they **collect** old clothes?	Yes, **they do**.
	No, **they don't**.

Die Wortstellung ist wie beim Aussagesatz. *Do* oder *does* stehen davor.

They **like** chocolate.
Do they **like** chocolate?

He **likes** chocolate.
Does he **like** chocolate?

Bei der dritten Person Singular musst du aufpassen: Wie bei der Verneinung wandert das *-s* zum *do* und macht daraus *does*.

Also **nicht**: *Does he like~~s~~ chocolate?*
sondern: *Does he like chocolate?*

Auch bei Fragen gilt:
He, she, it – das „s“ muss mit!
Doch sei klug – ein „s“ ist genug!

→ P 4, 5, 6, 7, 8, 9 (p. 95–97)

b Fragen mit Fragewörtern

Fragen mit Fragewörtern bildet man wie die Entscheidungsfragen (s. oben). Das Fragewort steht am Anfang.

Questions with question words

Question word	*do/ does*	Subject	Verb
What	do	you	**buy** at a supermarket?
When	does	the shop	**open**?
Where	do	you	**buy** clothes?
Why	do	you	**like** Marco clothes?

→ P 12, 13 (p. 98)

c **Das *simple present* bei aufeinander folgenden Handlungen**

Man verwendet das *simple present* auch, um mehrere aufeinander folgende Handlungen zu beschreiben. In solchen Sätzen findet man oft Wörter wie *first, then* und *after that (danach).*

Simple present after *first, then, after that*

First Debbie **tries on** the dress. **Then** she **buys** it. **After that** she **goes** to Jenny's house.

In dieser Unit hast du gelernt ...

- auf bestimmte Dinge hinzuweisen.
  ▶ This blouse is pretty, but those blouses there are nice, too.
- zu sagen, dass jemand oder etwas gut oder nicht gut aussieht.
  ▶ Jimmy looks great, but those jeans don't look very good on him.
- jemanden nach seinen Gewohnheiten, Hobbys und Vorlieben zu fragen.
  ▶ When do you usually get up in the mornings? Do you collect stamps? Do you like films about pets?
- über aufeinander folgende Handlungen zu sprechen.
  ▶ First I go to Assembly. Then I do music. After that I go to Geography.
- zu sagen, was du haben willst.
  ▶ I want a new dress.

Unit 7

1 **Wortstellung**
a **Nebensätze**

Nebensätze werden meistens durch Wörter wie *when, where* und *because* eingeleitet.
Die Wortstellung in solchen Nebensätzen ist genauso wie in Hauptsätzen:
Subjekt – Verb (– Objekt) = SVO

Word order
Subordinate clauses

Hauptsatz				Nebensatz		
Subject	Verb	Object		**Subject**	**Verb**	Object
Debbie	likes	zoos	because	**she**	**loves**	animals.

I always watch when **they feed** the lions.
..., wenn **sie** die Löwen **füttern**.
This is the cage where **they feed** the lions.
..., wo **sie** die Löwen **füttern**.
I often go to the zoo because **I love** animals.
..., weil **ich** Tiere **liebe**.

→ P 1, 2 (p. 112)

Du baust im Englischen keine Unfälle, wenn du die Straßen-Verkehrs-Ordnung (SVO) beachtest!

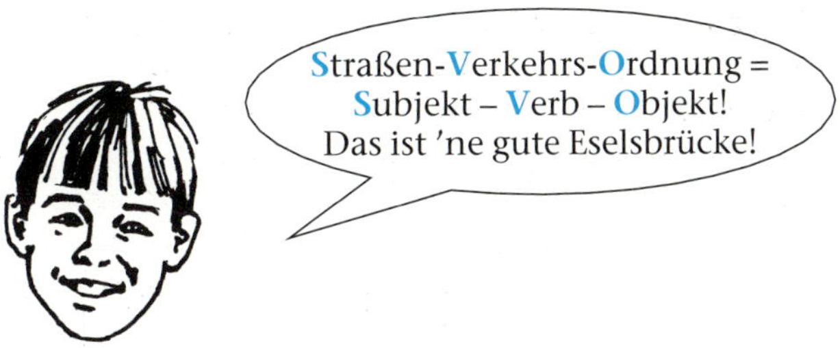

b Orts- und Zeitangaben

Ortsangaben (*to Kingsway High School, in room 4*) und Zeitangaben (*now, after school*) stehen meist am Satzende. Sie stehen nie zwischen Verb und Objekt.
Treten in einem Satz Orts- und Zeitangaben auf, dann gilt: Ort vor Zeit.

Place and time phrases

I go **to Kingsway High School**.
Ich gehe zur Kingsway High School.
I must do my homework **now**.
Ich muss jetzt meine Hausaufgaben machen.

The stamp club meets **in room 4** **after school**.
...**nach der Schule** **in Raum 4**.
Debbie and Nick walk **to school** **every day**.
...**jeden Tag** **zur Schule**.

Wie du schon gemerkt hast, können dir kleine Reime und Merksprüche beim Lernen helfen. Auch andere Eselsbrücken sind eine Hilfe. Am besten sind die, die du selbst erfindest!

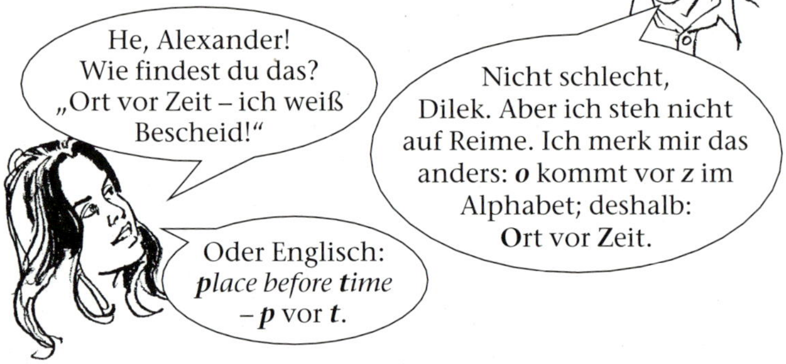

Manchmal will man die Zeitangabe an den Anfang des Satzes stellen. Die Wortstellung bleibt – anders als im Deutschen – **SVO**.

Ben goes to the computer club in the lunch break.
After school **he plays** football.
Nach der Schule **spielt er** Fußball.

→ P 7, 8 (p. 114/115)

2 Die einfache Form und die Verlaufsform der Gegenwart im Vergleich

Die einfache Form der Gegenwart drückt aus, dass jemand etwas wiederholt (regelmäßig, immer, jeden Tag, oft, manchmal usw.) oder nie tut.

Die Verlaufsform der Gegenwart drückt aus, dass jemand gerade dabei ist, etwas zu tun. Die Handlung ist also noch nicht zu Ende, sie ist noch im Gange.

Wörter wie *every day, always, usually, often, sometimes* und *never* zeigen, dass man die einfache Form der Gegenwart verwenden muss.

Wörter wie *now, at the moment* – manchmal auch *today, this morning* usw. – zeigen dagegen, dass die Verlaufsform angebracht ist.

The simple present and the present progressive in contrast

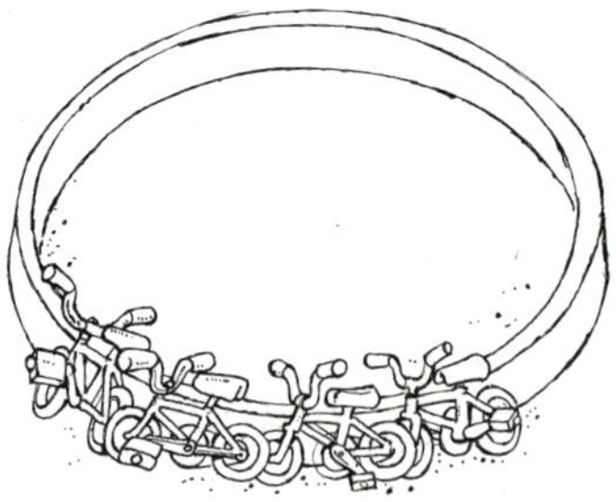

The clowns at Circus Grammaticus **ride** bikes.

They**'re riding** their bikes.

The lions **eat** lunch at 3 o'clock **every day**.

The lions **are eating** their lunch **now**.

3 Verben, die nicht im *present progressive* stehen

Es gibt eine Reihe von Verben, die nicht Tätigkeiten beschreiben, sondern Zustände oder Sinneswahrnehmungen. Diese Verben werden normalerweise nicht im *present progressive* verwendet.
Zu diesen Verben gehören:

be	*like*
believe	*love*
hate	*need*
hear	*see*
know	*want*

Verbs not used in the present progressive

Zustände
I **want** a new dress.
Ben **hates** the country.
I **don't know** Miss Hunt's phone number.

Sinneswahrnehmungen
Dad is home. I **hear** his car in the garage.
Do you **see** that girl there?

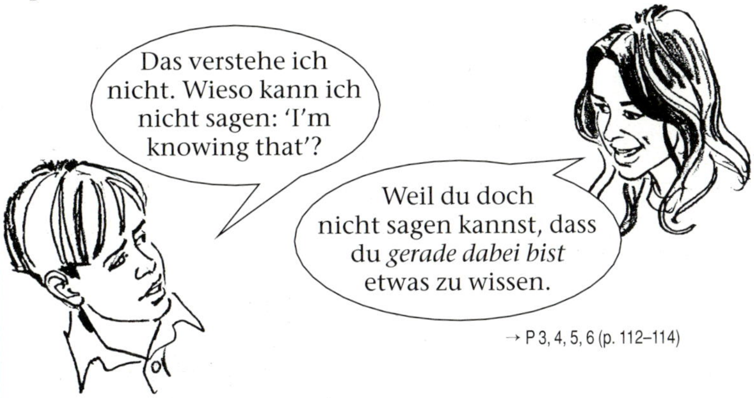

→ P 3, 4, 5, 6 (p. 112–114)

In dieser Unit hast du gelernt ...

- deine Meinung zu begründen. ▶ I like English because I've got a great teacher.
- zu sagen, wo und wann jemand etwas tut. ▶ The stamp club meets in room 4 on Mondays.

Damit geht unser Zirkus für den Sommer wieder auf Wanderschaft. Viel Spaß in den Ferien – auf ein Wiedersehen im neuen Schuljahr!
— Euer Circus Grammaticus

VOCABULARY

Dein Englischbuch hat zwei Wörterverzeichnisse:
das *VOCABULARY* (S. 145–171) und das *DICTIONARY* (S. 172–180).

Mit dem *VOCABULARY* (Vokabelverzeichnis) lernst du die neuen englischen Vokabeln. Es enthält die neuen Wörter dieses Buches in der Reihenfolge, in der sie in den Units vorkommen. Im *DICTIONARY* – einer alphabetischen Wörterliste – kannst du englische Wörter nachschlagen, deren Bedeutung du vergessen hast.

Vor- und Nachnamen, Ortsnamen und Ländernamen findest du auf der Seite 182 und auf der hinteren Umschlaginnenseite. **Grammatische Fachbegriffe** stehen gesammelt auf Seite 125. Außerdem gibt es auf Seite 184 noch eine Liste von Ausdrücken, die du häufig im Englischunterricht hören – und benutzen – wirst *(Classroom phrases)*.

Der folgende Ausschnitt zeigt dir, wie das *VOCABULARY* aufgebaut ist.

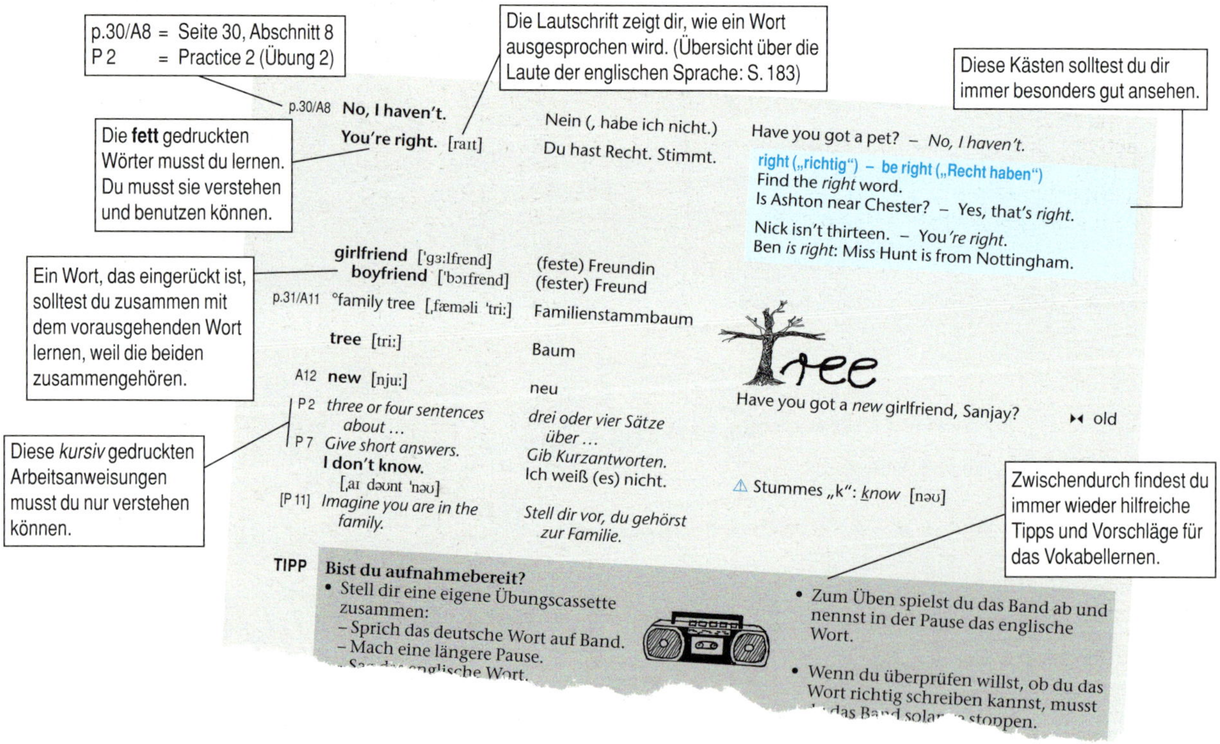

Symbole

° Wörter und Ausdrücke mit einem **Kringel** sind nur in der Unit wichtig, in der sie vorkommen. *Beispiel:* °family tree

[ ] **Eckige Klammern** bedeuten, dass dieser Teil der Unit nicht Pflicht ist. Dein Lehrer/Deine Lehrerin wird dir sagen, ob du die Wörter lernen sollst.

⧓ Dieses Symbol in der dritten Spalte weist dich auf ein bekanntes Wort mit **gegensätzlicher Bedeutung** hin. *Beispiel:* **new ⧓ old**

⚠ Das **Warndreieck** weist dich auf **Besonderheiten der englischen Sprache** hin, bei denen man leicht Fehler macht, oder auf **Unterschiede zum Deutschen**.

Abkürzungen

p. = page *(Seite)*
jd. = jemand • jm. = jemandem • jn. = jemanden
no pl = *no plural* (kein Plural) • *pl* = *plural*

Englische Wörter wie *computer, T-shirt, hamburger*, die du ohne weiteres verstehst, werden nicht im *VOCABULARY* aufgeführt. Alle diese Wörter findest du aber mit Angabe ihrer Aussprache im *DICTIONARY*.

TIPP **Vokabeln lernen – gewusst wie!**

- Lerne nur 5 bis 10 Vokabeln auf einmal!
- Aber lerne regelmäßig Vokabeln, nicht nur, wenn es deine Hausaufgabe ist. **Lieber jeden Tag 10 Minuten als einmal 2 Stunden pro Woche.**

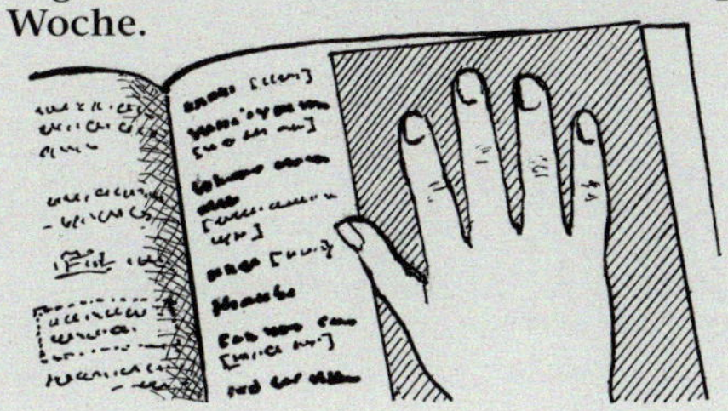

- So prägst du dir Vokabeln gut ein:
  - Lies das englische Wort laut.
  - Sieh dir die deutsche Übersetzung und die Beispiele in der rechten Spalte an.
  - Decke die deutsche Spalte ab: Weißt du die deutschen Bedeutungen noch?
  - Und nun decke die englische Spalte ab: Wie heißen die deutschen Wörter auf Englisch?
- Du kannst auch mit Freunden oder jemandem aus der Familie zusammen lernen. Das macht Spaß und erspart das Abdecken.

▶▶▶ Welcome

p.6/7	**welcome** ['welkəm]	willkommen
	We speak English. [ˌwi spiːk‿'ɪŋglɪʃ]	Wir sprechen Englisch.
	in Germany [ɪn 'dʒɜːməni]	in Deutschland
	activity [æk'tɪvəti]	Aktivität, Tätigkeit
	I [aɪ]	ich
	a little [ə 'lɪtl]	ein bisschen, ein wenig
	And you? [ənd 'juː]	Und du?
p.8	**Hello.** [hə'ləʊ]	Hallo. / Guten Tag.
	What's your name? [ˌwɒts jɔː 'neɪm]	Wie heißt du? (*wörtlich:* Was ist dein Name?)
	My name is … . [ˌmaɪ 'neɪm‿ɪz]	Mein Name ist … . / Ich heiße … .
	Where are you from? [ˌweər‿ə jʊ 'frɒm]	Wo kommst du her?
	I'm from … . ['aɪm frəm]	Ich bin aus … . / Ich komme aus … .
	I'm from Berlin, **too.** [tuː]	Ich komme auch aus Berlin.
	My mum and dad are … . [ˌmʌm‿ən 'dæd]	Meine Mutter und mein Vater sind … .
	now [naʊ]	nun, jetzt
	song [sɒŋ]	Lied
	Good morning. [gʊd 'mɔːnɪŋ]	Guten Morgen. / Guten Tag. *(vormittags)*
	How are you? [ˌhaʊ‿'ɑː jʊ]	Wie geht es dir? / Wie geht es euch?
	I'm fine. [ˌaɪm 'faɪn]	Mir geht's gut. / Es geht mir gut.
	thanks [θæŋks]	danke
	Can you count? [ˌkæn jʊ 'kaʊnt]	Kannst du zählen? / Könnt ihr zählen?
	How old …? [ˌhaʊ‿'əʊld]	Wie alt …?
p.9	**Can you spell** (your name)? [spel]	Kannst du (deinen Namen) buchstabieren?
	alphabet ['ælfəbet]	Alphabet
	please [pliːz]	bitte *(in Fragen und Aufforderungen)*

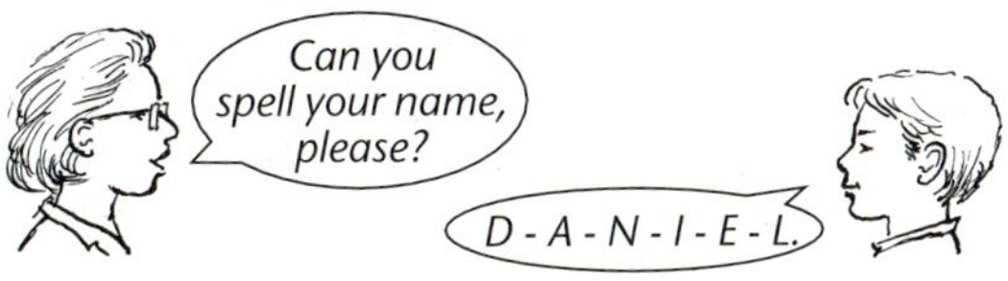

	the [ðə]	der, die, das; die
	letter ['letə]	Buchstabe
	number ['nʌmbə]	Zahl, Ziffer
	box [bɒks]	Kasten, Kiste
	teacher ['tiːtʃə]	Lehrer, Lehrerin

p.10	**What's this in English?** [ðɪs]	Wie heißt das auf Englisch?
	It's a classroom. [ˌɪts‿ə 'klɑːsruːm]	Das ist ein Klassenzimmer. / Es ist ein Klassenzimmer.
	boy [bɔɪ], boys [bɔɪz]	Junge, Jungen
	girl [gɜːl], girls [gɜːlz]	Mädchen, Mädchen
	board [bɔːd]	(Wand-)Tafel
	book [bʊk]	Buch
	chair [tʃeə]	Stuhl
	bin [bɪn]	Papierkorb, Mülleimer
	desk [desk]	Schreibtisch, Schülertisch
	school bag ['skuːlbæg]	Schultasche
	rubber ['rʌbə]	Radiergummi
	felt-tip ['felttɪp]	Filzstift
	biro ['baɪrəʊ]	Kugelschreiber
	pen [pen]	Füller
	ruler ['ruːlə]	Lineal
	pencil ['pensl]	Bleistift
	pencil-case ['penslkeɪs]	Federmäppchen
	Find the classroom words.	*Such die „Klassenzimmer-Wörter".*

⚠ *auf* Englisch = *in* English

one *boy* and one *girl* — two *boys* — two *girls*

bags [bægz]

p.11	**What colour is it?** [ˌwɒt 'kʌlər‿ɪz‿ɪt]	Welche Farbe hat es (er, sie)?
	it's [ɪts]	es ist (*bei Sachen und Tieren auch:* er/sie ist)
	yellow ['jeləʊ]	gelb
	red [red]	rot
	green [griːn]	grün
	blue [bluː]	blau
	white [waɪt]	weiß
	black [blæk]	schwarz
	Goodbye. [ˌgʊd'baɪ]	Auf Wiedersehen.
	How many words can you make?	*Wie viele Wörter kannst du bilden?*
	Let's go. [ˌlets 'gəʊ]	Auf geht's! (*wörtlich:* Lass uns gehen.)

What colour is …

… your *chair*?	– **It**'s yellow.	= *Er* ist gelb.
… your *school bag*?	– **It**'s red.	= *Sie* ist rot.
… your *ruler*?	– **It**'s green.	= *Es* ist grün.

TIPP **Abschreiben erwünscht!**

Am besten behält man, was man aufschreibt. Dein Lehrer/Deine Lehrerin hat dir bestimmt gesagt, wo du deine Vokabeln aufschreiben sollst. Das solltest du dann regelmäßig und systematisch tun:

- Schreib das englische Wort (Rechtschreibung überprüfen!) und daneben die deutsche Übersetzung.
- Füge nun einen Beispielsatz hinzu – die rechte Spalte des Vokabelverzeichnisses wird dir helfen. Du kannst auch ein Bild malen.

▸▸▸ Unit 1: Hello, Form 7CH

p.12/13	**form** [fɔ:m]	*(englische)* (Schul-) Klasse	Jenny is in *Form 7CH.* ⚠ „CH" = Christine Hunt (die Klassenlehrerin)
	This is … . [ðɪs‿ɪz]	Dies ist … .	*This is* my pencil-case. It's old. 
	she's [ʃi:z] = **she is** [ʃi:‿ɪz]	sie ist	Mandy is twelve. *She's* from Chemnitz.
	town [taʊn]	Stadt	
	her [hə, *betont:* hɜ:]	ihr, ihre	Dilek is from Berlin. *Her* dad is from Turkey.
	sister ['sɪstə]	Schwester	
	brother ['brʌðə]	Bruder	Mike and Sue are *brother and sister.* (= Geschwister)
	twins [twɪnz]	Zwillinge	
	they're [ðeə] = **they are** [ðeɪ‿ɑ:]	sie sind	

„SIE"

This is Jenny. **She**'s eleven.	Das ist Jenny. **Sie** ist elf.
This is my school bag. **It**'s red.	Das ist meine Schultasche. **Sie** ist rot.
Debbie and Nick are twins. **They**'re eleven.	Debbie und Nick sind Zwillinge. **Sie** sind elf.
How old are **you**?	Wie alt sind **Sie**?

	he's [hi:z] = **he is** [hi:‿ɪz]	er ist	
	tortoise ['tɔ:təs]	Schildkröte	
	Start a scrapbook.	*Fang ein Sammelalbum an.*	
p.14/A1	**Miss** Hunt [ˌmɪs 'hʌnt]	Fräulein/Frau Hunt *(Anrede für unverheiratete Frauen)*	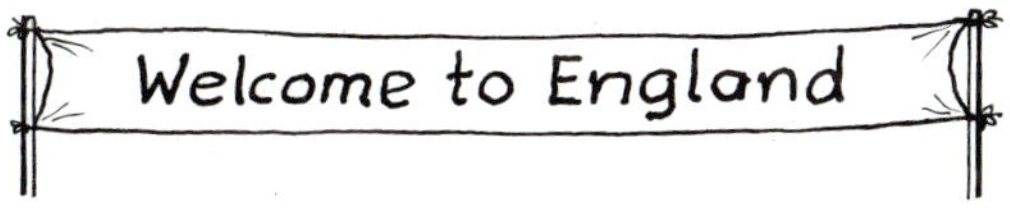
	Welcome to … . [tə, *betont:* tu:]	Willkommen in … .	
	school [sku:l]	Schule	
	new [nju:]	neu	▸◂ old
	your *(pl)* [jɔ:]	euer, eure	
A2	**you're** [jʊə, jɔ:] = **you are** [ju:‿ɑ:]	du bist; ihr seid; Sie sind	⚠ Aussprache: *you* [ju:] – *you're* [jʊə, jɔ:] – *your* [jɔ:]

you're – your

You're Jenny.	This is **your** new teacher, Jenny.
Du bist *Jenny.*	*Dies ist* ***deine*** *neue Lehrerin, Jenny.*
And **you're** Nick and Debbie.	This is **your** classroom, Nick and Debbie.
Und ***ihr seid*** *Nick und Debbie.*	*Dies ist* ***euer*** *Klassenzimmer, Nick und Debbie.*
And **you're** Miss Hunt.	This is **your** new form, Miss Hunt.
Und ***Sie sind*** *Miss Hunt.*	*Dies ist* ***Ihre*** *neue Klasse, Miss Hunt.*

	yes [jes]	ja	
A3	**village** ['vɪlɪdʒ]	Dorf	
	near [nɪə]	in der Nähe von, nahe (bei)	The boy is *near* the board. 
	but [bət, *betont:* bʌt]	aber	Jenny is from Chester, *but* Ben is from Ashton.
	German ['dʒɜ:mən]	deutsch; Deutsch; Deutsche(r)	Ina and Maik are *German.* They're from Celle in Germany. They speak *German* – and English, too.
	not [nɒt]	nicht	I'm *not* from Chester. I'm from Ashton. ⚠ I'm *not* from Chester. = Ich bin *nicht* aus Chester. I'm *not* German. = Ich bin *kein* Deutscher/*keine* Deutsche.
	British ['brɪtɪʃ]	britisch; Brite, Britin	Ben is *British.*
	Thank you. ['θæŋk jʊ]	Danke (schön).	How are you? – I'm fine, *thank you.*
A4	**nice** [naɪs]	schön, nett	'Sita' is a *nice* name. And Sita is *nice,* too.
	Indian ['ɪndiən]	indisch; Inder, Inderin	

p.15/A5	°Hi there.	Hallo.	
A6	**friend** [frend] **we're** [wɪə] = **we are** [wiː‿ɑː]	Freund, Freundin wir sind	
A7	**You're lucky.** ['lʌki]	Du hast Glück. / Du bist gut dran.	
	Let's swap. [swɒp]	Lass uns tauschen.	
	very funny [ˌveri 'fʌni]	sehr witzig, sehr komisch	
	Find forms on pages 14 and 15 like: …	*Such Formen auf den Seiten 14 und 15 wie: …*	
p.16/A8	**here** [hɪə] **under** ['ʌndə] **Open** your books **at page 5.** ['əʊpən], [peɪdʒ]	hier unter Schlagt Seite 5 auf.	Oh, *here*'s my book – *under* the desk. 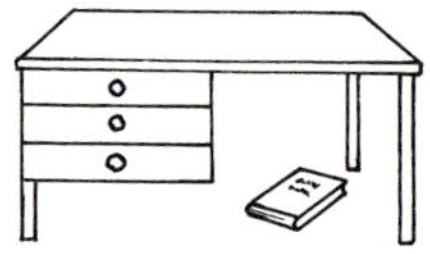
	(to)[1] **open** **page** **no** [nəʊ]	öffnen, aufmachen (Buch-, Heft-)Seite nein	⚠ Abkürzung: *page* 5 = p.5 (S.5) ▸◂ yes
A9	**on the floor** [ˌɒn ðə 'flɔː]	auf dem Fußboden	Julia, your pencil-case is *on the floor*. 

what

What's on the floor?	**Was** liegt auf dem Fußboden?
What's this?	**Was** ist das hier?
What's this in English?	**Wie** heißt dies auf Englisch?
What's 'Fußboden' in English?	**Was** heißt „Fußboden" auf Englisch?
What colour is your school bag?	**Welche** Farbe hat deine Schultasche?

A10	**year** [jɪə]	Jahr; Jahrgangsstufe	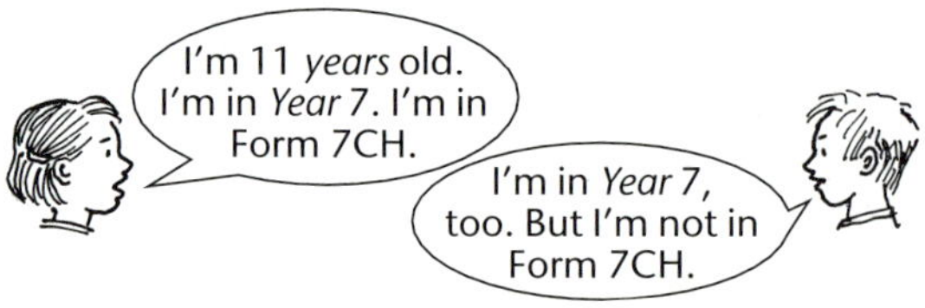
	we aren't [wiː‿ɑːnt] = **we are not**	wir sind nicht; wir sind keine	*We aren't* 11, and *we aren't* German. We're 12, and we're English.
p.17/A11	**clever** ['klevə] **silly** ['sɪli] *negative short forms*	schlau, klug albern, dumm *verneinte Kurzformen*	
A14	**of course** [əv 'kɔːs]	natürlich, selbstverständlich	Is Trundle clever? – Yes, *of course* he is.
	questions and short answers	*Fragen und Kurzantworten*	
P3	**questionnaire** [ˌkwestʃə'neə] **partner** ['pɑːtnə] *Copy … into your exercise book.* *Talk to … .* *Complete … .* *Now tell your form.*	Fragebogen Partner, Partnerin *Übertrage … in dein Übungsheft.* *Rede mit … .* *Vervollständige … .* *Nun berichte deiner Klasse.*	
P4	**at** Kingsway High School [ət, *betont:* æt] *Use 'we're …'.*	an/auf der Kingsway High School *Gebrauche/Verwende „we're …".*	

[1] Mit dem vorangestellten „(to)" kennzeichnen wir den Infinitiv (die Grundform) des Verbs.

P 6	*Listen to the cassette/CD and say the plural.*	*Hör dir die Cassette/CD an und sag den Plural.*	
P 7	**right** [raɪt]	richtig	Trundle is nice. – *Right*! Sanjay is nice. *Right*, Debbie? (= *Nicht wahr, …?*)
	wrong [rɒŋ]	falsch	⚠ Stummes „w": *wrong* [rɒŋ] ◂▸ right
	sentences	*Sätze*	
P 8	*chart*	*Tabelle*	
P 9	**question** ['kwestʃn]	Frage	
	answer ['ɑ:nsə]	Antwort	⚠ Stummes „w": *answer* ['ɑ:nsə] ◂▸ question
	Match the answers to the questions.	*Ordne die Antworten den Fragen zu.*	
P 10	**card** [kɑ:d]	Karte	*cards* 
	Write the words on cards.	*Schreib die Wörter auf Karten.*	
[P 11]	*Look at the pictures.*	*Schau dir die Bilder an.*	
	Listen again.	*Hör noch einmal zu.*	
	Write … .	*Schreib … .*	
	Match the numbers to the letters.	*Ordne die Ziffern den Buchstaben zu.*	
P 12	*Write … and ask your partner.*	*Schreib … und frag deine/n Partner/in.*	
P 13	**word group(s)** ['wɜ:d gru:p(s)]	Wortgruppe(n)	
	Make two groups: …	*Bilde zwei Gruppen: …*	
	people *(pl)* ['pi:pl]	Leute, Menschen	The *people* in Chester are very nice.

Home from school

p.22	**We're home.** [həʊm]	Wir sind (wieder) zu Hause.	
	Well, … [wel]	Nun, …; Also, …	
	great [greɪt]	großartig, toll	Miss Hunt is a *great* teacher!
	the same [ðə 'seɪm]	der-/die-/dasselbe, dieselben	Sita and Sanjay are at *the same* school, but they aren't in *the same* form.
	who? [hu:]	wer?	⚠ *Who*'s your teacher? = *Wer* ist dein/e Lehrer/in? *Where*'s your teacher? = *Wo* ist dein/e Lehrer/in?
	for [fə, *betont:* fɔ:]	für	The German word *for* 'who' is 'wer'.
	our ['aʊə]	unser, unsere	We're twins. *Our* names are Nick and Debbie.
	°Geography [dʒi'ɒgrəfi]	Geographie, Erdkunde	
	kid [kɪd]	Kind, Jugendliche(r)	
	his [hɪz]	sein, seine	Here's my friend Michael. And here's *his* sister. 
p.23	**tea** [ti:]	Tee	
	Correct the mistakes.	*Verbessere die Fehler.*	
	story ['stɔ:ri]	Geschichte, Erzählung	⚠ one *story* – two *stories*

TIPP

Alles im Kasten!
Eine **Vokabelkartei** ist ein prima Hilfsmittel fürs Vokabellernen:

- Du brauchst einen Kasten (z.B. einen Schuhkarton), den du in vier Fächer unterteilst, und Karteikarten.
- So beschriftest du deine Vokabelkarten:

Vorderseite / Rückseite

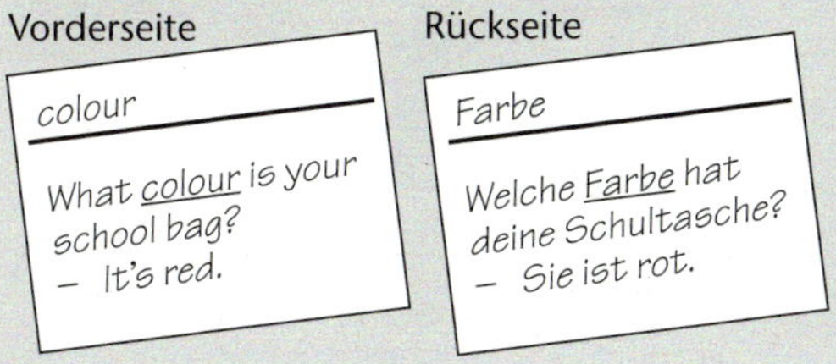

- Am Anfang benutzt du nur zwei Fächer: Das vordere Fach ist für Karten mit Wörtern, die du noch lernen musst. Wenn ein Wort „sitzt", kommt die Karte ins zweite Fach.
- Wiederhole auch die Vokabelkarten im zweiten Fach regelmäßig. Wenn du ein Wort vergessen hast, kommt die Karte wieder ins erste Fach.
- Welche Wörter du auf Karteikarten schreiben sollst, sagt dir dein Lehrer/deine Lehrerin.
- Ein Vorteil der Vokabelkartei: Du kannst auch ein paar Karten mitnehmen und unterwegs lernen.

▶▶▶ Topic 1: English in the classroom

p. 24/1	*Swap things with … .*	*Tausche Dinge mit … .*	
	Look at the picture.	*Schau dir das Bild an.*	
	°your rubber for my pen	dein Radiergummi gegen meinen Füller	
2	(to) **see** [si:]	sehen	Can you *see* my ruler? – It's under your chair.
	network	*(Wörter-)Netz, „Wörter-spinne"*	
	picture	*Bild*	
	Fill in: …	*Setze ein: …*	
	door [dɔ:]	Tür	
	window ['wɪndəʊ]	Fenster	
	cupboard ['kʌbəd]	Schrank	
	notice board ['nəʊtɪs bɔ:d]	Anschlagtafel, schwarzes Brett	
3	(to) **hear** [hɪə]	hören	*Look.* Can you *see* the tortoise? *Look at* the board. What can you *see*? *Look at* page 17. Can you *see* Ben?
	(to) **look (at)** [lʊk]	(an)schauen, (an)sehen	anschauen, ansehen, hingucken = (to) **look**; sehen, erkennen = (to) **see**
	picture ['pɪktʃə]	Bild	⚠ What can you see *in the picture*? (= *auf* dem Bild)
	more sentences	*weitere Sätze*	
	quiet ['kwaɪət]	ruhig, leise, still	Sita is a *quiet* girl.
p. 25/4	(to) **say** [seɪ]	sagen	Can you *say* 'Schildkröte' in English?
6	*ladder*	*(die) Leiter*	
	wall	*Wand*	
	or	*oder*	

TIPP

Mit *networks* kommt alles in Ordnung!
Man behält neue Vokabeln leichter, wenn man sie ordnet und in Gruppen lernt – zum Beispiel mithilfe eines Wörternetzes (*vocabulary network*).

Sieh dir dieses Wörternetz einmal an: Alexander und Dilek haben überlegt, was man alles mit *words* machen kann.
Erinnerst du dich noch, was die englischen Wörter – es sind alles Verben – bedeuten?

Übertrage das *network* in dein Vokabelheft und ergänze dort die deutschen Bedeutungen. (Die alphabetische Wörterliste – S. 172 – 180 – wird dir helfen, falls du nicht weiterweißt.)

Vielleicht kannst du jetzt ein *network* mit dem Titel *„in my school bag"* machen?

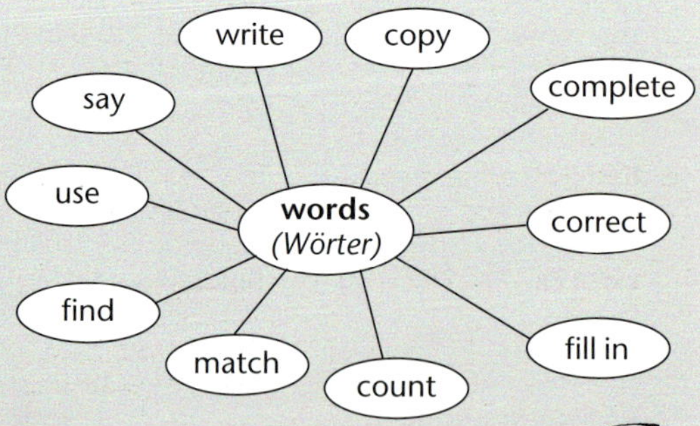

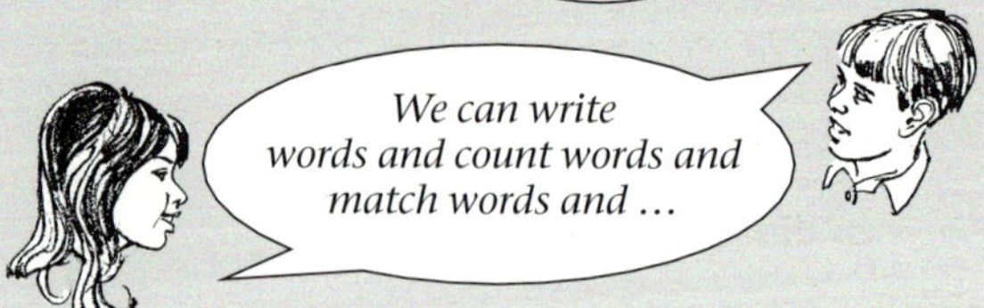

▶▶▶ Unit 2: My family and my pets

⚠ one famil<u>y</u> – two famil<u>ies</u>

p.26/27	**family** ['fæməli]	Familie	
	pet [pet]	Haustier	Here's Michael *with* his pet.
	with [wɪð]	mit (… zusammen), bei	Ben's mum is in Berlin *with* her German family.
	grandma ['grænmɑ:]	Oma	
	grandpa ['grænpɑ:]	Opa	

	cat [kæt]	Katze, Kater	 a dog, a cat → **it** Aber mit Namen: my dog Diana → **she** my cat Charles → **he**
	dog [dɒg]	Hund	
	aunt [ɑːnt]	Tante	
	uncle ['ʌŋkl]	Onkel	
	Bring ... to school and write about it.	*Bring ... mit zur Schule und schreib darüber.*	
	happy ['hæpi]	glücklich, froh	⚠ She's *happy*. = Sie ist glücklich. She's *lucky*. = Sie hat Glück.
	rabbit ['ræbɪt]	Kaninchen	
	little ['lɪtl]	klein, jung	
	hamster ['hæmstə]	Hamster	
	budgie ['bʌdʒi]	Wellensittich	
	a verse about ...	*ein Vers über ...*	
	goldfish ['gəʊldfɪʃ]	Goldfisch	⚠ one *goldfish* – two *goldfish* 
p.28/A1	**Mrs** Snow ['mɪsɪz]	Frau Snow *(Anrede für verheiratete Frauen)*	
	Mr Snow ['mɪstə]	Herr Snow	
	nurse [nɜːs]	Krankenschwester, Krankenpfleger	⚠ Aussprache Plural: one *nurse* [nɜːs] – two *nurses* ['nɜːsɪz]
	That's right. [ˌðæts 'raɪt]	Das ist richtig. / Das stimmt.	Is Ben from Ashton? – Yes, *that's right*.
A2	**their** [ðeə]	ihr, ihre *(Plural)*	Debbie and Nick are twins. They're 11. Lulu is *their* dog. ⚠ *their* [ðeə] = ihr, ihre – *they're* [ðeə] = sie sind
	garden ['gɑːdn]	Garten	
	its [ɪts]	sein, seine *(bei Sachen und Tieren auch:* ihr, ihre*)*	 What's *its* name? (*sein* Name) |  What's *its* name? (*ihr* Name) ⚠ *its* = sein, seine; ihr, ihre – *it's* = er/sie/es ist
	cage [keɪdʒ]	Käfig	⚠ Aussprache Plural: one *cage* [keɪdʒ] – two *cages* ['keɪdʒɪz]
A3	**I've got ... .** [ˌaɪv 'gɒt] = **I have got ... .** [həv, *betont:* hæv]	Ich habe ... . / Ich besitze	
	nothing ['nʌθɪŋ]	nichts	I've got a cat. – That's *nothing*. I've got a dog, a hamster and a budgie.
	champion ['tʃæmpiən]	Champion, Meister/in, Wettkampfsieger/in	
A4	**he/she/it has got** [həz, *betont:* hæz]	er/sie/es hat, besitzt	
	basket ['bɑːskɪt]	Korb	
	kitchen ['kɪtʃɪn]	Küche	
	poor [pɔː, pʊə]	arm	Marmalade has got a basket. *Poor* Trundle has got a cage in the garden. (= *Der arme* Trundle ...)
p.29/A5	**or** [ɔː]	oder	Are you in Form 7CH *or* in Form 7BW, Sita?
	Jenny **hasn't got** a hamster. ['hæznt] (**= has not got**)	Jenny hat keinen Hamster. (*wörtlich:* ... hat nicht einen Hamster.)	⧓ has got
A6	We **haven't got time.** [ˌhævnt gɒt 'taɪm] (**= have not got**)	Wir haben keine Zeit. (*wörtlich:* Wir haben nicht Zeit.)	⧓ have got
	mother ['mʌðə]	Mutter	
	father ['fɑːðə]	Vater	
	restaurant ['restrɒnt]	Restaurant	
	Talk about pets.	*Redet über Haustiere.*	
	forms of 'have got'	*Formen von „have got"*	

p.30/A7	**at** the restaurant	im Restaurant	

at

Sita and Sanjay are **at** the restaurant.	Sita und Sanjay sind **im** Restaurant.
Debbie is **at** school now.	Debbie ist jetzt **in** der Schule.
They're all **at** Kingsway High School.	Sie gehen alle **auf** die Kingsway High School.
Who's **at** the door?	Wer ist **an** der Tür?
Look **at** the board, please.	Sieh **an** die Tafel, bitte.

	problem ['prɒbləm]	Problem	
	all [ɔ:l]	alle; alles	Jenny, Debbie, Sita, Ben – they're *all* in Form 7CH. We're four kids – *all* girls. *All the* kids are home from school.
	What about Jenny? [ə'baʊt]	Was ist mit Jenny? / Und Jenny?	Ben has got a computer. *What about* Sita? Has she got a computer?
A8	**No, I haven't.**	Nein (, habe ich nicht.)	Have you got a pet? – *No, I haven't.* ◂▸ Yes, I have.
	You're right.	Du hast Recht. Stimmt.	**right („richtig") – be right („Recht haben")** Find the *right* word. Is Ashton near Chester? – Yes, that's *right*. Nick isn't thirteen. – You*'re right*. Ben *is right*: Miss Hunt is from Nottingham.
	Sorry. / I'm sorry. ['sɒri]	Entschuldigung. Tut mir Leid.	Have you got a ruler? – No, *I'm sorry*.
	girlfriend ['gɜ:lfrend]	(feste) Freundin	
	boyfriend ['bɔɪfrend]	(fester) Freund	
	Ask questions.	*Stell Fragen.*	

Susan and *a friend* Michael and *a friend*

p.31/A9	**parents** ['peərənts]	Eltern	
	together [tə'geðə]	zusammen	
	divorced [dɪ'vɔ:st]	geschieden	My parents aren't together. They're *divorced*.
	wife [waɪf]	Ehefrau	Mr and Mrs Miller
	husband ['hʌzbənd]	Ehemann	
	house [haʊs]	Haus	⚠ Aussprache Plural: one *house* [haʊs] – two *houses* ['haʊzɪz]

A11	°family tree [ˌfæməli 'tri:]	Familienstammbaum	
	tree [tri:]	Baum	
	room [ru:m]	Zimmer, Raum	I've got a computer in my *room*.
A12	**dead** [ded]	tot	My grandma and grandpa are *dead*.
	cousin ['kʌzn]	Cousin, Cousine	
	married ['mærid]	verheiratet	Mrs Scott is *married*. Miss Hunt isn't *married*.
P 2	*three or four sentences about …*	*drei oder vier Sätze über …*	
	You can put them in your scrapbook.	*Du kannst sie in dein Album tun.*	
P 3	(to) **make** [meɪk]	machen, bilden, bauen	Let's *make* a cage for our rabbit.
	sentence ['sentəns]	Satz	⚠ Aussprache Plural: one *sentence* ['sentəns] – two *sentences* ['sentənsɪz]
P 7	*Give short answers.*	*Gib Kurzantworten.*	
	I don't know. [ˌaɪ dəʊnt 'nəʊ]	Ich weiß (es) nicht.	⚠ Stummes „k": *know* [nəʊ]
P 9	*Read out loud.*	*Lies laut vor.*	
P 10	**exercise book** ['eksəsaɪz bʊk]	Übungsheft, Schulheft	
[P 12]	*Imagine you are in the family.*	*Stell dir vor, du gehörst zur Familie.*	

P 14	*Match the words.*	*Ordne die Wörter einander zu.*	

A cool new friend

p.36	**lonely** ['ləʊnli]	einsam	Mr Smith hasn't got a family. He's very *lonely*.
	a lot (of) [ə 'lɒt_əv]	eine Menge, viel, viele	I've got *a lot of* CDs. Have you got CDs? – Yes, *a lot*.
	°engineer [ˌendʒɪ'nɪə]	Ingenieur, Ingenieurin	
	so [səʊ]	deshalb, daher; also	Ben hasn't got a lot of friends, *so* he's *often* lonely.
	often ['ɒfn]	oft	
	(to) **be out** [bi_'aʊt]	weg sein, nicht da sein	Jenny is out *today*, so Trundle is lonely.
	today [tə'deɪ]	heute	
	really ['rɪəli]	wirklich	Grandma Scott is *really* great. But today she's out, so it's *boring*.
	boring ['bɔːrɪŋ]	langweilig	
	there [ðeə]	da, dort	⧓ here ⚠ [ðeə]: *there* = da, dort – *their* = ihr, ihre – *they're* = sie sind
	Good afternoon. [ˌɑːftə'nuːn]	Guten Tag. *(nachmittags)*	
	afternoon	Nachmittag	⚠ Let's look at my pictures *in the afternoon.* (= *am* Nachmittag)
p.37	(to) **answer** ['ɑːnsə]	antworten; beantworten	⚠ Stummes „w": *answer* ['ɑːnsə]
	°virus ['vaɪrəs]	Virus	

TIPP **Bist du aufnahmebereit?**

- Stell dir eine eigene Übungscassette zusammen:
  - Sprich das deutsche Wort auf Band.
  - Mach eine längere Pause.
  - Sag das englische Wort. (Achtung Aussprache!)

- Zum Üben spielst du das Band ab und nennst in der Pause das englische Wort.
- Wenn du überprüfen willst, ob du das Wort richtig schreiben kannst, musst du das Band solange stoppen.

▶▶▶ Topic 2: Numbers

p.38/3	°as always [əz_'ɔːlweɪz]	wie immer	
	late [leɪt]	(zu) spät	It's *late*. I'm *late* for school.
	°back to one [ˌbæk tə 'wʌn]	zurück zur Eins	
	again [ə'gen]	wieder, noch einmal	Can you say it *again*, please?
p.39/4	**(tele)phone number** ['teləfəʊn ˌnʌmbə]	Telefonnummer	We've got a new *(tele)phone*. And a new *(tele)phone number*, too.
	°double ['dʌbl]	Doppel-	
5	**five times nought** [ˌfaɪv taɪmz 'nɔːt]	fünf mal null	Five *times* nought is nought. (5 x 0 = 0)
6	*Draw a board on cardboard.*	*Zeichne ein Spielbrett auf Karton/auf Pappe.*	
	Cut it out.	*Schneide es aus.*	
	(to) colour	*bunt anmalen*	
	a dice and counters	*ein Würfel und Spielsteine*	
	Throw the dice, move your counter.	*Würfle, zieh deinen Spielstein.*	
	Go up the ladders and down the snakes.	*Zieh die Leitern hinauf und die Schlangen hinunter.*	

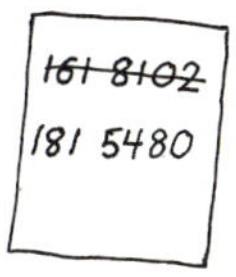

▶▶▶ Unit 3: Around the house

p.40/41	°Around the house. [ə'raʊnd]	Rund ums Haus.	
	garage ['gærɪdʒ]	Garage	⚠ Aussprache Plural: one *garage* ['gærɪdʒ] – two *garages* ['gærɪdʒɪz]

V

Unit 3

	small [smɔːl]	klein	
	big [bɪg]	groß	a small *car*  a big *car* 
	car [kɑː]	Auto	
	flat [flæt]	Wohnung	
	over the restaurant ['əʊvə]	über dem Restaurant	▸◂ under
	living-room ['lɪvɪŋruːm]	Wohnzimmer	
	bathroom ['bɑːθruːm]	Badezimmer	
	°hall [hɔːl]	Flur, Diele	
	bedroom ['bedruːm]	Schlafzimmer	
	bed [bed]	Bett	
	bookshelf ['bʊkʃelf]	Bücherregal	⚠ one *bookshel<u>f</u>* [-ʃelf] – two *bookshel<u>ves</u>* [-ʃelvz]
	radio ['reɪdiəʊ]	Radio	
	TV [ˌtiː'viː]	Fernsehgerät; Fernsehen	
	I think ... . [θɪŋk]	Ich glaube, ... / Ich meine, ... / Ich denke, ...	
p.42/A1	**at** six [ət 'sɪks]	um sechs	
	(to) **help** [help]	helfen	
	me [mi, *betont:* miː]	mir; mich	Help *me*, Nick. Nick, can you hear *me*?
	tidy ['taɪdi]	ordentlich, aufgeräumt	
A2	(to) **come** [kʌm]	kommen	
	Come here.	Komm her.	
	(to) **tidy up** [ˌtaɪdi‿'ʌp]	aufräumen	*Tidy up* your room, Debbie. – But it is tidy, Mum!
	(to) **clean** [kliːn]	sauber machen	*Clean* the bathroom, please, Nick.
	clean [kliːn]	sauber	– But it is *clean*, Mum!
	Go away. [ˌgəʊ‿ə'weɪ]	Geh weg.	 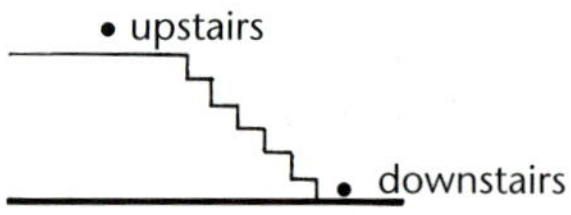
	upstairs [ˌʌp'steəz]	nach oben; oben	Come *upstairs*, please.
	downstairs [ˌdaʊn'steəz]	nach unten; unten	My room is *upstairs*, but my sister's room is *downstairs*.
[p.42]	**[Activity]**		
	Listen to the rap and move to the music.	*Hör dir den Rap an und beweg dich zur Musik.*	
	Raise your arms – and up and down.	*Heb deine Arme – und auf und ab.*	
	Snap your fingers.	*Schnips mit den Fingern.*	
	Clap your hands.	*Klatsch in die Hände.*	
	Close your eyes.	*Schließ deine Augen.*	
p.42	**Game**		
	(to) **put** [pʊt]	legen, stellen, *(etwas wohin)* tun	*Put* the books on the desk, please. *Put* the words together and make sentences.
	Sit down. [ˌsɪt 'daʊn]	Setz dich hin. / Setzt euch hin.	
	(to) **sit** [sɪt]	sich (hin)setzen; sitzen	*Sit* on your desk now. The dog can *sit* here.

wo? – wohin?

WO?				WOHIN?
Here is Lulu.	*hier*	**here**	*hierher*	Come **here**, Lulu.
There's Marmalade.	*da, dort*	**there**	*dahin, dorthin*	Put the books on the desk. And put the basket **there**, too.
Where's Trundle?	*wo*	**where**	*wohin*	**Where** can we put the old desk?
Nick is **upstairs**.	*oben*	**upstairs**	*nach oben*	Go **upstairs**, Debbie.
Trundle is **under** the chair.	*unter dem Stuhl*	**under**	*unter den Stuhl*	Put the cage **under** the chair.
Nick is **home** from school.	*zu Hause*	**home**	*nach Hause*	Let's go **home**, Sita.

p.43/A3	**Don't do** that. [ˌdəʊnt 'duː ðæt]	Tu das nicht. / Lass das.	

(to) do – (to) make

(to) **do** (tun, machen)	(to) **make** (machen, bilden, zubereiten)
Can you **do** exercise 3?	Let's **make** a poster/a video/a cage/... . **Make** sentences/questions/two groups/... .
You're silly, Lulu. Don't **do** that.	Can you **make** the beds, please?
I can clean the bathroom. What can you **do**?	Let's **make** hamburgers/tea/... .

	(to) **take** [teɪk]	nehmen; mitnehmen; (weg)bringen	Thanks for the book, Ben. Can I *take* it with me? Please *take* the old chair upstairs, Debbie.
	into ['ɪntə, *betont:* 'ɪntuː]	in (... hinein)	*into* 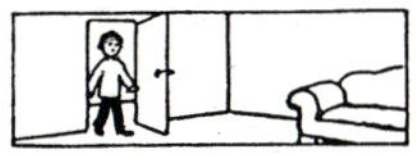 *in* 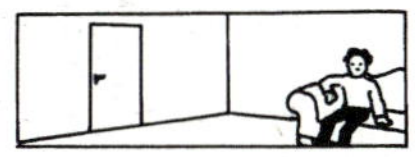
	dirty ['dɜːti]	schmutzig	⧓ clean
	(to) **run** [rʌn]	laufen, rennen	
	Go **to** your basket.	Geh zu deinem Korb.	

(to) go = gehen; fahren

Go *into* the bathroom.	Geh *ins* Bad.
Go *to* your cage.	Geh *zu* deinem Käfig.
Go *to* school, Ben.	Geh *zur* Schule, Ben.
Let's *go to* Ashton today.	Lass uns heute *nach* Ashton *fahren.*

	Collect sentences like	*Sammle Sätze wie ... .*	
	a list of ...	*eine Liste von ...*	
	(to) **wear** [weə]	tragen, anhaben *(Kleidung)*	Can I *wear* your red T-shirt, Sally? – Yes, OK.
	(to) **draw** [drɔː]	zeichnen	
A4	(to) **read** [riːd]	lesen	 He*'s reading.*
A5	(to) **play** [pleɪ]	spielen	 She*'s playing* football.
p.44/A6	(to) **work** [wɜːk]	arbeiten	 He*'s washing* a pullover.
	(to) **wash** [wɒʃ]	waschen	
	Close your eyes and imagine	*Schließ deine Augen und stell dir vor, ...*	
A7	six **o'clock** [ˌsɪks‿ə'klɒk]	sechs Uhr	It's *six o'clock* now. 
	(to) **pack** [pæk]	packen	
	weekend [ˌwiːk'end]	Wochenende	Can we go to Ashton at the *weekend*? ⚠ *at* the weekend = *am* Wochenende; *in* the afternoon = *am* Nachmittag
A8	**letter (to)** ['letə]	Brief (an)	Trundle is writing a *letter to* Jenny. ⚠ *letter* = **1.** Buchstabe; **2.** Brief
p.45/A10	(to) **wait (for)** ['weɪt fɔː]	warten (auf)	*Don't wait for* Trundle – he's late.
	at home [ət 'həʊm]	zu Hause, daheim	Nick and Debbie are going home. *At home* their mum is waiting for them.
A11	**dinner** ['dɪnə]	Abendessen, Abendbrot	
	(to) **watch TV** [ˌwɒtʃ tiː'viː]	fernsehen	Susan and Michael *are watching TV.* 
	(to) **watch** [wɒtʃ]	beobachten, sich *(etwas)* ansehen	

(to) look – (to) see – (to) watch

Look. Can you **see** Lulu? – Yes, I can **see** Lulu.	**Guck** mal. Kannst du Lulu **sehen**? – ...
What is she doing? – She**'s watching** Trundle.	... – Sie **beobachtet** Trundle.
What are Jenny and Sally doing? – They**'re watching TV**.	... – Sie **sehen fern**.

(to) **wash the dishes** ['dɪʃɪz]	das Geschirr abwaschen	
why? [waɪ]	warum?	It's 9 o'clock. *Why* are you late, Peter?
(to) **sleep** [sliːp]	schlafen	
Have a nice weekend.	Schönes Wochenende.	
a telephone dialogue	*ein Dialog am Telefon*	

	these or other words	*diese oder andere Wörter*	
	Act the dialogue	*Spiel den Dialog ... .*	
P 1	*(to) put in*	*einsetzen*	 
	(to) **listen (to)** ['lɪsn]	*(jm.)* zuhören; sich *(etwas)* anhören; horchen	*Listen to* the song. / *Listen*. Can you hear Lulu? She's in the garden. ⚠ *(to) listen (to)* = zuhören, sich anhören; *(to) hear* = hören (können)
	(to) write **on** the board	an die Tafel schreiben	
P 4	*mistake*	*Fehler*	
P 5	*Mind the spelling.*	*Gib Acht auf die Schreibung.*	
P 6	**Spot the difference.** [ˌspɒt ðə 'dɪfrəns]	Entdecke den Unterschied.	⚠ Aussprache Plural: *difference* ['dɪfrəns] – *differences* ['dɪfrənsɪz]
	(to) write down	*aufschreiben*	
	(to) find out	*herausfinden*	
P 7	*Mime an activity in front of your form.*	*Spiele deiner Klasse eine Tätigkeit vor.*	
	(to) guess	*raten*	
P 8	**Sorry?** ['sɒri]	Wie bitte?	
[P 10]	*a piece of paper*	*ein Stück Papier*	
	Fill in the boxes.	*Fülle die Kästchen aus.*	
	Give them out to your form.	*Verteile sie an deine Klasse.*	
P 12	**dream house** ['dri:m haʊs]	Traumhaus	
	the text about ...	*der Text über ...*	

The tree house

p.50	**Saturday** ['sætədeɪ, 'sætədi]	Samstag, Sonnabend	
	day [deɪ]	Tag	⚠ Guten *Tag*. = Hello./Good morning./Good afternoon. (*nicht:* ~~Good day~~.)
	(to) **talk (to)** [tɔ:k]	reden (mit), sich unterhalten (mit)	Susan *is talking to* Sandra. The two girls *are talking*. 
	°rope [rəʊp]	Seil	
	°(to) pull [pʊl]	ziehen	
	up [ʌp]	hinauf, herauf, nach oben	 *up* the tree
	down [daʊn]	hinunter, herunter, nach unten	 *down* the tree ⚠ Wortstellung: *up* the tree = den Baum *hinauf*
	a piece of [ə 'pi:s‿əv]	ein Stück	*a piece of* wood 
	°wood [wʊd]	Holz	
	one more [ˌwʌn 'mɔ:]	noch ein(e), ein(e) weitere(r, s)	*two more pieces* of wood ['pi:sɪz] 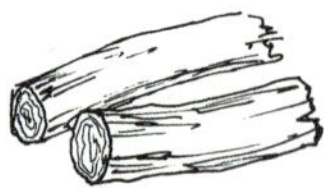
	child [tʃaɪld], *pl* **children** ['tʃɪldrən]	Kind	
	wall [wɔ:l]	Wand; Mauer	A room has got four *walls*.
	°roof [ru:f]	Dach	
	you're **too** little [tu:]	du bist zu klein	**too** [tu:] The flat is *too* big. – *zu* groß; The garden is big, *too*. – *auch* groß; **two** [tu:] The *two* girls are sisters. – *zwei*
	Be careful. ['keəfl]	Sei vorsichtig.	
p.51	(to) **fly** [flaɪ]	fliegen	
	city ['sɪti]	Stadt, Großstadt	⚠ one *city* – two *cities*
	°river ['rɪvə]	Fluss	
	°cathedral [kə'θi:drəl]	Kathedrale, Dom	

(to) **move** [muːv]	(sich) bewegen	*Don't move.*

just [dʒʌst]	nur, bloß	Is Nick your boyfriend, Debbie? – No, he's *just* my brother.
then	*dann*	
in the right order	*in der richtigen Reihenfolge*	

▶▶▶ Topic 3: The time and date

p.52/1 **date** [deɪt]	Datum	
What time is it? [ˌwɒt ˈtaɪm‿ɪz‿ɪt]	Wie spät ist es?	
quarter past eight [ˌkwɔːtə pɑːst‿ˈeɪt]	Viertel nach acht (8.15/20.15)	
half past eight [ˌhɑːf pɑːst‿ˈeɪt]	halb neun (8.30/20.30)	
quarter to nine [ˌkwɔːtə tə ˈnaɪn]	Viertel vor neun (8.45/20.45)	
Read out the times.	*Lies die Uhrzeiten vor.*	
2 **when?** [wen]	wann?	Let's watch 'The pet show'. – *When* is it?
3.50 **to** 5.30	3 Uhr 50 bis 5 Uhr 30	

What *time* is it?	Wie spät ist es?
What *time* is the film?	Wann fängt der Film an?

p.53/3 **calendar** [ˈkælɪndə]	Kalender
month [mʌnθ]	Monat

The months

January [ˈdʒænjʊəri]	**April** [ˈeɪprəl]	**July** [dʒʊˈlaɪ]	**October** [ɒkˈtəʊbə]
February [ˈfebrʊəri]	**May** [meɪ]	**August** [ˈɔːgəst]	**November** [nəʊˈvembə]
March [mɑːtʃ]	**June** [dʒuːn]	**September** [sepˈtembə]	**December** [dɪˈsembə]

Write: *1st January* – Say: ***the** first **of** January*

week [wiːk]	Woche

The days of the week

Monday [ˈmʌndeɪ, ˈmʌndi]	**Friday** [ˈfraɪdeɪ, -di]
Tuesday [ˈtjuːzdeɪ, -di]	**Saturday** [ˈsætədeɪ, -di]
Wednesday [ˈwenzdeɪ, -di]	**Sunday** [ˈsʌndeɪ, -di]
Thursday [ˈθɜːzdeɪ, -di]	

What's the date on the first Friday in May, 2020?
Welches Datum haben wir am ersten Freitag …?
What day is 1st January, 2020?
Was für ein Tag ist der 1. Januar 2020?

on – in

on 12th January
on Monday
Write *on* the board.

on the floor/*on* the chair/…
Put the books *on* the desk.
Write *on* cards.

on → am, an / auf

in the morning
in the afternoon

in the picture
in English

in → am / auf / in, im

in England/*in* Form 7CH/*in* the classroom/…
in November
Write *in* your exercise book.

tomorrow [təˈmɒrəʊ]	morgen	Let's play *tomorrow* afternoon.
next Monday [nekst]	(am) nächsten Montag	⚠ *next Monday/next week* aber: *the next day* = am nächsten Tag

to**morrow**
morgen

birthday [ˈbɜːθdeɪ]	Geburtstag

It's my *birthday* next week.	Ich habe nächste Woche Geburtstag.
When's your *birthday*? – It's on 1st March.	Wann hast du Geburtstag? – Am 1. März.

4 **evening** [ˈiːvnɪŋ]	Abend
night [naɪt]	Nacht, (später) Abend

TIPP **Verbindungen herstellen**
Wenn du ein neues Wort lernst, schließ die Augen, sag das Wort leise und stell dir etwas vor, was du mit dem Wort verbinden kannst:
- ein Bild (vielleicht ein witziges),
- die Zeichnung in der rechten Spalte,
- ein Ereignis aus deinem Englischbuch,
- etwas, was du selbst erlebt hast,
- einen bestimmten Ort,
- eine Farbe, ein Geräusch, einen Geruch oder Geschmack.

Dadurch wird jedes Wort etwas Besonderes für dich und es fällt dir später leichter wieder ein.

▶▶▶ Unit 4: Happy birthday!

p.54/55	(to) **dream (about)** ['driːm‿əˌbaʊt]	träumen (von)	⚠ *dream* = **1.** träumen; **2.** Traum

about

Let's talk **about** pets.	Lass uns **über** Haustiere sprechen.
Mrs Walker is writing a book **about** dogs.	Frau Walker schreibt gerade ein Buch **über** Hunde.
The story **is about** Lulu, Trundle, Marmalade and C1B1.	Die Geschichte **handelt von** Lulu, Trundle, Marmalade und C1B1.
Trundle is dreaming **about** a new cage.	Trundle träumt **von** einem neuen Käfig.
Answer three questions **about** your English book.	Beantworte drei Fragen **über** dein/**zu** deinem Englischbuch.

	candle ['kændl]	Kerze	candle
	cake [keɪk]	Kuchen, Torte	a *cake* with *candles* 
	orange juice ['ɒrɪndʒ dʒuːs]	Orangensaft	
	present ['preznt]	Geschenk	a *present* 
	chips *(pl)* [tʃɪps]	Pommes frites	 *chips* and *ice-cream*
	ice-cream [ˌaɪs'kriːm]	(Speise-)Eis	
	lots (of) ['lɒts‿əv]	eine Menge, viel, viele	I've got *lots of* videos. Have you got videos? – Yes, *lots*.
	(to) add of your favourite star	*hinzufügen, ergänzen deines Lieblingsstars*	
p.56/A1	(to) **have a party** ['pɑːti]	eine Party veranstalten, feiern	Let's *have a* birthday *party*!
	You **can't** … . [kɑːnt] (= You **cannot** … .) ['kænɒt]	Du kannst nicht … . / Du darfst nicht … .	▸◂ you can
	idea [aɪ'dɪə]	Idee, Einfall	Let's make cakes for our party. – That's a good *idea*.
	Nick can **have** a video. ['vɪdiəʊ]	Nick kann ein Video haben/bekommen.	Ben has got lots of videos. Nick can *have* a video for his birthday.
A2	**invitation** [ˌɪnvɪ'teɪʃn]	Einladung	
	Must we …? [mʌst]	Müssen wir …?	
	(to) **tell (about)** [tel]	erzählen (von), berichten (über)	*Tell* me *about* your pets, please. ⚠ *tell* braucht immer ein Objekt – sag immer, wem du etwas erzählst oder berichtest.
A3	*Make notes.*	*Mach dir Notizen.*	football
	football ['fʊtbɔːl]	Fußball	
	(to) **ride a bike** [ˌraɪd‿ə 'baɪk]	Rad fahren	Lulu can run, but she can't *ride a bike*. Sita can't *ride her bike* now – she must help at home. Let's *ride our bikes* to school, Nick. (= mit dem Rad zur Schule fahren)
	(to) **sing** [sɪŋ]	singen	
	Fill it in.	*Füll es aus.*	

p.57/A4	(to) **look for** ['lʊk fɔ:]	suchen	I can't find my school bag. Can you *look for* it, Nick?
	a box of chocolates ['tʃɒkləts]	eine Schachtel Pralinen	⚠ *chocolate* = **1.** Praline; **2.** Schokolade

Mengenangaben mit „of"

a **box of** chocolates	eine **Schachtel** Pralinen
a **piece of** chocolate	ein **Stück** Schokolade
a small **number of** children	eine kleine **Anzahl** Kinder/**von** Kindern
a lot of/lots of pencils	**eine Menge** Bleistifte, **viele** Bleistifte
a **group of** girls	eine **Gruppe (von)** Mädchen
in **groups of** four	in Vierer**gruppen**

	watch [wɒtʃ]	Armbanduhr	⚠ *watch* = **1.** beobachten, sich *(etwas)* ansehen; **2.** Armbanduhr
	expensive [ɪk'spensɪv]	teuer	€ 60,- for a T-shirt? That's too *expensive*.
	cheap [tʃi:p]	billig, preiswert	◂▸ expensive
	scarf [skɑ:f], *pl* **scarves** [skɑ:vz]	Schal	⚠ one *scarf* [skɑ:f] – two *scarves* [skɑ:vz] 
	What about a calendar**?**	Wie wär's mit einem Kalender?	
	°class [klɑ:s]	*(deutsche)* (Schul-) Klasse	
A5	**still** [stɪl]	(immer) noch	Is Lulu *still* playing? – Yes, she's *still* in the garden.
	mouse [maʊs], *pl* **mice** [maɪs]	Maus	
p.58/A6	°director [də'rektə]	Regisseur/in	
	(to) **stand** [stænd]	stehen; sich (hin)stellen	 Maik *is standing* on a chair. 
	in front of [ɪn 'frʌnt‿əv]	vor	 *in front of* the wall
	behind [bɪ'haɪnd]	hinter	 *behind* the wall
	man [mæn], *pl* **men** [men]	Mann	
	woman ['wʊmən], *pl* **women** ['wɪmɪn]	Frau	
	back [bæk]	zurück	You can go, but please come *back*.
	bench [bentʃ]	Bank *(zum Sitzen)*	
	next to [nekst]	neben	*next to* the book 
	between [bɪ'twi:n]	zwischen	*between* the books 

Where is the rabbit?

in front of the cage	**behind** the cage	**in** the cage	**between** the girls	**near** the cat	**next to** the cat

A7	*Imagine …*	*Stellt euch vor, …*	
	one of you	*eine/r von euch*	
p.59/A8	(to) **act** [ækt]	spielen, schauspielern	⚠ *(to) act* = (eine Rolle, einen Dialog) *spielen*; *(to) play* = (ein Spiel) *spielen*
	(to) **dance** [dɑ:ns]	tanzen	
	(to) **climb** [klaɪm]	klettern; hinaufklettern (auf)	Can cats *climb*? – Yes, they can. They *climb* trees and walls. ⚠ Stummes „b": *climb* [klaɪm], *climbing* ['klaɪmɪŋ]
A9	**them** [ðəm, *betont:* ðem]	sie; ihnen	There are the twins. I can see *them*. Let's help *them*.
	us [əs, *betont:* ʌs]	uns	We're here. Can you see *us*?

	you	dich/dir; euch; Sie/Ihnen	I can see *you*, I can hear *you* – but I can't help *you*.
	her [hə, *betont:* hɜː]	sie; ihr	There's Sita. I can see *her*. Let's help *her*.
	him [hɪm]	ihn; ihm	There's Ben. I can see *him*. Let's help *him*.
	because he's the director [bɪˈkɒz]	weil er der Regisseur ist	Wash your pullover, please. – Why? – *Because* it's dirty!
	on the bus [bʌs]	im Bus	
p.60/A10	**there are** [ðər‿ə, ðeər‿ɑː]	es sind (vorhanden); es gibt	
	there's [ðəz, ðeəz] = **there is**	es ist (vorhanden); es gibt	

there is, there's – there are

Du kennst bereits *there* (= da, dort): Jenny isn't *there*. / Sit *there*, please.

Mit *there is* und *there are* kannst du auch sagen, dass etwas vorhanden ist.
Im Deutschen benutzt man meist „Es gibt", „Es ist/sind" oder Sätze mit „liegen", „stehen".
In solchen Sätzen ist die Aussprache von *there* meist [ðə].

There's a good film on TV.	**Es gibt** einen guten Film im Fernsehen.
There isn't a film for children today.	Heute **gibt es keinen** Film für Kinder.
Is there an Indian restaurant in your town?	**Gibt es** ein indisches Restaurant in deiner Stadt?
– Yes, **there is**. / No, **there isn't**.	– Ja (, **gibt es**). / Nein (, **gibt es nicht**).
There's a boy at the door.	An der Tür **ist** ein Junge.
There's a card for you on the desk.	Auf dem Schreibtisch **liegt** eine Karte für dich.
There are lots of chairs in the kitchen.	In der Küche **stehen** viele Stühle.

	sandwich [ˈsænwɪdʒ]	*(zusammengeklapptes)* belegtes Brot, Sandwich	*sandwiches* 
	table [ˈteɪbl]	Tisch	
A11	**only** [ˈəʊnli]	nur, bloß; erst	There aren't two CDs on the desk, there's *only* one. Sanjay isn't sixteen – he's *only* fourteen.
A12	a picture **of** Chester [ə ˈpɪktʃər‿əv]	ein Bild von Chester	Can one *of* you (= eine/r von euch) draw a picture *of* your school and one *of* you draw the teachers?
	°part [pɑːt]	Teil	
	(to) **laugh (at)** [lɑːf]	lachen (über); *(jn.)* auslachen	Don't *laugh at* Ben. He isn't silly. He's nice. 
P 5	*for two minutes*	*zwei Minuten (lang)*	
	(to) close	*schließen, zumachen*	
	list [lɪst]	Liste	
P 6	**homework** *(no pl)* [ˈhəʊmwɜːk]	Hausaufgabe(n)	⚠ Hausaufgaben *sind* langweilig. = Homework *is* boring.
P 7	(to) **ask** [ɑːsk]	fragen	Let's play a game: you must *ask questions* (= Fragen stellen), and I must answer them.
P 9	*paper*	*Papier*	
	line	*Linie*	
P 13	*combination*	*Kombination, Verbindung*	
[P 14]	*the day of the mice*	*der Tag der Mäuse*	
	a copy of	*eine Kopie von*	
	(to) draw in	*einzeichnen*	
P 15	*classmate*	*Klassenkamerad/in*	

Twelve little cakes

p.66	(to) **put down** (-tt-)[1] [ˌpʊt ˈdaʊn]	hinstellen, hinlegen	*Put down* the cake, Sally. It isn't for you.
	(to) **eat** [iːt]	essen	
	(to) **drink** [drɪŋk]	trinken	
	°witch [wɪtʃ]	Hexe	

[1] Die Angabe „(-tt-)" zeigt, dass der Endkonsonant bei der Bildung der *-ing*-Form verdoppelt wird: *putting*.

	alone [ə'ləʊn]	allein	⚠ *alone* = allein – *lonely* = einsam (und unglücklich)
	(to) **give** [gɪv]	geben	⧓ (to) take
p.67	**then** [ðen]	dann, danach	
	supermarket ['su:pəmɑ:kɪt]	Supermarkt	
	(to) **be in trouble** ['trʌbl]	in Schwierigkeiten sein; Ärger kriegen	Nick hasn't got his homework. He*'s in trouble* now.
	the other [ði‿'ʌðə]	der/die/das andere, die anderen	Ben is at home. *The other* children are at school.
	the missing dialogue	*der fehlende Dialog*	
	line	*Zeile*	
	You can start like this:	*So kannst du beginnen:*	

TIPP

Wiederholung macht den Meister!

- Es gibt sicherlich Wörter, die du bereits gelernt, aber dann doch wieder vergessen hast. Um dir Wörter richtig fest einzuprägen, solltest du sie regelmäßig wiederholen. Sieh dir immer wieder die Wörter der letzten Units an. Kannst du sie noch?
- Die rechte Spalte des Vokabelverzeichnisses hilft dir nicht nur beim Lernen, sondern auch beim Wiederholen. Decke die deutsche und die englische Spalte ab und sieh dir die englischen Beispielsätze und die Zeichnungen an: Wie heißt das Wort auf Deutsch?

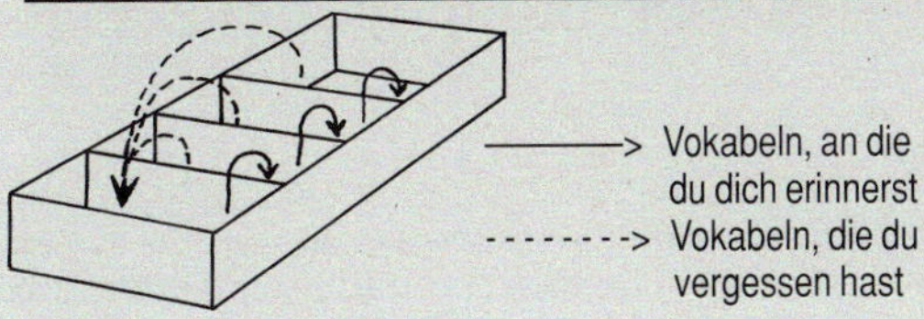

Arbeitest du mit einer **Vokabelkartei**? Dann solltest du ab jetzt alle vier Fächer benutzen:

- Gehe regelmäßig alle Fächer durch. Aber nicht alle auf einmal – verteile die Arbeit lieber auf mehrere Tage.
- Vokabeln, die „sitzen", wandern immer ein Fach weiter nach hinten.
- Vokabeln, die du vergessen hast, wandern immer zurück ins erste Fach.
- Karten, die im vierten Fach angekommen sind, kannst du aus der Kartei herausnehmen – aber mache erst noch einen Prüfdurchgang, ob du die Vokabeln wirklich noch kannst!

Viermal gekonnt ist wirklich gekonnt!

Wenn du regelmäßig wiederholst, reichen 20 bis 30 Karten pro Durchgang!

▶▶▶ Topic 4: Money, money, money

p.68/1	**money** ['mʌni]	Geld	
	pound (£) [paʊnd]	Pfund *(brit. Währung)*	
	pence *(pl)* [pens]	Pence	10*p* [pi:] = 10 *pence*
	penny ['peni]	*kleinste britische Münze*	1*p* [pi:] = 1 *penny*
	You say … [ˌjʊ 'seɪ]	Du sagst / Man sagt …	
	euro (€) ['jʊərəʊ]	Euro	
2	**How much is/are …?** [ˌhaʊ 'mʌtʃ]	Was kostet/kosten …? Wie viel kostet/kosten …?	*How much is* the green biro? And *how much are* the pencils?
	the felt-tip **is** £1	der Filzstift kostet £1	The green biro *is* £2.25, the pencils *are* 35p.
p.69/3	(to) **buy** [baɪ]	kaufen	I must *buy* a nice present for my dad's birthday.
	(to) read to	*vorlesen*	
	Ask … for the exchange rate.	*Frage … nach dem Wechselkurs.*	
	things	*Dinge, Sachen*	
4	**May I help you?** [meɪ]	Sie wünschen? (*wörtlich:* Darf ich Ihnen helfen?)	*May I help you?* – Yes, please. I'm looking for a new cage for my hamster.

„dürfen"

Can I watch TV now? – Yes, you **can**. / No, you **can't**. — *Darf* ich jetzt fernsehen?

Wenn man besonders höflich um Erlaubnis bitten möchte, benutzt man *may* statt *can*:

May I use your computer, please? – Yes, you **may**. / No, you **may** not. — *Darf* ich bitte/*Dürfte* ich deinen Computer benutzen?

assistant [ə'sɪstənt]	Verkäufer/in	
customer ['kʌstəmə]	Kunde, Kundin	
I'm just looking.	Ich sehe mich nur um.	

▸▸▸ Unit 5: Kingsway High School

p.70/71	**uniform** ['ju:nɪfɔ:m]	Uniform	⚠ Aussprache ['ju:nɪfɔ:m], daher: <u>a</u> *uniform, the uniform* [ðə 'ju:nɪfɔ:m]
	grey [greɪ]	grau	
	pupil ['pju:pl]	Schüler, Schülerin	There are 28 *pupils* in my form – 16 girls, 12 boys.
	canteen [kæn'ti:n]	Kantine, Schulmensa	
	lunch [lʌntʃ]	Mittagessen	Pupils can buy *lunch* in the school canteen.
	break [breɪk]	Pause	Lunch *break* is at 12.20 at Kingsway High.
	lesson ['lesn]	Unterrichtsstunde	Today our first *lesson* is English.
	lessons *(pl)*	Unterricht	English *lessons* are great! (= Der Englischunterricht ist toll!)
	in the morning(s)	am Morgen, morgens	

Zeit-angaben (1)

in the morning(s)	am Morgen, morgens	**this morning**	heute Morgen
in the afternoon(s)	am Nachmittag, nachmittags	**this afternoon**	heute Nachmittag
in the evening(s)	am Abend, abends	**this evening**	heute Abend
⚠ **at night**	in der Nacht, nachts	⚠ **tonight** [tə'naɪt]	heute Nacht, heute Abend

	Assembly [ə'sembli]	Schulversammlung (oft mit Andacht)	
	every ['evri]	jede, jeder, jedes	There are chips for lunch *every* day in the canteen!
	drama ['drɑ:mə]	Drama, Schauspiel	
	club [klʌb]	Klub; Verein	
	sport [spɔ:t]	Sport, Sportart	*Sport* is good for you!
	(to) **go with**	passen zu	
	(to) **go together**	zusammenpassen	
	information	*Informationen*	
	(to) take photos	*Fotos machen*	
p.72/A1	**brochure** ['brəʊʃə]	Prospekt, Broschüre	
A2	**information** *(no pl)* [ˌɪnfə'meɪʃn]	Information(en); Auskunft, Auskünfte	All the *information* about Chester is in the brochure. ⚠ Nie: *information*~~s~~ / Nie: ~~*an information*~~
A3	**from** Monday **to** Friday	von Montag bis Freitag	

from

aus	Ben is **from** Ashton. a football team **from** Chester a letter **from** Germany words **from** the box a page **from** the school brochure	**von**	**from** Monday to Friday a football team **from** Kingsway High a letter **from** Ben ⚠ a letter **from** Jenny with a picture **of** Trundle *ein Brief **von** Jenny mit einem Bild **von** Trundle*

	(to) **start** [stɑ:t]	anfangen, beginnen (mit)	The twins *start* lessons at 8.45 every morning. Lessons *start* at 8.45 in Chester.
	(to) **finish** ['fɪnɪʃ]	beenden, zu Ende machen; enden	Let's *finish* the exercise and read the text again. Lessons *finish* at 3.30. ⧓ (to) start
	(to) **bring** [brɪŋ]	(mit-, her)bringen	⚠ *(to) bring* = herbringen | *(to) take* = hinbringen

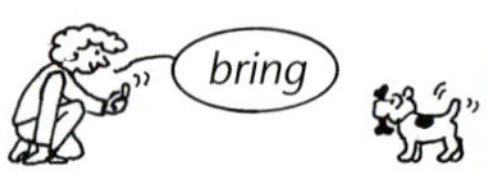

A4	**after** ['ɑ:ftə]	nach *(zeitlich)*	Don't play in the garden *after* 9 o'clock, please.
	before [bɪ'fɔ:]	vor *(zeitlich)*	The English lesson is *before* lunch. ⧓ after

„vor" – „nach"

vor	Can we watch TV ***before*** school? *aber in Uhrzeiten:* It's ten **to** three.	**nach**	Let's play tennis ***after*** school. *aber in Uhrzeiten:* It's ten **past** three.

	judo ['dʒu:dəʊ]	Judo	
p.73/A5	**timetable** ['taɪmteɪbl]	Stundenplan	

School and sport

School subjects ['sʌbdʒɪkts]	Schulfächer	Sports	Sportarten
English ['ɪŋglɪʃ]	Englisch	**badminton** ['bædmɪntən]	Badminton, Federball
French [frentʃ]	Französisch	**basketball** ['bɑ:skɪtbɔ:l]	Basketball
Geography [dʒi'ɒgrəfi]	Geographie, Erdkunde	**football** ['fʊtbɔ:l]	Fußball
		hockey ['hɒki]	Hockey
Maths *(sing)* [mæθs]	Mathematik	**judo** ['dʒu:dəʊ]	Judo
Music ['mju:zɪk]	Musik	**volleyball** ['vɒlibɔ:l]	Volleyball

⚠ You *play* football/hockey/…, but you *do* judo.

Dear Katrin and Julia, … [dɪə]	Liebe Katrin, liebe Julia, …	
(to) **try** [traɪ]	versuchen, (aus)probieren	Collect words and *try* and make sentences. (= … versuche, Sätze zu bilden.)

Verben auf „-y"

1. Vor dem *-y* steht ein **Konsonant**:

try – he/she/it is **trying** / he/she/it **tries**

Ebenso: **fly** – **flying, flies**
tidy up – **tidying up, tidies up**

2. Vor dem *-y* steht ein **Vokal**:

play – he/she/it is **playing** / he/she/it **plays**

Ebenso: **say** – **saying, says**
buy – **buying, buys**

Zeitangaben (2)

on Monday	am Montag	**at the weekend**	am Wochenende
on Mondays (= every Monday)	montags, jeden Montag	**at weekends**	an Wochenenden
on Monday morning	am Montagmorgen		
on Monday evenings (= every Monday evening)	montagabends/ montags abends		

	(to) **like** [laɪk]	mögen, gern haben	
	favourite ['feɪvərɪt]	Lieblings-	Nick's *favourite* sport is football.
	different ['dɪfrənt]	verschieden, unterschiedlich; anders; andere(r, s)	Nick and Debbie are in the same form. Sita and Sanjay are in *different* forms. Cats and dogs are *different* – cats can climb, dogs can't.
	Love, … [lʌv]	Viele liebe Grüße (von) …	
A6	**stamp** [stæmp]	Briefmarke	
	(to) **collect** [kə'lekt]	sammeln	You can *collect* stamps, stickers, comics, posters, … .
	play [pleɪ]	Theaterstück	⚠ *play* = **1.** spielen; **2.** Theaterstück
	chess [tʃes]	Schach	
	(to) **meet** [mi:t]	sich treffen; *(jn.)* treffen	Play chess with us – we *meet* on Mondays. Can you *meet* us after school?
	(to) **take photos** ['fəʊtəʊz]	Fotos machen, fotografieren	Come to the camera club and *take photos.* ⚠ *auf* dem Foto = *in* the photo
	(to) **learn** [lɜ:n]	lernen	*Learn* about cameras in the camera club.
	gym [dʒɪm]	Sporthalle, Turnhalle	
p.74/A8	(to) **love** [lʌv]	lieben, sehr mögen	
A9	(to) **hate** [heɪt]	hassen, gar nicht mögen	◂▸ (to) love

***do* als Vollverb, *do* als Hilfsverb**

Du kennst bereits das Vollverb „(to) **do**" (= tun, machen):

I can't **do** exercise 4. Can you **do** it?
Sanjay **does** judo on Wednesdays.

„**do**" kann auch Hilfsverb sein. Als Hilfsverb steht es zusammen mit einem Vollverb:

Sit on your chair, please. **Don't** sit on your desk.
Marmalade likes tennis, but she **doesn't** like chess.
Sanjay **doesn't** do judo on Fridays.

Hilfsverb **Vollverb**

p.75/A11	**au pair** [ˌəʊ 'peə]	Aupair(mädchen, -junge)	

	always ['ɔːlweɪz]	immer	
	never ['nevə]	nie, niemals	⧓ always
	(to) **get up** (-tt-) [ˌget_'ʌp]	aufstehen	I always *get up* at 7.30. I never *get up* before 7.30.
	breakfast ['brekfəst]	Frühstück	What's for *breakfast* this morning? ⚠ Aussprache: *breakfast* ['brekfəst] – *break* [breɪk]
	at work [wɜːk]	bei der Arbeit, am Arbeitsplatz	⚠ *work* = **1.** arbeiten; **2.** Arbeit
	(to) **fetch (from)** [fetʃ]	holen, abholen (von)	Can you *fetch* me *from* school today, Mum?
	usually ['juːʒuəli]	meistens, gewöhnlich, normalerweise	never – sometimes – often – usually – always
	sometimes ['sʌmtaɪmz]	manchmal	
	Yours, [jɔːz]	dein/deine; euer/eure; Ihr/Ihre *(Briefschluss)*	
P 4	**around** Ashton [ə'raʊnd]	in Ashton umher, durch Ashton	Let's ride our bikes *around* the village.
P 5	**match** [mætʃ]	Spiel, Wettkampf	Football *matches* are usually on Saturdays.
P 7	*pronunciation*	*Aussprache*	
	ending	*Endung*	
P 13	*correct*	*korrekt, richtig*	
[P 17]	*before*	*bevor*	
	What is the group's new play about?	*Wovon handelt das neue Stück der Gruppe?*	
	face	*Gesicht*	
	scene	*Szene*	
	king	*König*	
	prince	*Prinz*	
	dancing girl	*Tänzerin*	
P 19	*the following words*	*die folgenden Wörter*	

The Saturday match

p.83	*before*	*bevor*	
	(to) **sleep late** [ˌsliːp 'leɪt]	lange schlafen	I usually *sleep late* at the weekend. ⚠ Nicht: ~~*sleep long*~~, sondern: *sleep late*.
	today's match	das heutige Spiel	*Today's* lunch in the canteen is pizza and chips.
	(to) **be special** ['speʃl]	etwas Besonderes sein	Tortoises can't talk – but Trundle *is special*.
	°rival ['raɪvl]	Rivale, Rivalin	
	on the radio	im Radio	There's a football match *on the radio*. What's *on TV*?
	°goal [gəʊl]	Tor *(im Sport)*	
	one nil **to** …	eins zu null für …	

to

Welcome **to** Chester.	Willkommen **in** Chester.
Let's go **to** Chester.	Lass uns **nach** Chester fahren.
Go **to** your cage, Trundle.	Geh **zu** deinem Käfig, Trundle.
one nil **to** Chester	eins zu null **für** Chester
a letter **to** Ben	ein Brief **an** Ben
It's quarter **to** nine.	Es ist Viertel **vor** neun.
from 3.30 **to** 5.15	von 3.30 **bis** 5.15
Don't talk **to** Debbie.	Sprich nicht **mit** Debbie.

half-time [ˌhɑːf'taɪm]	Halbzeitpause	the break between two halves of a football match
half [hɑːf], *pl* **halves** [hɑːvz]	Hälfte, Hälften	⚠ *die erste Halbzeit = the first half*

„Stumme" Buchstaben

l: half
w: answer, write, wrong
k: know
b: climb
d: sandwich

orange ['ɒrɪndʒ]	Apfelsine, Orange	
What are they talking about?	Worüber reden sie?	Ben is talking about computers. *What are Nick and Debbie talking about?*
(to) **take off** [ˌteɪk_'ɒf]	ausziehen *(Kleidung)*	*Take off* my new T-shirt, Jenny!
shoe [ʃuː]	Schuh	

p.84	°whistle ['wɪsl]	(An-)Pfiff; (Triller-)Pfeife	
	terrible ['terəbl]	schrecklich, furchtbar	
	so lonely [səʊ]	so einsam	Poor Ben! He's *so* lonely. ⚠ *so* = **1.** so; **2.** deshalb; also

TIPP

Schwierige Vokabeln – leicht gelernt!

- Schreib die Wörter, die du dir nicht so gut merken kannst, **groß** auf Papier.
- Hänge die Wörter an deine Pinnwand, deine Zimmertür, an den Spiegel, an die Wand neben deinem Kopfkissen … – jedenfalls so, dass du sie immer wieder vor Augen hast.

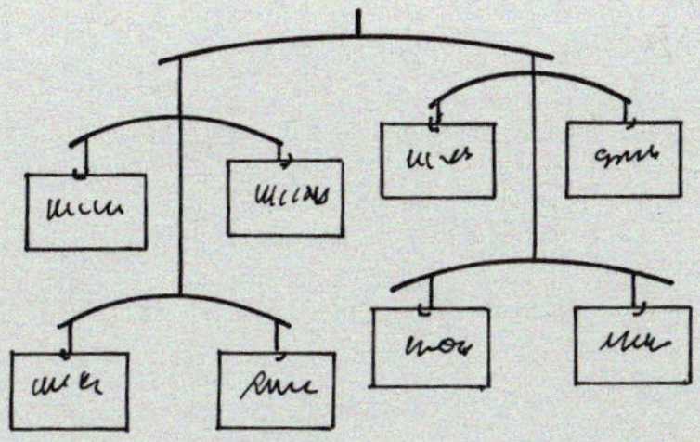

- Du kannst dir auch ein Vokabel-Mobile basteln – mit Kleiderbügeln geht das ganz leicht. Befestige kleine Haken an den Fäden, sodass du jede Woche neue Wörter aufhängen kannst.

▶▶▶ Unit 6: Out shopping

p.88/89	**shopping** ['ʃɒpɪŋ]	Einkaufen; Einkäufe

shopping

Ben's mum and dad *are out **shopping***.
Sita doesn't often *go **shopping***.
Debbie *goes to the **shops*** every week.
She *loves **shopping***.
Ben doesn't *like **shopping***. He *hates **shopping***.

Every Friday we *do the **shopping*** for the weekend.

Where can you buy pets? – At the pet ***shop***.

(to) **go shopping** / (to) **go to the shops** = einkaufen gehen
(to) **like shopping** = gern einkaufen gehen
(to) **love shopping** = sehr gern einkaufen gehen
(to) **hate shopping** = gar nicht gern einkaufen gehen
(to) **do the shopping** = Einkäufe machen/erledigen, einkaufen
shop = Laden, Geschäft

magazine [ˌmægə'ziːn]	Zeitschrift	I don't read books, but I read *magazines*.
clothes *(pl)* [kləʊðz, kləʊz]	Kleidung, „Klamotten"	My new *clothes* are great! ⚠ *Kleidung ist* teuer. = *Clothes are* expensive.
fashion ['fæʃn]	Mode	
beach [biːtʃ]	Strand	
swimsuit ['swɪmsuːt]	Badeanzug	

Der *s*-Genitiv

Ben's clothes are by Marco.	Bens Kleidung ist von Marco.
The Scotts' car is great.	Das Auto der Scotts ist toll.
Girls' swimsuits by Fun Fashions	Mädchenbadeanzüge/Badeanzüge für Mädchen von Fun Fashions
a special shop for **men's clothes**	ein Spezialgeschäft für Herrenbekleidung
Today's football match is great.	Das Fußballspiel heute/Das heutige Fußballspiel ist toll.

bright [braɪt]	leuchtend, hell	
by [baɪ]	von	Miss Hunt likes songs *by* The Beatles. ⚠ a song *by* The Beatles (ein Lied *von* den Beatles) a photo *of* Madonna (ein Foto *von* Madonna) a letter *from* Madonna (ein Brief *von* Madonna)
swimming-trunks *(pl)* ['swɪmɪŋtrʌŋks]	Badehose	Nick's new *swimming-trunks* are nice. ⚠ Nie: ~~*a swimming-trunk*~~
shorts *(pl)* [ʃɔːts]	Shorts, kurze Hose	Ben's new *shorts* are nice.

V Unit 6	**sandal** ['sændl]	Sandale	
	shirt [ʃɜːt]	(Ober-)Hemd	
	tartan ['tɑːtn]	Schottenstoff, Schottenmuster	
	jacket ['dʒækɪt]	Jacke; Jackett, Sakko	
	skirt [skɜːt]	Rock	⚠ *skirt* = Rock – *shirt* = Hemd
	(to) **show** [ʃəʊ]	zeigen	Can you *show* me your stamps?
	pretty ['prɪti]	hübsch	 a *pretty blouse*
	blouse [blaʊz]	Bluse	
	(to) **look** great	toll aussehen	Look, Sita has got a new dress. She *looks great*.
	trousers *(pl)* ['traʊzəz]	(lange) Hose	Are your *trousers* new? (= Ist deine Hose neu?) – Yes, they are. ⚠ Nie: ~~a trouser~~

Plural nouns

Clothes are expensive.	Kleidung ist teuer.
Nick's *swimming-trunks are* nice. *They're* red.	Nicks Badehose ist schön. Sie ist rot.
My *trousers are* new. *They're* black.	Meine Hose ist neu. Sie ist schwarz.
My *jeans are* blue. *They're* old.	Meine Jeans ist blau. Sie ist alt.

	sock [sɒk]	Socke, Strumpf	
	Yuck! [jʌk]	Igitt! / Bäh!	
	interesting	*interessant*	
p.90/A1	**these** [ðiːz]	diese, die (hier)	 This is my pen. *These* are my books.
A2	**on the right** [raɪt]	rechts, auf der rechten Seite	Here are my pets. Diana, my dog, is *on the right*. My cat Charles is *on the left*.  
	on the left [left]	links, auf der linken Seite	
	(to) **need** [niːd]	brauchen, benötigen	Can I use your pen, please? – No, sorry. I *need* it.
	long [lɒŋ]	lang	▸◂ short [ʃɔːt]
	those [ðəʊz]	die (da), jene (dort)	
A3	**price** [praɪs]	(Kauf-)Preis	What's the *price* of the car? = How much is the car?
	(to) **go up** [ˌgəʊ‿'ʌp]	steigen	Prices usually *go up* (↗), not down (↘).
	maybe ['meɪbi]	vielleicht	Those shoes are too expensive. – *Maybe* you're right. But they're nice!
	still [stɪl]	trotzdem, dennoch	The shoes are expensive, but I *still* like them. ⚠ *still* = **1.** (immer) noch; **2.** trotzdem, dennoch
	(to) **want** [wɒnt]	(haben) wollen	I *don't want* a black dress, I *want* a red dress.
	expression	*Ausdruck*	
	advert	*Anzeige, Reklame*	
	slogan	*Slogan, Werbespruch*	**FUN** Ben and Grandma always *have fun* with C1B1. Shopping *is fun*. (= … macht Spaß.) Football is boring. – No, it isn't! It*'s fun*.
	(to) **have fun** [fʌn]	Spaß haben, sich amüsieren	
p.91/A4	**class** [klɑːs]	Klasse, Kurs	On Saturdays Grandma Scott goes to her judo *class*.
	some [səm, *betont:* sʌm]	einige, ein paar; etwas	I've got *some* questions. = … *einige* Fragen. I've got *some* money. = … *etwas* Geld.
	toy [tɔɪ]	Spielzeug	*some toys* 
A5	*things*	*Sachen*	

Questions and answers

Meist antwortet man im Englischen auf Entscheidungsfragen *(Yes/No questions)* mit einer so genannten Kurzantwort.

Are you twins? –	**Yes, we are. / No, we aren't.**
Has your sister got a pet? –	**Yes, she has. / No, she hasn't.**
Can your parents sing? –	**Yes, they can. / No, they can't.**
Are you waiting for me? –	**Yes, I am. / No, I'm not.**
Do you watch TV after dinner? –	**Yes, I do. / No, I don't.**

Es gibt aber auch andere Möglichkeiten, auf Entscheidungsfragen zu antworten.

Are you twins? –	**Yes, that's right. / No, that's wrong.**
Can your parents sing? –	**Yes, of course (they can).**
Can your computer sing? –	**No, of course not.**
Do you watch TV after dinner? –	**Yes, sometimes. / No, never.**
Do you often sleep late? –	**No, only on Sundays.**

p.92/A6	(to) **try on** [ˌtraɪ_ˈɒn]	anprobieren *(Kleidung)*	Can I *try on* your new dress? – You can *try* it *on*, but be careful, please.
A7	Does this shirt **look good on** me?	Steht mir dieses Hemd?	
	stupid [ˈstjuːpɪd]	blöd, dämlich	◂▸ clever
	like [laɪk]	wie	Can you make a sound *like* a cat? Start *like this*: Take a felt-tip, … (= Fang *so* an: …) ⚠ *like* = **1.** mögen, gern haben; **2.** wie
A8	**the wrong way round** [ðə ˌrɒŋ weɪ ˈraʊnd]	verkehrt herum	
p.93/A9	**first** [fɜːst]	zuerst, als Erstes	
	(to) **phone** [fəʊn]	anrufen	Can you *phone* me tomorrow? Here's my number.
A10	**thing** [θɪŋ]	Ding, Sache	You can buy lots of *things* at a supermarket.
	food [fuːd]	Essen; Lebensmittel; Futter	The *food* in our school canteen is terrible!
	(to) **pay (for)** [peɪ]	bezahlen	⚠ ein Sandwich *bezahlen* = *pay for* a sandwich

„bezahlen"

Thanks for your work. Can I **pay** you next week?	… Kann ich dich nächste Woche bezahlen?
Where's my money? I can't **pay for** the T-shirt!	… Ich kann das T-Shirt nicht bezahlen!
I'm sorry, I can't **pay £120 for** your old computer.	…, ich kann nicht 120 Pfund für deinen alten Computer bezahlen.

A11	**department store** [dɪˈpɑːtmənt stɔː]	Kaufhaus	
	everything [ˈevriθɪŋ]	alles	◂▸ nothing ⚠ You can't have *everything*. (one word) You can't play football *every day*. (two words)

TIPP

Nicht vergessen – MEMORY spielen!

- Arbeite mit einem Partner/einer Partnerin. Beschriftet 10 bis 15 Kartenpaare:
  - **ENTWEDER** englisches Wort – deutsche Bedeutung *(chair – Stuhl; garden – Garten)*
  - **ODER** Gegensätze *(big – small; question – answer)*
  - **ODER** englisches Wort – Bild
  - **ODER** Teile von Wörtern *(book – shelf → bookshelf)*.

- Legt die Karten verdeckt auf den Tisch. Ihr müsst zusammengehörige Karten finden: Deckt abwechselnd zwei Karten auf. Wenn sie zusammenpassen, dürft ihr sie behalten.
- Vielleicht könnt ihr mehrere solcher Spiele für eure Klasse anfertigen.

P 4	*out of cardboard*	*aus Pappe, aus Karton*	
P 5	(to) **know** [nəʊ]	kennen	*Do* you *know* Ben Scott? – Yes, of course. He's from Ashton. ⚠ *(to) know* = **1.** wissen; **2.** kennen ⚠ Stummes „k": <u>k</u>*now* [nəʊ]
	true	*wahr*	
	point [pɔɪnt]	Punkt	Three *points* for the right answer!
[P 10]	*police*	*Polizei*	
P 11	*poem*	*Gedicht*	
	°easy [ˈiːzi]	leicht	
P 13	°around the world [wɜːld]	rund um die Welt	
P 15	*some*	*einige, ein paar*	
	(to) compare	*vergleichen*	

Why, Gillian, why?

p.101	**street** [stri:t]	Straße *(in einer Stadt)*	The kids are playing *in the street.* (= *auf* der Straße)
	(to) **worry (about)** ['wʌri]	sich Sorgen machen (wegen, um)	Sometimes I come home late – and my mum always *worries about* me.
	size [saɪz]	Größe	What *size* are you, Katrin? – I'm *size* 36 in Germany. That's *size* 10 in Britain, I think.
p.102	**Excuse me.** [ɪk'skju:z]	Entschuldigung. / Entschuldigen Sie.	

Excuse me – Sorry

Excuse me, what time is it, please?
Excuse me, does this bus go to Chester?

You're late, Nick. – *I'm sorry.*
Can you come at three o'clock? – *Sorry,* I can't.

• Wenn ich etwas von jemandem möchte:
Excuse me, ... = *Entschuldigen Sie, ...*

• Wenn ich mich für etwas entschuldige:
Sorry. / I'm sorry. = *Entschuldigung. Tut mir Leid.*

	(to) **stop (-pp-)** [stɒp]	anhalten, stoppen	*Stop* the car here, please. – But we can't *stop* here! ▸◂ (to) start
	What's happening? ['hæpənɪŋ]	Was ist los? / Was geht hier vor?	All the pupils are in front of the school. *What's happening?*
	(to) **happen (to)** ['hæpən]	*(jm.)* geschehen, passieren	Oh no, I'm late! Why *does* it always *happen to* me?
	Shut up. [ˌʃʌt_'ʌp]	Halt den Mund!	*Shut up,* Debbie. I'm watching this film.
p.103	**minute** ['mɪnɪt]	Minute	It's three *minutes* to six. 
	shoplifter ['ʃɒplɪftə]	Ladendieb, Ladendiebin	
	thief [θi:f], *pl* **thieves** [θi:vz]	Dieb, Diebin	⚠ Plurale auf *-ves*: *thief – thieves, half – halves, scarf – scarves, shelf – shelves*
	(to) **believe** [bɪ'li:v]	glauben	Ben's mum really is from Berlin. You can *believe* me.
	proof *(no pl)* [pru:f]	Beweis(e), Nachweis(e)	Is Sita really a thief? We need *proof.* (= Beweise) ⚠ Nie: ~~a proof~~
	police *(pl)* [pə'li:s]	Polizei	⚠ „police" ist immer Plural:  Where *are* the *police*? We must fetch *them.* (Wo ist die Polizei? Wir müssen sie holen.)
	I don't care. [keə]	Das ist mir egal.	But that dress is so expensive, Debbie! – *I don't care.*
	bad [bæd]	schlecht, schlimm	▸◂ good

▶▶▶ Unit 7: A trip to the zoo

p.106/107	**trip (to)** [trɪp]	Ausflug, Reise (nach)	
	zoo [zu:]	Zoo, Tierpark	Form 7CH is on a *trip to* the *zoo.*
	(to) **adopt** [ə'dɒpt]	adoptieren, die Patenschaft übernehmen für	People sometimes *adopt* children.
	animal ['ænɪml]	Tier	
	elephant ['elɪfənt]	Elefant	
	tiger ['taɪgə]	Tiger	
	danger ['deɪndʒə]	Gefahr	A lot of animals are in *danger.* The people at Chester zoo try and *save* them.
	(to) **save** [seɪv]	retten	
	(to) **feed** [fi:d]	füttern	(to) *feed* an animal = (to) give it food
	bird [bɜ:d]	Vogel	
	lion ['laɪən]	Löwe	
	monkey ['mʌŋki]	Affe	
	giraffe [dʒə'rɑ:f]	Giraffe	
	zebra ['zebrə]	Zebra	
	penguin ['peŋgwɪn]	Pinguin	
	sea lion ['si: laɪən]	Seelöwe	
	80 kilos (of) ['ki:ləʊz]	80 Kilo(gramm)	We need 2 *kilos of* oranges for the orange juice.
	bread *(no pl)* [bred]	Brot	
	meat [mi:t]	Fleisch	Some people don't eat *meat* because they love animals.

Wörter mit gleicher Aussprache

[miːt] (to) **meet** *(treffen)* – **meat** *(Fleisch)*	[baɪ] (to) **buy** *(kaufen)* – **Bye** *(Tschüs)* – **by** *(von)*
[nəʊ] (to) **know** *(wissen; kennen)* – **no** *(nein)*	[raɪt] **right** *(richtig)* – **write** *(schreiben)*
[hɪə] (to) **hear** *(hören)* – **here** *(hier)*	[ðeə] **their** *(ihr/e)* – **there** *(dort)* – **they're** *(sie sind)*
[weə] (to) **wear** *(tragen, anhaben)* – **where** *(wo)*	[tuː] **too** *(auch; zu)* – **two** *(zwei)*

tomato [tə'mɑːtəʊ], *pl* **tomatoes** [-z] — Tomate

210 litres (of) ['liːtəz] — 210 Liter

⚠ *2 litres of* juice (2 Liter Saft)
10 kilos of meat (10 Kilo Fleisch)
Can you buy 2 litres of *milk* for the baby, please?

milk [mɪlk] — Milch
(to) stick — *kleben*
onto — *auf*

TIPP

Lernen wie im Flug – mit dem „Vokabelfalter"

- Nimm ein DIN-A4-Blatt.
- Schreib die englischen Wörter und Wendungen, die du lernen oder wiederholen willst, ganz links untereinander hin. (Rechtschreibung überprüfen!)
- Daneben schreibst du die deutschen Bedeutungen.

- Falte die englischen Wörter nach hinten weg, sodass du nur die deutschen Wörter und Wendungen siehst. Weißt du, wie die deutschen Wörter auf Englisch heißen? Schreib sie wieder daneben.
- Mach abwechselnd so weiter, bis das Blatt voll ist.

- Am besten ist es, wenn du die Arbeit mit dem Vokabelfalter auf mehrere Tage aufteilst.

p.108/A1 **quick** [kwɪk] — schnell — We're late, Debbie! Be *quick*!
ham [hæm] — Schinken
cheese [tʃiːz] — Käse
apple ['æpl] — Apfel

banana [bə'nɑːnə] — Banane

A2 (to) **run around** [ə'raʊnd] — umherrennen, herumrennen

around

The animals can't run **around** in their cages.	… in ihren Käfigen **umher**laufen.
Don't stand **around** there. Come in and sit down.	Steh nicht da **rum**. …
Don't run **around** the classroom. Sit down.	… **im** Klassenzimmer **herum**. …
Miss Hunt rides her bike **around** Chester.	… **in** Chester **umher/durch** Chester.
I like my work at the zoo with all the animals **around** me.	… mit all den Tieren **um** mich **herum**.
Look **around** you. What can you see?	Sieh dich **um**. …

Karen is standing *in front of* the bus.

John is sitting *at the front*.

at the front [frʌnt] — vorn

when [wen] — wenn

When Mr Scott comes home, he makes tea.
⚠ *when* = **1.** wann (*When* does he come home?)
2. wenn (*When* he comes home, he …)

A3	**at the moment** ['məʊmənt]	im Moment, gerade, zurzeit	now
	tune	*Melodie*	
p.109/A4	**feeding times** ['fi:dɪŋ taɪmz]	Fütterungszeiten	
A5	**for example** [ˌfər‿ɪg'zɑ:mpl]	zum Beispiel	Nick likes ball games – football, *for example*.
	(to) **find out** [ˌfaɪnd‿'aʊt]	herausfinden	How can we *find out* where the elephants are?
	(to) ask for help	*um Hilfe bitten*	
	dangerous ['deɪndʒərəs]	gefährlich	Be careful. This is a *dangerous* street.
	sharp [ʃɑ:p]	scharf	
	tooth [tu:θ], *pl* **teeth** [ti:θ]	Zahn	Trundle hasn't got very sharp *teeth*.
	during ['djʊərɪŋ]	während	Sanjay never sleeps *during* lessons.
	fast [fɑ:st]	schnell	
p.110/A6	**farm** [fɑ:m]	Bauernhof, Farm	 
	cow [kaʊ]	Kuh	
	sheep, *pl* **sheep** [ʃi:p]	Schaf	
	pig [pɪg]	Schwein	
	(to) **live** [lɪv]	leben, wohnen	The Guptas *live* in Chester.
	country ['kʌntri]	Land	The Scotts live *in the country*. *(= auf dem Land)*
	field [fi:ld]	Feld, Wiese, Weide	You can't play *in these fields* (= *auf …*). They're for the cows.
A7	**finished** ['fɪnɪʃt]	fertig, vollendet	Go and fill in your questionnaires. Then meet me here with the *finished* questionnaires.
A8	**before** [bɪ'fɔ:]	bevor	Finish your homework *before* you play chess. ⚠ *before* = **1.** vor (*before* lunch) **2.** bevor (*before* you eat)
	°Tropical House ['trɒpɪkl haʊs]	Tropenhaus	
	°snark [snɑ:k]	Snark	 
	ear [ɪə]	Ohr	
	eye [aɪ]	Auge	
	°tail [teɪl]	Schwanz	
p.111/A9	**bacon** ['beɪkən]	Schinkenspeck	
	lettuce ['letɪs]	(Kopf-)Salat	*lettuce*
	vegetarian [ˌvedʒə'teəriən]	Vegetarier, Vegetarierin	Sita doesn't eat meat. She's a *vegetarian*.
A10	**real** [rɪəl]	echt, wirklich	A snark isn't a *real* animal.

Wörter mit „-ea-“

1. -ea- [i:]: beach, cheap, clean, dream, (to) eat, ice-cream, meat, please, (to) read, (to) speak, tea, teacher
2. -ea- [e]: bread, breakfast, dead
3. -ea- [eɪ]: break, great
4. -ea(r)- [ɪə]: dear, ear, (to) hear, near, year, idea, real
   ⚠ [ɜ:]: (to) learn
   ⚠ [eə]: (to) wear

	°it keeps the twins quiet [ki:ps]	*etwa:* es sorgt dafür, dass die Zwillinge keinen Ärger machen	
[p.111]	**[Activity]**		
	half an apple	*ein halber Apfel*	
	100 grammes of … [græmz]	*100 Gramm …*	

	grape [greɪp]	*Weintraube*	
	cocktail stick ['kɒkteɪl stɪk]	*Holzspießchen*	
	bowl [bəʊl]	*Schüssel, Schale*	
	saucepan ['sɔ:spən]	*Kochtopf*	
	hot [hɒt]	*heiß*	
	water ['wɔ:tə]	*Wasser*	
	(to) melt [melt]	*schmelzen*	
	(to) coat [kəʊt]	*überziehen, bestreichen*	
	(to) choose [tʃu:z]	*auswählen*	
	foot [fʊt], *pl feet* [fi:t]	*Fuß, Füße*	
	head [hed]	*Kopf*	
P 1	*word order*	*Wortstellung*	
P 2	*(to) understand*	*verstehen*	
	joke	*Witz*	

s-Genitiv – of

P 4

Der **s-Genitiv** wird bei **Personen** und oft auch bei Tieren verwendet:

Ben**'s** computer	Bens Computer
the cat**'s** name	der Name der Katze
my sister**'s** favourite colour	die Lieblingsfarbe meiner Schwester
the girls**'** room	das Zimmer der Mädchen
the Scotts**'** car	das Auto der Scotts

Bei **Sachen** wird die ***of*-Fügung** verwendet:

the name **of** the street	der Name der Straße
the colour **of** the wall	die Farbe der Wand
the door **of** room 3	die Tür von Raum 3

	imagination	*Fantasie, Vorstellungskraft*	
P 5	**robot** ['rəʊbɒt]	Roboter	
	(to) do jobs	*Arbeiten erledigen*	
P 8	(to) **guess** [ges]	raten, erraten	How old are you? – *Guess.* – 12? – No, I'm 13.
	(to) read out	*vorlesen*	
[P 9]	*zoo keeper*	*Tierwärter, Tierwärterin*	
	plan	*Plan*	
P 10	*(to) check*	*prüfen, überprüfen, kontrollieren*	
P 16	*both lists*	*beide Listen*	
P 17	*preposition*	*Präposition*	
	more [mɔ:]	mehr, weitere	There are *more* apples in the basket.

The end-of-term party

p.118	°end-of-term party [ˌend‿əv 'tɜ:m]	*Party am Ende eines Schulhalbjahres*	
	costume ['kɒstju:m]	Kostüm, Verkleidung	
	the best ... [best]	der/die/das beste ...	*The best* animal in the zoo is the elephant, I think.
	DJ [ˌdi:'dʒeɪ], **disc jockey** ['dɪsk dʒɒki]	Diskjockey	
	ticket ['tɪkɪt]	Eintrittskarte	*Tickets* for the party are £1.50.
	°fancy-dress party [ˌfænsi'dres]	Kostümfest	
	prize [praɪz]	Preis, Gewinn	⚠ *prize* = Preis, Gewinn *(bei einem Wettbewerb)* *price* = Preis *(, den man für etwas bezahlt)*
p.119	°(to) annoy [ə'nɔɪ]	ärgern, belästigen	
	slow [sləʊ]	langsam	◂▸ quick, fast
	all alone [ˌɔ:l‿ə'ləʊn]	ganz allein	Ben is often *all alone* at home.
	It's me – Sita.	Ich bin es – Sita.	⚠ Für „ich" wird in kurzen Antworten und nach *be* statt *I* meist *me* verwendet: Who's at the door? – *Me.* / It's *me*, Julia.
	(to) **think of**	halten von, denken über	What do you *think of* my new jacket? – It's great.
	°microphone ['maɪkrəfəʊn]	Mikrofon	
	(to) **cheer** [tʃɪə]	jubeln, Beifall klatschen	Let's all *cheer* – it's the end of the book!

DICTIONARY Alphabetical list of words

Das *DICTIONARY* enthält den Wortschatz dieses Bandes. Wörter, die mit einem kleinen Kringel (°) markiert sind, gehören nicht zum Lernwortschatz.

Abkürzungen: jm. = jemandem jn. = jemanden *pl = plural* *no pl = no plural* (kein Plural)

A

a, an [ə, ən] ein, eine **a little** [ə 'lɪtl] ein bisschen, ein wenig • **a lot (of)** [ə 'lɒt_əv] eine Menge, viel, viele
about [ə'baʊt] über • **a question about your book** eine Frage über dein Buch/zu deinem Buch • **this book is about** dieses Buch handelt von • **dream about** träumen von • **tell about** erzählen von, berichten über **What about a calendar?** Wie wär's mit einem Kalender? • **What about Jenny?** Was ist mit Jenny? / Und Jenny?
act [ækt] spielen, schauspielern
activity [æk'tɪvəti] Aktivität, Tätigkeit
°**add** [æd] hinzufügen, ergänzen
adopt [ə'dɒpt] adoptieren, die Patenschaft übernehmen für
°**advert** ['ædvɜːt] Anzeige, Reklame
after ['ɑːftə] nach *(zeitlich)* **after that** danach
afternoon [ˌɑːftə'nuːn] Nachmittag • **Good afternoon.** Guten Tag. *(nachmittags)* **in the afternoon(s)** am Nachmittag, nachmittags **this afternoon** heute Nachmittag • **tomorrow afternoon** morgen Nachmittag
again [ə'gen] wieder, noch einmal
all [ɔːl] alle; alles • **all the kids** alle Kinder • **all alone** ganz allein
alone [ə'ləʊn] allein
alphabet ['ælfəbet] Alphabet
always ['ɔːlweɪz] immer °**as always** wie immer
an [ən] ein, eine
and [ənd, *betont:* ænd] und **And you?** Und du?
animal ['ænɪml] Tier
°**annoy** [ə'nɔɪ] ärgern, belästigen
answer ['ɑːnsə] **1.** antworten; beantworten; **2.** Antwort
apple ['æpl] Apfel
April ['eɪprəl] April
are [ə, *betont:* ɑː] bist; sind; seid • **How much are ...?** Was kosten ...? / Wie viel kosten ...?
around [ə'raʊnd] um ... herum; in ... umher **around Ashton** in Ashton umher, durch Ashton °**around the house** rund ums Haus • °**around the world** rund um die Welt **Look around (you).** Sieh dich um. • **run around** umherrennen, herumrennen **stand around** herumstehen
°**as always** [əz_'ɔːlweɪz] wie immer
ask [ɑːsk] fragen • **ask questions** Fragen stellen °**ask for** bitten um
Assembly [ə'sembli] Schulversammlung *(oft mit Andacht)*
assistant [ə'sɪstənt] Verkäufer/in
at [ət, *betont:* æt] an, bei • **at home** zu Hause, daheim **at Kingsway High School** an/auf der Kingsway High School • **at night** in der Nacht, nachts • **at school** in der Schule • **at six** um sechs • **at the door** an der Tür • **at the front** vorn **at the moment** im Moment, gerade, zurzeit **at the restaurant** im Restaurant • **at the weekend** am Wochenende **at weekends** an Wochenenden • **at work** bei der Arbeit, am Arbeitsplatz **laugh at** lachen über; auslachen • **look at** anschauen, ansehen • **Open your books at page 5.** Schlagt Seite 5 auf.
au pair [ˌəʊ 'peə] Aupair (-mädchen, -junge)
August ['ɔːgəst] August
aunt [ɑːnt] Tante
away [ə'weɪ] weg, fort

B

back [bæk] zurück • °**back to one** zurück zur Eins
bacon ['beɪkən] Schinkenspeck
bad [bæd] schlecht, schlimm
badminton ['bædmɪntən] Badminton, Federball
bag [bæg] Tasche
ball [bɔːl] Ball
banana [bə'nɑːnə] Banane
basket ['bɑːskɪt] Korb
basketball ['bɑːskɪtbɔːl] Basketball
bathroom ['bɑːθruːm] Badezimmer
be [bi, *betont:* biː] sein **Be careful.** Sei vorsichtig. **be in trouble** in Schwierigkeiten sein; Ärger kriegen **be late** zu spät sein/kommen • **be late for school** zu spät zur Schule kommen **be out** weg sein, nicht da sein • **be right** Recht haben
beach [biːtʃ] Strand
because [bɪ'kɒz] weil
bed [bed] Bett
bedroom ['bedruːm] Schlafzimmer
before [bɪ'fɔː] **1.** vor *(zeitlich)*; **2.** bevor
behind [bɪ'haɪnd] hinter
believe [bɪ'liːv] glauben
bench [bentʃ] Bank *(zum Sitzen)*
best [best]: **the best ...** der/die/das beste ..., die besten ...
between [bɪ'twiːn] zwischen
big [bɪg] groß
bike [baɪk] Fahrrad • **ride a bike** Rad fahren
bikini [bɪ'kiːni] Bikini
bin [bɪn] Papierkorb, Mülleimer
°**biology** [baɪ'ɒlədʒi] Biologie
bird [bɜːd] Vogel

biro ['baɪrəʊ] Kugelschreiber
birthday ['bɜːθdeɪ] Geburtstag • **birthday card** Geburtstagskarte • **Happy birthday!** Herzlichen Glückwunsch zum Geburtstag! • **It's my birthday next week.** Ich habe nächste Woche Geburtstag. **When's your birthday?** Wann hast du Geburtstag?
black [blæk] schwarz
blouse [blaʊz] Bluse
blue [bluː] blau
board [bɔːd] **1.** (Wand-)Tafel; °**2.** Spielbrett • **write on the board** an die Tafel schreiben • **notice board** Anschlagtafel, schwarzes Brett
book [bʊk] Buch • **exercise book** Übungs-, Schulheft
bookshelf ['bʊkʃelf], *pl* **bookshelves** ['bʊkʃelvz] Bücherregal
boring ['bɔːrɪŋ] langweilig
°**both lists** [bəʊθ] beide Listen
boutique [buː'tiːk] Boutique
box [bɒks] Kasten, Kiste **a box of chocolates** eine Schachtel Pralinen
boy [bɔɪ] Junge
boyfriend ['bɔɪfrend] (fester) Freund
bread *(no pl)* [bred] Brot
break [breɪk] Pause
breakfast ['brekfəst] Frühstück • **for breakfast** zum Frühstück
bright [braɪt] leuchtend, hell
bring [brɪŋ] (mit-, her)bringen
British ['brɪtɪʃ] britisch **He's/She's British.** Er ist Brite./Sie ist Britin.
brochure ['brəʊʃə] Prospekt, Broschüre
brother ['brʌðə] Bruder
budgie ['bʌdʒi] Wellensittich
bus [bʌs] Bus • **on the bus** im Bus
but [bət, *betont:* bʌt] aber
buy [baɪ] kaufen
by [baɪ] von
Bye bye! [baɪ 'baɪ] Tschüs!

C

cage [keɪdʒ] Käfig
cake [keɪk] Kuchen, Torte
calendar ['kælɪndə] Kalender
camcorder ['kæmkɔːdə] Camcorder *(Videokamera mit eingebauter Abspielfunktion)*
camera ['kæmərə] Kamera, Fotoapparat
can [kən, *betont:* kæn] **1.** können; **2.** dürfen • **You can't ... .** [kɑːnt] (= **You cannot ... .**) ['kænɒt] Du kannst nicht ... . / Du darfst nicht ... .
candle ['kændl] Kerze
canteen [kæn'tiːn] Kantine, Schulmensa
car [kɑː] Auto
card [kɑːd] Karte
°**cardboard** ['kɑːdbɔːd] Pappe, Karton
care [keə]: **I don't care.** Das ist mir egal.
careful ['keəfl] vorsichtig
cassette [kə'set] Cassette
cat [kæt] Katze, Kater
°**cathedral** [kə'θiːdrəl] Kathedrale, Dom
CD [ˌsiː'diː] CD
chair [tʃeə] Stuhl
champion ['tʃæmpiən] Champion, Meister/in, Wettkampfsieger/in
°**chart** [tʃɑːt] Tabelle
cheap [tʃiːp] billig, preiswert
°**check** [tʃek] prüfen, überprüfen, kontrollieren
cheer [tʃɪə] jubeln, Beifall klatschen
cheese [tʃiːz] Käse
chess [tʃes] Schach
child [tʃaɪld], *pl* **children** ['tʃɪldrən] Kind
chips *(pl)* [tʃɪps] Pommes frites
chocolate ['tʃɒklət] **1.** Schokolade; **2.** Praline **a box of chocolates** eine Schachtel Pralinen
city ['sɪti] Stadt, Großstadt
class [klɑːs] **1.** Klasse, Kurs; °**2.** *(deutsche)* (Schul-)Klasse °**classmate** ['klɑːsmeɪt] Klassenkamerad/in, Mitschüler/in • **classroom** ['klɑːsruːm] Klassenzimmer **classroom phrases** [ˌklɑːsruːm 'freɪzɪz] *Redewendungen für das Klassenzimmer; Unterrichtssprache*
clean [kliːn] **1.** sauber; **2.** sauber machen
clever ['klevə] schlau, klug
climb [klaɪm] klettern; hinaufklettern (auf)
°**close** [kləʊz] schließen, zumachen
clothes *(pl)* [kləʊðz, kləʊz] Kleidung, „Klamotten"
club [klʌb] Klub; Verein
cola ['kəʊlə] Cola
collect [kə'lekt] sammeln
colour ['kʌlə] **1.** Farbe; °**2.** bunt anmalen • **What colour is it?** Welche Farbe hat es (er, sie)?
°**combination** [ˌkɒmbɪ'neɪʃn] Kombination, Verbindung
come [kʌm] kommen **Come here.** Komm her.
comic ['kɒmɪk] Comic-Heft
°**compare** [kəm'peə] vergleichen
complete [kəm'pliːt] vervollständigen, ergänzen
computer [kəm'pjuːtə] Computer, Rechner
cool [kuːl] cool, scharf, stark
copy ['kɒpi] übertragen, kopieren, abschreiben
correct [kə'rekt] **1.** verbessern, korrigieren; °**2.** korrekt, richtig
costume ['kɒstjuːm] Kostüm, Verkleidung
count [kaʊnt] zählen
°**counters** ['kaʊntəz] Spielsteine
country ['kʌntri] Land • **in the country** auf dem Land
course: **of course** [əv 'kɔːs] natürlich, selbstverständlich
cousin ['kʌzn] Cousin/Cousine
cow [kaʊ] Kuh • **cowboy** ['kaʊbɔɪ] Cowboy
cupboard ['kʌbəd] Schrank
customer ['kʌstəmə] Kunde, Kundin
°**cut out** (-tt-) [ˌkʌt_'aʊt] ausschneiden

D

dad [dæd] Vati, Papa; Vater
dance [dɑːns] tanzen
danger ['deɪndʒə] Gefahr **dangerous** ['deɪndʒərəs] gefährlich
date [deɪt] Datum • **What's the date?** Welches Datum haben wir?
day [deɪ] Tag • **the next day** der nächste Tag; am nächsten Tag • **What day is 1st January?** Was für ein Tag ist der 1. Januar?
dead [ded] tot
Dear Katrin and Julia, ... [dɪə] Liebe Katrin, liebe Julia, ...
December [dɪ'sembə] Dezember
department store [dɪ'pɑːtmənt stɔː] Kaufhaus

desk [desk] Schreibtisch, Schülertisch
°**dialogue** ['daɪəlɒg] Dialog
°**dice**, *pl* **dice** [daɪs] Würfel
dictionary ['dɪkʃənri] Wörterbuch, *(alphabetisches)* Wörterverzeichnis
difference ['dɪfrəns] Unterschied • **different** ['dɪfrənt] verschieden, unterschiedlich; anders; andere(r, s)
dinner ['dɪnə] Abendessen, Abendbrot • **for dinner** zum Abendbrot
°**director** [də'rektə] Regisseur/in
dirty ['dɜːti] schmutzig
disc jockey ['dɪsk dʒɒki] Diskjockey
disco ['dɪskəʊ] Disko
dishes *(pl)* ['dɪʃɪz] Geschirr **wash the dishes** das Geschirr abwaschen
divorced [dɪ'vɔːst] geschieden
DJ [ˌdiː'dʒeɪ], **disc jockey** ['dɪsk dʒɒki] Diskjockey
do [duː] tun, machen **do homework** die Hausaufgabe(n) machen, Schularbeiten machen • °**do jobs** Arbeiten erledigen • **do the shopping** Einkäufe machen/erledigen, einkaufen **Don't do that.** Tu das nicht. / Lass das.
dog [dɒg] Hund
door [dɔː] Tür • **at the door** an der Tür
°**double** ['dʌbl] Doppel-
down [daʊn] hinunter, herunter, nach unten **down the tree** den Baum hinunter • **put down** hinstellen, hinlegen • **Sit down.** Setz dich hin. / Setzt euch hin. • °**write down** aufschreiben
downstairs [ˌdaʊn'steəz] nach unten; unten
drama ['drɑːmə] Drama, Schauspiel
draw [drɔː] zeichnen
dream [driːm] **1.** Traum **dream house** Traumhaus; **2. dream (about)** träumen (von)
dress [dres] Kleid
drink [drɪŋk] trinken
during ['djʊərɪŋ] während

E

ear [ɪə] Ohr
°**easy** ['iːzi] leicht
eat [iːt] essen
elephant ['elɪfənt] Elefant
°**end-of-term party** [ˌend‿əv 'tɜːm] *Party am Ende eines Schulhalbjahres*
°**ending** ['endɪŋ] Endung
°**engineer** [ˌendʒɪ'nɪə] Ingenieur/Ingenieurin
England ['ɪŋglənd] England
English ['ɪŋglɪʃ] englisch; Englisch • **He's/She's English.** Er ist Engländer./Sie ist Engländerin. • **We speak English.** Wir sprechen Englisch. • **in English** auf Englisch • **What's this in English?** Wie heißt das auf Englisch?
euro (€) ['jʊərəʊ] Euro *(europäische Währungseinheit)*
evening ['iːvnɪŋ] Abend **Good evening.** Guten Abend. • **in the evening(s)** am Abend, abends • **this evening** heute Abend **tomorrow evening** morgen Abend
every ['evri] jede, jeder, jedes
everything ['evriθɪŋ] alles
example [ɪg'zɑːmpl] Beispiel **for example** zum Beispiel
°**exchange rate** [ɪks'tʃeɪndʒ reɪt] Wechselkurs
Excuse me. [ɪk'skjuːz] Entschuldigung. / Entschuldigen Sie.
exercise ['eksəsaɪz] Übung **exercise book** Übungsheft, Schulheft
expensive [ɪk'spensɪv] teuer
°**expression** [ɪk'spreʃn] Ausdruck
eye [aɪ] Auge

F

family ['fæməli] Familie °**family tree** Familienstammbaum
fan [fæn] Fan
°**fancy-dress party** [ˌfænsi'dres] Kostümfest
farm [fɑːm] Bauernhof, Farm
fashion ['fæʃn] Mode
fast [fɑːst] schnell
father ['fɑːðə] Vater
favourite ['feɪvərɪt] Lieblings-
February ['februəri] Februar
feed [fiːd] füttern • **feeding times** Fütterungszeiten
felt-tip ['felttɪp] Filzstift
fetch (from) [fetʃ] holen, abholen (von)
field [fiːld] Feld, Wiese, Weide • **in the field** auf dem Feld, der Wiese, der Weide
fill in [ˌfɪl‿'ɪn] **1.** einsetzen; °**2.** ausfüllen
film [fɪlm] Film
find [faɪnd] finden; suchen **find out** herausfinden
fine: I'm fine. [ˌaɪm 'faɪn] Mir geht's gut. / Es geht mir gut.
finish ['fɪnɪʃ] beenden, zu Ende machen; enden **finished** fertig, vollendet
first [fɜːst] **1.** erste(r, s); **2.** zuerst, als Erstes
fish, *pl* **fish** [fɪʃ] Fisch
flat [flæt] Wohnung
floor [flɔː] Fußboden
fly [flaɪ] fliegen
°**following** ['fɒləʊɪŋ]**: the following words** die folgenden Wörter
food [fuːd] Essen; Lebensmittel; Futter
football ['fʊtbɔːl] Fußball
for [fə, *betont:* fɔː] für • **for breakfast/lunch/dinner** zum Frühstück/Mittagessen/Abendbrot • **for example** zum Beispiel • °**for two minutes** zwei Minuten (lang) • °**your rubber for my pen** dein Radiergummi gegen meinen Füller **look for** suchen • **wait for** warten auf
form [fɔːm] **1.** *(englische)* (Schul-)Klasse; °**2.** Form
French [frentʃ] französisch; Französisch
Friday ['fraɪdeɪ, 'fraɪdi] Freitag
friend [frend] Freund/Freundin
from [frəm, *betont:* frɒm] aus; von • **I'm from ...** Ich bin aus ... / Ich komme aus ... **Where are you from?** Wo kommst du her? • **from Monday to Friday** von Montag bis Freitag
front [frʌnt]**: at the front** vorn • **in front of** [ɪn 'frʌnt‿əv] vor
fun [fʌn]**: have fun** Spaß haben, sich amüsieren **Have fun!** Viel Spaß! **Shopping is (great) fun.** Einkaufen macht (viel/großen) Spaß. • **funny** ['fʌni] witzig, komisch

G

game [geɪm] Spiel
garage ['gærɪdʒ] Garage
garden ['gɑːdn] Garten
Geography [dʒi'ɒgrəfi] Geographie, Erdkunde
German ['dʒɜːmən] deutsch; Deutsch; Deutsche(r)
Germany ['dʒɜːməni] Deutschland
get up **(-tt-)** [ˌget_'ʌp] aufstehen
giraffe [dʒə'rɑːf] Giraffe
girl [gɜːl] Mädchen
girlfriend ['gɜːlfrend] (feste) Freundin
give [gɪv] geben
go [gəʊ] gehen; fahren **Go away.** Geh weg. • **go shopping/go to the shops** einkaufen gehen • **Let's go.** Auf geht's! • **Let's go to Ashton today.** Lass(t) uns heute nach Ashton fahren. **go together** zusammenpassen • **go up** steigen **go with** passen zu
°**goal** [gəʊl] Tor *(im Sport)*
goldfish, *pl* **goldfish** ['gəʊldfɪʃ] Goldfisch
good [gʊd] gut • **Good morning/afternoon/evening.** Guten Morgen/Tag/Abend. • **Goodbye.** [ˌgʊd'baɪ] Auf Wiedersehen.
got [gɒt]: **have got** haben, besitzen
grandfather ['grænfɑːðə] Großvater
grandma ['grænmɑː] Oma
grandmother ['grænmʌðə] Großmutter
grandpa ['grænpɑː] Opa
great [greɪt] großartig, toll **look great** toll aussehen
green [griːn] grün
grey [greɪ] grau
group [gruːp] Gruppe • **a group of girls** eine Gruppe (von) Mädchen • **in groups of four** in Vierergruppen
guess [ges] raten, erraten
gym [dʒɪm] Sporthalle, Turnhalle

H

half [hɑːf], *pl* **halves** [hɑːvz] Hälfte • **the first half** die erste Hälfte/Halbzeit • **half past eight** halb neun (8.30/20.30) • **half-time** [ˌhɑːf'taɪm] Halbzeitpause
°**hall** [hɔːl] Flur, Diele
ham [hæm] Schinken
hamburger ['hæmbɜːgə] Hamburger
hamster ['hæmstə] Hamster
happen (to) ['hæpən] *(jm.)* geschehen, passieren **What's happening?** Was ist los? / Was geht hier vor?
happy ['hæpi] glücklich, froh **Happy birthday!** Herzlichen Glückwunsch zum Geburtstag!
has [həz, *betont:* hæz]: **he/she/it has got** er/sie/es hat, besitzt • **Jenny hasn't got a hamster. (= has not got)** Jenny hat keinen Hamster.
hate [heɪt] hassen, gar nicht mögen • **hate shopping** gar nicht gern einkaufen gehen
have [hæv]: **have a party** eine Party veranstalten, feiern • **have fun** Spaß haben, sich amüsieren • **Have fun!** Viel Spaß! • **Nick can have a video.** Nick kann ein Video haben/bekommen. **Have a nice weekend.** Schönes Wochenende.
have got haben, besitzen **We haven't got time. (= have not got)** Wir haben keine Zeit.
he [hi, *betont:* hiː] er • **he's** [hiːz] = **he is** [hiː_ɪz] er ist
hear [hɪə] hören
Hello. [hə'ləʊ] Hallo. / Guten Tag.
help [help] **1.** helfen; °**2.** Hilfe • **May I help you?** Sie wünschen?
her [hə, *betont:* hɜː] **1.** ihr, ihre; **2.** sie; ihr
here [hɪə] hier; hierher
°**Hi there.** Hallo.
him [hɪm] ihn; ihm
his [hɪz] sein, seine
hit [hɪt] Hit
hobby ['hɒbi] Hobby
hockey ['hɒki] Hockey
home [həʊm] **1.** Heim, Zuhause; **2.** nach Hause **at home** zu Hause, daheim **We're home.** Wir sind (wieder) zu Hause.
homework *(no pl)* ['həʊmwɜːk] Hausaufgabe(n) **do homework** die Hausaufgabe(n) machen, Schularbeiten machen
house [haʊs] Haus
how? [haʊ] wie? • **How are you?** Wie geht es dir/euch/Ihnen? • **How old are you?** Wie alt bist du/seid ihr/sind Sie? • °**how many?** [ˌhaʊ 'meni] wie viele? • **How much is/are ...?** [ˌhaʊ 'mʌtʃ] Was kostet/kosten ...? / Wie viel kostet/kosten ...?
husband ['hʌzbənd] Ehemann

I

I [aɪ] ich • **I don't know.** Ich weiß (es) nicht. • **I'm fine.** Mir geht's gut. / Es geht mir gut.
ice-cream [ˌaɪs'kriːm] (Speise-)Eis
idea [aɪ'dɪə] Idee, Einfall
°**imagination** [ɪˌmædʒɪ'neɪʃn] Fantasie, Vorstellungskraft °**imagine** [ɪ'mædʒɪn] sich *etwas* vorstellen
in [ɪn] in • **in English** auf Englisch • **in front of** vor **in Germany** in Deutschland **in November** im November • **in the country** auf dem Land • **in the field** auf dem Feld/der Wiese/der Weide • **in the morning(s)/afternoon(s)/evening(s)** am Morgen, morgens/am Nachmittag, nachmittags/am Abend, abends • **in the photo** auf dem Foto • **in the picture** auf dem Bild • **in the street** auf der Straße
Indian ['ɪndiən] indisch; Inder/in
information *(no pl)* [ˌɪnfə'meɪʃn] Information(en); Auskunft, Auskünfte
°**interesting** ['ɪntrəstɪŋ] interessant
interview ['ɪntəvjuː] Interview
into ['ɪntə, *betont:* 'ɪntuː] in (... hinein)
invitation [ˌɪnvɪ'teɪʃn] Einladung
is [ɪz] ist • **How much is ...?** Was kostet ...? / Wie viel kostet ...? • **the felt-tip is 65p** der Filzstift kostet 65 Pence

it [ɪt] es (*bei Sachen und Tieren auch:* er, sie) • **its** [ɪts] sein, seine (*bei Sachen und Tieren auch:* ihr, ihre)
it's [ɪts] es ist (*bei Sachen und Tieren auch:* er/sie ist)
It's me – Sita. Ich bin es – Sita.

J

jacket ['dʒækɪt] Jacke; Jackett, Sakko
January ['dʒænjʊəri] Januar
jeans *(pl)* [dʒi:nz] Jeans
job [dʒɒb] Beruf, Arbeit, Job
°**do jobs** Arbeiten erledigen
°**joke** [dʒəʊk] Witz
judo ['dʒu:dəʊ] Judo
juice [dʒu:s] Saft
July [dʒʊ'laɪ] Juli
June [dʒu:n] Juni
just [dʒʌst] nur, bloß • **I'm just looking.** Ich sehe mich nur um.

K

°**keep** [ki:p]: **it keeps the twins quiet** *etwa:* es sorgt dafür, dass die Zwillinge keinen Ärger machen
kid [kɪd] Kind, Jugendliche(r)
kilo ['ki:ləʊ] Kilo(gramm)
2 kilos of meat 2 Kilo Fleisch
kindergarten ['kɪndəgɑ:tn] Kindergarten; Vorschule
kitchen ['kɪtʃɪn] Küche
know [nəʊ] **1.** wissen; **2.** kennen • **I don't know.** Ich weiß (es) nicht.

L

°**ladder** ['lædə] *(die)* Leiter
language ['læŋgwɪdʒ] Sprache
late [leɪt] spät; zu spät • **be late** zu spät sein/kommen
I'm late for school. Ich komme zu spät zur Schule.
sleep late lange schlafen
laugh [lɑ:f] lachen • **laugh at** lachen über; auslachen
learn [lɜ:n] lernen
left [left]: **on the left** links, auf der linken Seite
lesson ['lesn] Unterrichtsstunde • **lessons** *(pl)* Unterricht
Let's ... [lets] Lass(t) uns ...
Let's swap. Lass uns tauschen. / Tauschen wir.
Let's go. Auf geht's!
letter ['letə] **1.** Buchstabe; **2. letter (to)** Brief (an)
lettuce ['letɪs] (Kopf-)Salat
like [laɪk] wie • **Start like this: ...** Fang so an: ...
like [laɪk] mögen, gern haben • **like shopping** gern einkaufen gehen
°**line** [laɪn] **1.** Linie; **2.** Zeile
link [lɪŋk]: **word link** Wortverbindung
lion ['laɪən] Löwe
list [lɪst] Liste
listen ['lɪsn] zuhören; horchen • **listen to** *jm.* zuhören; sich *etwas* anhören
litre ['li:tə] Liter • **2 litres of milk** 2 Liter Milch
little ['lɪtl] klein, jung • **a little** ein bisschen, ein wenig
live [lɪv] leben, wohnen
living-room ['lɪvɪŋru:m] Wohnzimmer
lonely ['ləʊnli] einsam
long [lɒŋ] lang
look [lʊk] **1.** schauen, sehen; **2.** aussehen • **I'm just looking.** Ich sehe mich nur um. • **look at** anschauen, ansehen • **Look at the board.** Sieh an die Tafel.
Look at the picture. Sieh dir das Bild an. • **look great** toll aussehen • **Does this shirt look good on me?** Steht mir dieses Hemd?
look for suchen
lot: **lots (of)/a lot (of)** [ə 'lɒt‿əv, 'lɒts‿əv] eine Menge, viel, viele
°**loud** [laʊd] laut
love [lʌv] lieben, sehr mögen
love shopping sehr gern einkaufen gehen • **Love, ...** Viele liebe Grüße (von) ...
love [lʌv] null *(Tennis)*
lucky ['lʌki]: **You're lucky.** Du hast Glück. / Du bist gut dran.
lunch [lʌntʃ] Mittagessen
for lunch zum Mittagessen

M

magazine [,mægə'zi:n] Zeitschrift
make [meɪk] machen, bilden, bauen; zubereiten
man [mæn], *pl* **men** [men] Mann
°**many** ['meni]: **how many?** wie viele?
March [mɑ:tʃ] März
married ['mærid] verheiratet
match [mætʃ] **1.** Spiel, Wettkampf; **2.** zuordnen
°**Match the answers to the questions.** Ordne die Antworten den Fragen zu.
Maths *(sing)* [mæθs] Mathematik
May [meɪ] Mai
may [meɪ] dürfen • **May I help you?** Sie wünschen?
maybe ['meɪbi] vielleicht
me [mi, *betont:* mi:] mir; mich • **It's me – Sita.** Ich bin es – Sita.
meat [mi:t] Fleisch
meet [mi:t] sich treffen; *jn.* treffen
mega ['megə] mega-; Mega-
°**microphone** ['maɪkrəfəʊn] Mikrofon
milk [mɪlk] Milch
°**mime** [maɪm] vorspielen, pantomimisch darstellen
°**Mind the spelling.** [maɪnd] Gib Acht auf die Schreibung.
minute ['mɪnɪt] Minute
Miss Hunt [,mɪs 'hʌnt] Fräulein/Frau Hunt *(Anrede für unverheiratete Frauen)*
°**missing** ['mɪsɪŋ] fehlend
°**mistake** [mɪ'steɪk] Fehler
moment ['məʊmənt]: **at the moment** im Moment, gerade, zurzeit
Monday ['mʌndeɪ, 'mʌndi] Montag
money ['mʌni] Geld
monkey ['mʌŋki] Affe
month [mʌnθ] Monat
more [mɔ:] mehr, weitere
one more noch ein(e), ein(e) weitere(r, s)
morning ['mɔ:nɪŋ] Morgen, Vormittag • **Good morning.** Guten Morgen. / Guten Tag. *(vormittags)*
in the morning(s) am Morgen, morgens • **this morning** heute Morgen
tomorrow morning morgen früh, morgen Vormittag
mother ['mʌðə] Mutter
mouse [maʊs], *pl* **mice** [maɪs] Maus
move [mu:v] (sich) bewegen
°**Move your counter.** Zieh deinen Spielstein.
Mr Snow ['mɪstə] Herr Snow

Mrs Snow ['mɪsɪz] Frau Snow *(Anrede für verheiratete Frauen)*
much: How much is/are …? [ˌhaʊ 'mʌtʃ] Was kostet/kosten …? Wie viel kostet/kosten …?
mum [mʌm] Mutti, Mama; Mutter
music ['mjuːzɪk] Musik
must [məst, *betont:* mʌst] müssen
my [maɪ] mein, meine **My name is … .** Mein Name ist … . / Ich heiße … .

N

name [neɪm] Name • **My name is … .** Mein Name ist … . / Ich heiße … . • **What's your name?** Wie heißt du?
near [nɪə] in der Nähe von, nahe (bei)
need [niːd] brauchen, benötigen
network ['netwɜːk] (Wörter-) Netz, „Wörterspinne"
never ['nevə] nie, niemals
new [njuː] neu
next [nekst] nächste(r, s) *(zeitlich; Reihenfolge)* • **next Monday** (am) nächsten Montag • **next week** in der nächsten Woche, nächste Woche • **the next day** der nächste Tag; am nächsten Tag • **next to** neben
nice [naɪs] schön, nett
night [naɪt] Nacht, (später) Abend • **at night** in der Nacht, nachts
nil [nɪl] null • **one nil to Kingsway** eins zu null für Kingsway
no [nəʊ] nein
not [nɒt] nicht • **I'm not from Chester.** Ich bin nicht aus Chester. • **I'm not German.** Ich bin kein Deutscher/keine Deutsche.
°**notes** [nəʊts] Notizen
nothing ['nʌθɪŋ] nichts
notice board ['nəʊtɪs bɔːd] Anschlagtafel, schwarzes Brett
nought [nɔːt] null
November [nəʊ'vembə] November
now [naʊ] nun, jetzt
number ['nʌmbə] Zahl, Ziffer **a small number of children** eine kleine Anzahl Kinder/von Kindern
nurse [nɜːs] Krankenschwester, Krankenpfleger

O

o'clock [ə'klɒk]**: six o'clock** sechs Uhr
October [ɒk'təʊbə] Oktober
Odd word out [ˌɒd wɜːd_'aʊt] *etwa:* Das unpassende Wort raus
of [əv, *betont:* ɒv] von • **a picture of Chester** ein Bild von Chester • **a group of girls** eine Gruppe (von) Mädchen • **a small number of children** eine kleine Anzahl Kinder/von Kindern **in groups of four** in Vierergruppen • **one of you** eine/r von euch • **the name of the street** der Name der Straße • **2 kilos of meat** 2 Kilo Fleisch • **2 litres of milk** 2 Liter Milch • **a piece of** ein Stück • **lots of/a lot of** eine Menge, viel, viele **think of** halten von, denken über • **of course** natürlich, selbstverständlich
off: take off [ˌteɪk_'ɒf] ausziehen
often ['ɒfn] oft
old [əʊld] alt • **How old are you?** Wie alt bist du/seid ihr/sind Sie?
on [ɒn] auf • **on the bus** im Bus • **on the floor** auf dem Fußboden • **on the left** links, auf der linken Seite **on the right** rechts, auf der rechten Seite • **on the radio** im Radio • **on TV** im Fernsehen • **on 12th January** am 12. Januar • **on Monday** am Montag • **on Mondays** montags, jeden Montag **on Monday morning/afternoon/evening** am Montagmorgen/-nachmittag/-abend **write on the board** an die Tafel schreiben
one [wʌn]**: one more** noch ein(e), ein(e) weitere(r, s) **one of you** eine/r von euch
only ['əʊnli] nur, bloß; erst
°**onto** ['ɒntə, *betont:* 'ɒntuː] auf
open ['əʊpən] öffnen, aufmachen • **Open your books at page 5.** Schlagt Seite 5 auf.
or [ɔː] oder
orange ['ɒrɪndʒ] Apfelsine, Orange • **orange juice** Orangensaft
°**order** ['ɔːdə] Reihenfolge
other ['ʌðə] andere • **the other** der/die/das andere, die anderen
our ['aʊə] unser, unsere
out: be out [bi_'aʊt] weg sein, nicht da sein
°**out of cardboard** [ˌaʊt_əv 'kɑːdbɔːd] aus Pappe, aus Karton
over ['əʊvə] über, oberhalb von • **over the restaurant** über dem Restaurant

P

pack [pæk] packen
page [peɪdʒ] (Buch-, Heft-) Seite • **on page 25** auf Seite 25 • **Open your books at page 5.** Schlagt Seite 5 auf.
°**paper** ['peɪpə] Papier
parents ['peərənts] Eltern
°**part** [pɑːt] Teil
partner ['pɑːtnə] Partner/Partnerin
party ['pɑːti] Party • **have a party** eine Party veranstalten, feiern
past: half past eight [ˌhɑːf pɑːst_'eɪt] halb neun (8.30/20.30) • **quarter past eight** [ˌkwɔːtə pɑːst_'eɪt] Viertel nach acht (8.15/20.15)
pay (for) [peɪ] bezahlen
pen [pen] Füller
pence (p) *(pl)* [pens, piː] Pence
pencil ['pensl] Bleistift
pencil-case ['penslkeɪs] Federmäppchen
penguin ['peŋgwɪn] Pinguin
penny ['peni] *kleinste britische Münze*
people *(pl)* ['piːpl] Leute, Menschen
°**person** ['pɜːsn] Person
pet [pet] Haustier
phone [fəʊn] **1.** anrufen; **2.** Telefon • **(tele)phone number** ['telɪfəʊn ˌnʌmbə] Telefonnummer
photo ['fəʊtəʊ] Foto • **in the photo** auf dem Foto • **take photos** Fotos machen, fotografieren
picture ['pɪktʃə] Bild **a picture of Chester** ein Bild von Chester • **in the picture** auf dem Bild

piece: a piece of [ə 'pi:s_əv] ein Stück
pig [pɪg] Schwein
play [pleɪ] **1.** spielen; **2.** Theaterstück
please [pli:z] bitte *(in Fragen und Aufforderungen)*
°**poem** ['pəʊɪm] Gedicht
point [pɔɪnt] Punkt
police *(pl)* [pə'li:s] Polizei
poor [pɔ:, pʊə] arm • **poor Trundle** der arme Trundle
popcorn ['pɒpkɔ:n] Popcorn
poster ['pəʊstə] Poster
pound (£) [paʊnd] Pfund *(britische Währung)*
practice *(no pl)* ['præktɪs] Praxis, Übung(en)
present ['preznt] Geschenk
pretty ['prɪti] hübsch
price [praɪs] (Kauf-)Preis
prize [praɪz] Preis, Gewinn
problem ['prɒbləm] Problem
professor [prə'fesə] Professor, Professorin
project ['prɒdʒekt] Projekt
°**pronunciation** [prə,nʌnsi'eɪʃn] Aussprache
proof *(no pl)* [pru:f] Beweis(e), Nachweis(e)
°**pull** [pʊl] ziehen
pullover ['pʊləʊvə] Pullover
pupil ['pju:pl] Schüler, Schülerin
put (-tt-) [pʊt] legen, stellen, *(etwas wohin)* tun
put down hinstellen, hinlegen • °**put in** einsetzen

Q

quarter past eight [,kwɔ:tə pɑ:st_'eɪt] Viertel nach acht (8.15/20.15) • **quarter to nine** [,kwɔ:tə tə 'naɪn] Viertel vor neun (8.45/20.45)
question ['kwestʃn] Frage
ask questions Fragen stellen
questionnaire [,kwestʃə'neə] Fragebogen
quick [kwɪk] schnell
quiet ['kwaɪət] ruhig, leise, still

R

rabbit ['ræbɪt] Kaninchen
radio ['reɪdiəʊ] Radio • **on the radio** im Radio
rap [ræp] Rap *(rhythmischer Sprechgesang)*
read [ri:d] lesen • °**read out** vorlesen • °**Read out loud.** Lies laut vor. • °**read to** *jm.* vorlesen
real [rɪəl] echt, wirklich
really ['rɪəli] wirklich
red [red] rot
reporter [rɪ'pɔ:tə] Reporter/in
restaurant ['restrɒnt] Restaurant • **at the restaurant** im Restaurant
revision [rɪ'vɪʒn] Wiederholung *(des Lernstoffs)*
ride a bike [,raɪd_ə 'baɪk] Rad fahren • **Let's ride our bikes to school.** Lass(t) uns mit dem Rad zur Schule fahren.
right [raɪt] richtig • **That's right.** Das stimmt. / Das ist richtig. • **be right** Recht haben • **You're right.** Du hast Recht. / Stimmt. **Right, Debbie?** Nicht wahr, Debbie? • **on the right** rechts, auf der rechten Seite
°**rival** ['raɪvl] Rivale/Rivalin
°**river** ['rɪvə] Fluss
robot ['rəʊbɒt] Roboter
°**roof** [ru:f] Dach
room [ru:m] Zimmer, Raum
°**rope** [rəʊp] Seil
round: the wrong way round [ðə ,rɒŋ weɪ 'raʊnd] verkehrt herum
rubber ['rʌbə] Radiergummi
ruler ['ru:lə] Lineal
run (-nn-) [rʌn] laufen, rennen • **run around** umherrennen, herumrennen

S

same: the same [ðə 'seɪm] der-/die-/dasselbe, dieselben
sandal ['sændl] Sandale
sandwich ['sænwɪdʒ] *(zusammengeklapptes)* belegtes Brot, Sandwich
Saturday ['sætədeɪ, 'sætədi] Samstag, Sonnabend
save [seɪv] retten
say [seɪ] sagen • **You say** Du sagst / Man sagt
scarf [skɑ:f], *pl* **scarves** [skɑ:vz] Schal
school [sku:l] Schule • **at school** in der Schule
school bag ['sku:lbæg] Schultasche • **school subject** ['sku:l ,sʌbdʒɪkt] Schulfach
°**scrapbook** ['skræpbʊk] Sammelalbum
sea lion ['si: laɪən] Seelöwe
second ['sekənd] zweite(r, s)
see [si:] sehen
sentence ['sentəns] Satz
September [sep'tembə] September
sharp [ʃɑ:p] scharf
she [ʃi, *betont:* ʃi:] sie • **she's** [ʃi:z] = **she is** [ʃi:_ɪz] sie ist
sheep, *pl* **sheep** [ʃi:p] Schaf
shelf [ʃelf], *pl* **shelves** [ʃelvz] Regal
shirt [ʃɜ:t] (Ober-)Hemd
shoe [ʃu:] Schuh
shop [ʃɒp] **1.** Laden, Geschäft; **2.** einkaufen gehen
shopping ['ʃɒpɪŋ] *(das)* Einkaufen; Einkäufe • **go to the shops/go shopping** einkaufen gehen • **do the shopping** einkaufen, Einkäufe machen/erledigen
like shopping gern einkaufen gehen • **hate shopping** gar nicht gern einkaufen gehen • **shoplifter** ['ʃɒplɪftə] Ladendieb, Ladendiebin
short [ʃɔ:t] kurz
shorts *(pl)* [ʃɔ:ts] Shorts, kurze Hose
show [ʃəʊ] zeigen
Shut up. [,ʃʌt_'ʌp] Halt den Mund!
silly ['sɪli] albern, dumm
sing [sɪŋ] singen
sister ['sɪstə] Schwester
sit (-tt-) [sɪt] sitzen; sich (hin)setzen • **Sit down.** Setz dich hin. / Setzt euch hin.
size [saɪz] Größe • **What size are you?** Welche Größe hast du/haben Sie?
skirt [skɜ:t] Rock
sleep [sli:p] schlafen
sleep late lange schlafen
°**slogan** ['sləʊgən] Slogan, Werbespruch
slow [sləʊ] langsam
small [smɔ:l] klein
°**snake** [sneɪk] Schlange
°**snark** [snɑ:k] Snark
so [səʊ] **1.** deshalb, daher; also; **2.** so • **so lonely** so einsam
sock [sɒk] Socke, Strumpf
sofa ['səʊfə] Sofa
some [səm, *betont:* sʌm] einige, ein paar; etwas
sometimes ['sʌmtaɪmz] manchmal
song [sɒŋ] Lied

Sorry. / I'm sorry. ['sɒri] Entschuldigung. Tut mir Leid. • **Sorry?** Wie bitte?
sound [saʊnd] Laut
speak [spi:k] sprechen **We speak English.** Wir sprechen Englisch.
special ['speʃl]: **be special** etwas Besonderes sein
spell [spel] buchstabieren °**spelling** ['spelɪŋ] (Recht-)Schreibung, Schreibweise
sport [spɔ:t] Sport, Sportart
spot [spɒt]: **Spot the difference.** Entdecke den Unterschied.
stamp [stæmp] Briefmarke
stand [stænd] stehen; sich (hin)stellen
star [stɑ:] (Film-, Pop-)Star
start [stɑ:t] anfangen, beginnen (mit)
°**stick** [stɪk] kleben
sticker ['stɪkə] Sticker, Aufkleber
still [stɪl] 1. (immer) noch; 2. trotzdem, dennoch
stop (-pp-) [stɒp] anhalten, stoppen
story ['stɔ:ri] Geschichte, Erzählung
street [stri:t] Straße *(in einer Stadt)* • **in the street** auf der Straße
stupid ['stju:pɪd] blöd, dämlich
subject ['sʌbdʒɪkt] (Unterrichts-)Fach
Sunday ['sʌndeɪ, 'sʌndi] Sonntag
super ['su:pə] super, toll
supermarket ['su:pəmɑ:kɪt] Supermarkt
swap (-pp-) [swɒp] tauschen
sweatshirt ['swetʃɜ:t] Sweatshirt
swimming-pool ['swɪmɪŋpu:l] Swimmingpool, Schwimmbad
swimming-trunks *(pl)* ['swɪmɪŋtrʌŋks] Badehose
swimsuit ['swɪmsu:t] Badeanzug

T

table ['teɪbl] Tisch
°**tail** [teɪl] Schwanz
take [teɪk] nehmen; mitnehmen; (weg)bringen **take off** ausziehen *(Kleidung)* • **take photos** Fotos machen, fotografieren
talk (to) [tɔ:k] reden (mit), sich unterhalten (mit)
tartan ['tɑ:tn] Schottenstoff, Schottenmuster
tea [ti:] Tee
teacher ['ti:tʃə] Lehrer/in
team [ti:m] Team, Mannschaft
telephone ['teləfəʊn] Telefon **telephone number** Telefonnummer
tell (about) [tel] erzählen (von), berichten (über)
tennis ['tenɪs] Tennis
terrible ['terəbl] schrecklich, furchtbar
test [test] Test, Prüfung, Klassenarbeit
text [tekst] Text
Thank you. ['θæŋk jʊ] Danke (schön). • **thanks** danke
that [ðæt] jene(r, s); das (dort) • **That's right.** Das ist richtig. / Das stimmt.
the [ðə] der, die, das; die **the next day** der nächste Tag; am nächsten Tag • **the same** der-/die-/dasselbe, dieselben • **the wrong way round** verkehrt herum
their [ðeə] ihr, ihre *(Plural)*
them [ðəm, *betont:* ðem] sie; ihnen
then [ðen] dann, danach
there [ðeə] da, dort; dahin, dorthin • °**Hi there.** Hallo. **there are** [ðər‿ə, ðeər‿ɑ:] es sind (vorhanden); es gibt **there's** [ðəz, ðeəz] = **there is** es ist (vorhanden); es gibt
these [ði:z] diese, die (hier)
they [ðeɪ] sie *(pl)* • **they're** [ðeə] = **they are** sie sind
thief [θi:f], *pl* **thieves** [θi:vz] Dieb, Diebin
thing [θɪŋ] Ding, Sache
think [θɪŋk] glauben, meinen, denken • **think of** halten von, denken über
third [θɜ:d] dritte(r, s)
this [ðɪs] diese(r, s); dies (hier) • **This is ... .** Dies ist ... . • **this morning/afternoon/evening** heute Morgen/Nachmittag/Abend
those [ðəʊz] die (da), jene (dort)
°**Throw the dice.** [θrəʊ] Würfle.
Thursday ['θɜ:zdeɪ, 'θɜ:zdi] Donnerstag
ticket ['tɪkɪt] Eintrittskarte
tidy ['taɪdi] ordentlich, aufgeräumt • **tidy up** aufräumen
tiger ['taɪgə] Tiger
time [taɪm] Zeit • **What time is it?** Wie spät ist es? **What time is the film?** Wann fängt der Film an? **feeding times** Fütterungszeiten • **five times nought** fünf mal null
timetable ['taɪmteɪbl] Stundenplan
to [tə, *betont:* tu:] zu, nach **letter to** Brief an • **Welcome to ...** Willkommen in ... • **quarter to nine** Viertel vor neun (8.45/20.45) • **3.50 to 5.30** 3 Uhr 50 bis 5 Uhr 30 **from Monday to Friday** von Montag bis Freitag **next to** neben • **one nil to Kingsway** eins zu null für Kingsway • **listen to** *jm.* zuhören; sich *etwas* anhören **talk to** reden mit, sich unterhalten mit
today [tə'deɪ] heute **today's match** das heutige Spiel
together [tə'geðə] zusammen • **go together** zusammenpassen
tomato [tə'mɑ:təʊ], *pl* **tomatoes** Tomate
tomorrow [tə'mɒrəʊ] morgen • **tomorrow morning/afternoon/evening** morgen Vormittag/Nachmittag/Abend
tonight [tə'naɪt] heute Nacht, heute Abend
too [tu:] 1. auch • **I'm from Berlin, too.** Ich komme auch aus Berlin. 2. **too little** zu klein
tooth [tu:θ], *pl* **teeth** [ti:θ] Zahn
topic ['tɒpɪk] Thema, Themenbereich
tortoise ['tɔ:təs] Schildkröte
town [taʊn] Stadt
toy [tɔɪ] Spielzeug
trainer ['treɪnə] Trainer/in
tree [tri:] Baum • °**family tree** Familienstammbaum
trend [trend] (Mode-)Trend
trip (to) [trɪp] Ausflug, Reise (nach, zu)
°**Tropical House** ['trɒpɪkl haʊs] Tropenhaus
trouble ['trʌbl]: **be in trouble** in Schwierigkeiten sein; Ärger kriegen
trousers *(pl)* ['traʊzəz] (lange) Hose
°**true** [tru:] wahr

try [traɪ] versuchen, (aus)probieren • **Try and make sentences.** Versuche, Sätze zu bilden. • **try on** anprobieren *(Kleidung)*
T-shirt ['ti:ʃɜ:t] T-Shirt
Tuesday ['tju:zdeɪ, 'tju:zdi] Dienstag
°**tune** [tju:n] Melodie
TV [ˌti:'vi:] Fernsehgerät; Fernsehen • **on TV** im Fernsehen • **watch TV** fernsehen
twins [twɪnz] Zwillinge

U

uncle ['ʌŋkl] Onkel
under ['ʌndə] unter
°**understand** [ˌʌndə'stænd] verstehen
uniform ['ju:nɪfɔ:m] Uniform
unit ['ju:nɪt] Kapitel, Lektion
up [ʌp] hinauf, herauf, nach oben • **up the tree** den Baum hinauf
upstairs [ˌʌp'steəz] nach oben; oben
us [əs, *betont:* ʌs] uns
use [ju:z] gebrauchen, verwenden, benutzen
usually ['ju:ʒʊəli] meistens, gewöhnlich, normalerweise

V

vegetarian [ˌvedʒə'teəriən] Vegetarier, Vegetarierin
°**verse** [vɜ:s] Vers
very ['veri] sehr • **very funny** sehr witzig, sehr komisch
video ['vɪdiəʊ] Video • **video recorder** ['vɪdiəʊ rɪˌkɔ:də] Videorecorder
village ['vɪlɪdʒ] Dorf
°**virus** ['vaɪrəs] Virus
vocabulary [və'kæbjələri] Vokabelverzeichnis, Wörterverzeichnis
volleyball ['vɒlibɔ:l] Volleyball

W

wait (for) ['weɪt fɔ:] warten (auf)
walkman ['wɔ:kmən] Walkman
wall [wɔ:l] Wand; Mauer
want [wɒnt] (haben) wollen
wash [wɒʃ] waschen • **wash the dishes** das Geschirr abwaschen
watch [wɒtʃ] **1.** Armbanduhr; **2.** beobachten, sich *etwas* ansehen • **watch TV** fernsehen
way: **the wrong way round** [ðə ˌrɒŋ weɪ 'raʊnd] verkehrt herum
we [wi, *betont:* wi:] wir
we're [wɪə] = **we are** [wi:‿ɑ:] wir sind • **we aren't** [wi:‿ɑ:nt] = **we are not** wir sind nicht; wir sind keine
wear [weə] tragen, anhaben *(Kleidung)*
Wednesday ['wenzdeɪ, 'wenzdi] Mittwoch
week [wi:k] Woche • **next week** nächste Woche, in der nächsten Woche
weekend [ˌwi:k'end] Wochenende • **at the weekend** am Wochenende **at weekends** an Wochenenden • **Have a nice weekend.** Schönes Wochenende.
welcome ['welkəm] willkommen • **Welcome to …** Willkommen in …
Well, … [wel] Nun, …; Also, …
what? [wɒt] **1.** was?; **2.** welche, welcher, welches? • **What about a calendar?** Wie wär's mit einem Kalender? • **What about Jenny?** Was ist mit Jenny? / Und Jenny? • **What are they talking about?** Worüber reden sie? • **What colour is it?** Welche Farbe hat es (er, sie)? • **What day is 1st January?** Was für ein Tag ist der 1. Januar? **What size are you?** Welche Größe hast du/haben Sie? **What time is it?** Wie spät ist es? • **What time is the film?** Wann fängt der Film an? • **What's the date?** Welches Datum haben wir? **What's this in English?** Wie heißt das auf Englisch? **What's your name?** Wie heißt du? / Wie heißen Sie?
when [wen] **1.** wann **When is it?** Wann fängt es an? • **When's your birthday?** Wann hast du Geburtstag? **2.** wenn
where? [weə] wo?; wohin? **Where are you from?** Wo kommst du her?
°**whistle** ['wɪsl] (An-)Pfiff; (Triller-)Pfeife
white [waɪt] weiß
who? [hu:] wer?
why? [waɪ] warum?
wife [waɪf], *pl* **wives** [waɪvz] Ehefrau
window ['wɪndəʊ] Fenster
°**witch** [wɪtʃ] Hexe
with [wɪð] mit (… zusammen), bei • **go with** passen zu
woman ['wʊmən], *pl* **women** ['wɪmɪn] Frau
°**wood** [wʊd] Holz
word [wɜ:d] Wort • **word group** Wortgruppe • **word link** Wortverbindung °**word order** Wortstellung
work [wɜ:k] **1.** arbeiten; **2.** Arbeit • **at work** bei der Arbeit, am Arbeitsplatz
worry (about) ['wʌri] sich Sorgen machen (wegen, um)
write [raɪt] schreiben **write on the board** an die Tafel schreiben • °**write down** aufschreiben
wrong [rɒŋ] falsch • **the wrong way round** verkehrt herum

Y

year [jɪə] Jahr; Jahrgangsstufe
yellow ['jeləʊ] gelb
yes [jes] ja
you [jʊ, *betont:* ju:] **1.** du; ihr; Sie; **2.** dich/dir; euch/euch; Sie/Ihnen • **you're** [jʊə, jɔ:] = **you are** [ju:‿ɑ:] du bist; ihr seid; Sie sind • **You say** Du sagst / Man sagt **You're right.** Du hast Recht. Stimmt. • **How are you?** Wie geht es dir/euch/Ihnen? • **Thank you.** Danke (schön).
your [jɔ:] dein/deine; euer/eure; Ihr/Ihre • **Yours,** [jɔ:z] dein/deine; euer/eure; Ihr/Ihre *(Briefschluss)*
Yuck! [jʌk] Igitt! / Bäh!

Z

zebra ['zebrə] Zebra
zero ['zɪərəʊ] null
zoo [zu:] Zoo, Tierpark

Bildquellen

Action Images, London (S. 39 Football);
Anthony Verlag, Starnberg (S. 7 unten);
Anna Baker, York (S. 122 unten);
Barnaby's Picture Library, London (S. 31 Grandpa Scott, Jeremy, Susan);
Bavaria Bildagentur, Gauting (S. 54/55; S. 88 Hintergrund);
Kirsten Bleck, Berlin (S. 38 door);
Russell Bruce, London (S. 40/41);
Allan Cash Photolibrary, London (S. 39 tennis; S. 55 cinema);
Chester City Council (S. 12/13; S. 85; S. 86 oben Mitte, oben rechts, Mitte links, unten links; S. 87 toy museum inside 2x, unten rechts);
Chester Zoo (S. 87 oben 3x; S. 106/107; S. 106 elephants, tigers; S. 107 sea lions, penguin);
Jutta Debo, Berlin (S. 31 Bernd Bauer, Stefanie Zimmer-Bauer);
David Dore, Guildford (S. 31 Edward Simpson);
Angelika Fischer, Berlin (S. 10 unten; S. 48; S. 111 unten; S. 122 unten rechts; S. 123);
Focus, Hamburg (S. 7 oben);
Malena Frau, Berlin (S. 31 Julia);
Gruner + Jahr, Hamburg (S. 6 unten; S. 6/7 oben);
John and Penny Hubley, Leeds (S. 6 oben);
IFA-Bilderteam, München (S. 39 Rakete);
Image Bank, Berlin (S. 38 football; S. 88 oben rechts);
Ute Klaphake, London (S. 6/7 unten; S. 10 oben; S. 12; S. 13 oben, Mitte; S. 14; S. 15; S. 17; S. 19; S. 22, 23; S. 26; S. 29; S. 31 Grandma Scott, David Scott, Richard Scott, Karin Scott, Ben; S. 38 bus, rooms, door 24; S. 39 Telefon, Tafel; S. 40; S. 52; S. 54; S. 55 Nick, hamburger; S. 57; S. 58; S. 65; S. 70, 71, 72; S. 77; S. 78; S. 86 unten rechts; S. 87 toy museum outside; S. 99; S. 111 oben; S. 117);
John Lally, York (S. 68);
Mainbild, Frankfurt/Main (S. 106 giraffe);
Mauritius, Mittenwald (S. 31 Claire Simpson; S. 75; S. 88 unten);
Susanne Meyer, Berlin (S. 26/27);
Lutz Neumann, Bad Dürkheim (S. 25);
Okapia, Berlin (S. 107 tortoise);
Oxfam, Oxford (S. 91);
Presse Fotos Günther Peters, Berlin (S. 106 monkeys; S. 107 zebras, lion);
Yvonne Petter-Zimmer, Berlin (S. 31 Oma Bauer);
Reinhard Tierfoto, Heiligkreuzsteinach/Eiterbach (S. 27);
Martina Reis, Hannover (S. 31 Katrin);
Sainsbury's, London (S. 122 oben links);
Cedric Sherratt, Berlin (S. 13 unten);
Stock Food, München (S. 55 popcorn, ice-cream);
D.C. Thomson, Dundee (S. 88 oben links, unten links, unten rechts; S. 89);
Rolf Wiesemes, Berlin (S. 31 Opa Bauer)

Umschlag Ute Klaphake, London

Liedquellen

Happy birthday to you 1935 by CL. F. Summy & Co. Chicago © Musikverlag Intersong GmbH, Hamburg
Money, money © Eldorado Musikverlag GmbH, Hamburg

Textquellen

Mice by Rose Fyleman. Reprinted by permission of The Society of Authors (UK);
Lazy Jane by Shel Silverstein. From: *Where The Sidewalk Ends.* © 1974 Evil Eye Music, Inc.

Nicht alle Copyrightinhaber konnten ermittelt werden; deren Urheberrechte werden hiermit vorsorglich und ausdrücklich anerkannt.

Many thanks to everyone who agreed to have their photograph taken, especially the staff and pupils of Kingsway High School, Chester. A special thanks to Karen Shipley for all the preparation and organization at Kingsway High School.

LIST OF NAMES

Girls / Women
(Mädchen / Frauen)

Ann [æn]
Bina ['bi:nə]
Carol ['kærəl]
Christine ['krɪsti:n]
Claire [kleə]
Debbie ['debi]
Gillian ['dʒɪliən]
Hannah ['hænə]
Helen ['helən]
Jane [dʒeɪn]
Jenny ['dʒeni]
Laurie ['lɒri]
Linda ['lɪndə]
Lynn [lɪn]
Nazma ['næzmə]
Pam [pæm]
Pat [pæt]
Rachel ['reɪtʃəl]
Rebecca [rɪ'bekə]
Sally ['sæli]
Sandra ['sɑ:ndrə]
Sarah ['seərə]
Sita ['si:tə]
Sue [su:]
Susan ['su:zn]
Tracy ['treɪsi]
Wendy ['wendi]

Boys / Men
(Jungen / Männer)

Alan ['ælən]
Andy ['ændi]
Asif ['æsif]
Ben [ben]
Brian ['braɪən]
Dave [deɪv]
David ['deɪvɪd]
Edward ['edwəd]
Jeff [dʒef]
Jeremy ['dʒerəmi]
Joe [dʒəʊ]
Joey ['dʒəʊi]
Lenny ['leni]
Mark [mɑ:k]
Mike [maɪk]
Nick [nɪk]
Paul [pɔ:l]
Peter ['pi:tə]
Richard ['rɪtʃəd]
Robby ['rɒbi]
Ron [rɒn]
Sanjay ['sændʒeɪ]
Tim [tɪm]
Tom [tɒm]
Zack [zæk]

Family names
(Familiennamen)

Baker ['beɪkə]
Ball [bɔ:l]
Bloggs [blɒgz]
Bond [bɒnd]
Cobb [kɒb]
Crick [krɪk]
Gregg [greg]
Gupta ['gʊptə]
Hunt [hʌnt]
Jam [dʒæm]
Keller ['kelə]
MacDonald [mək'dɒnəld]
Martin ['mɑ:tɪn]
Peterson ['pi:təsən]
Scott [skɒt]
Simpson ['sɪmpsn]
Smith [smɪθ]
Snow [snəʊ]
Williams ['wɪljəmz]
Wolf [wʊlf]

Place names
(Ortsnamen)

Africa ['æfrɪkə] *Afrika*
America [ə'merɪkə] *Amerika*
Ashton ['æʃtən]
Austria ['ɒstriə] *Österreich*
Belgium ['beldʒəm] *Belgien*
Berlin [bɜ:'lɪn]
Bosnia-Herzegovina [ˌbɒzniə ˌhɜ:tsəgə'vi:nə] *Bosnien-Herzegowina*
Bristol ['brɪstl]
Chester ['tʃestə]
Croatia [krəʊ'eɪʃə] *Kroatien*
the **Czech Republic** [ˌtʃek rɪ'pʌblɪk] *Tschechien, die Tschechische Republik*
Denmark ['denmɑ:k] *Dänemark*
England ['ɪŋglənd]
France [frɑ:ns] *Frankreich*
Germany ['dʒɜ:məni] *Deutschland*
Great Barrow [ˌgreɪt 'bærəʊ]
Great Britain [ˌgreɪt 'brɪtn] *Großbritannien*
Greece [gri:s] *Griechenland*
Hong Kong [ˌhɒŋ 'kɒŋ]
Hungary ['hʌŋgəri] *Ungarn*
India ['ɪndiə] *Indien*
Ireland ['aɪələnd] *Irland*
Istanbul [ˌɪstæn'bʊl]
Italy ['ɪtəli] *Italien*
London ['lʌndən]
the **Netherlands** ['neðələndz] *die Niederlande*
New York [ˌnju: 'jɔ:k]
Nottingham ['nɒtɪŋəm]
Oslo ['ɒzləʊ]
Poland ['pəʊlənd] *Polen*
Portugal ['pɔ:tʃʊgl] *Portugal*
Russia ['rʌʃə] *Russland*
Scotland ['skɒtlənd] *Schottland*
Shorewood ['ʃɔ:wʊd]
Slovakia [sləʊ'vɑ:kiə] *die Slowakei*
Slovenia [sləʊ'vi:niə] *Slowenien*
Spain [speɪn] *Spanien*
Sweden ['swi:dn] *Schweden*
Switzerland ['swɪtsələnd] *die Schweiz*
Turkey ['tɜ:ki] *die Türkei*
the **USA** [ˌju:‿es‿'eɪ] / the **United States of America** [ju:ˌnaɪtɪd ˌsteɪts‿əv‿ə'merɪkə] *die USA / die Vereinigten Staaten von Amerika*
Wisconsin [wɪ'skɒnsɪn]
Yugoslavia [ˌju:gəʊ'slɑ:viə] *Jugoslawien*

Other names
(Andere Namen)

Blacon High School [ˌbleɪkən 'haɪ sku:l]
Eastgate Street ['i:stgeɪt stri:t]
Kevin Costner [ˌkevɪn 'kɒstnə]
Kingsway High School [ˌkɪŋzweɪ 'haɪ sku:l]
Lulu ['lu:lu:]
Marco ['mɑ:kəʊ]
Marmalade ['mɑ:məleɪd]
Merlin ['mɜ:lɪn]
Millie ['mɪli]
Newton Road [ˌnju:tn 'rəʊd]
Odeon ['əʊdiən] *Kino in Chester*
Oxfam ['ɒksfæm] *britische wohltätige Organisation mit Secondhand- und Dritte-Welt-Läden*
Rambo ['ræmbəʊ]
Santa Claus ['sæntə klɔ:z] *der Weihnachtsmann*
Trundle ['trʌndl]
Wembley Stadium [ˌwembli 'steɪdiəm]

ENGLISH SOUNDS (Englische Laute)

In den Wörterverzeichnissen steht hinter jedem englischen Wort in eckigen Klammern die Lautschrift. Sie zeigt dir, wie das Wort ausgesprochen und betont wird. In der folgenden Übersicht findest du alle Lautzeichen.

TIPP Am besten kannst du dir die Aussprache der einzelnen Zeichen einprägen, wenn du dir zu jedem Zeichen ein einfaches Wort merkst – das [iː] ist der *green*-Laut, das [eɪ] ist der *name*-Laut usw.

Vokale (Vowels)

[iː]	green	[eɪ]	name
[i]	story	[aɪ]	my
[ɪ]	in	[ɔɪ]	boy
[e]	yes	[əʊ]	old
[æ]	black	[aʊ]	now
[ɑː]	partner	[ɪə]	here
[ɒ]	not	[eə]	where
[ɔː]	morning	[ʊə]	tour
[uː]	blue		
[ʊ]	book		
[ʌ]	mum		
[ɜː]	girl		
[ə]	a ruler		

Konsonanten (Consonants)

[p]	pen	[f]	fit
[b]	box	[v]	over
[t]	ten	[s]	sister
[d]	dad	[z]	has
[k]	cat	[tʃ]	teacher
[g]	good	[dʒ]	Germany
[m]	mum	[θ]	thanks
[n]	no	[ð]	this
[ŋ]	song	[ʃ]	she
[l]	hello	[ʒ]	television
[r]	red	[h]	he
[w]	we		
[j]	you		

[ː] zeigt, dass der vorangehende Vokallaut lang gesprochen wird.

Betonung
[ˈ] und [ˌ] sind Betonungszeichen. Sie stehen immer vor der betonten Silbe.
[ˈ] zeigt die Hauptbetonung, [ˌ] die Nebenbetonung.
Beispiel:
afternoon [ˌɑːftəˈnuːn]
Hauptbetonung auf der letzten Silbe: [-ˈnuːn]
Nebenbetonung auf der ersten Silbe: [ˌɑːftə-]

Bindebogen
Der Bindebogen [‿] gibt an, dass zwei Wörter beim Sprechen aneinander gebunden und wie ein Wort gesprochen werden.
Beispiel:
mum and dad [ˌmʌm‿ən ˈdæd]

Ein Spiel mit der Lautschrift:

Jeder wählt einen Laut und versucht, in fünf Minuten so viele Wörter wie möglich zu finden, in denen dieser Laut vorkommt. Ihr müsst vorher vereinbaren, ob ihr in der alphabetischen Liste (S. 172–180) nachsehen dürft oder nicht.

Ihr könnt das Spiel zu zweit, in Gruppen oder mit der ganzen Klasse spielen. Alle Mitspieler und Mitspielerinnen sollten entweder einen Vokal oder einen Konsonanten wählen.

THE ENGLISH ALPHABET (Das englische Alphabet)

a [eɪ]	e [iː]	i [aɪ]	m [em]	q [kjuː]	u [juː]	y [waɪ]
b [biː]	f [ef]	j [dʒeɪ]	n [en]	r [ɑː]	v [viː]	z [zed]
c [siː]	g [dʒiː]	k [keɪ]	o [əʊ]	s [es]	w [ˈdʌbljuː]	
d [diː]	h [eɪtʃ]	l [el]	p [piː]	t [tiː]	x [eks]	

CLASSROOM PHRASES

What YOU can say in the classroom

You need help
What's '…' in English/in German?
What does '…' mean?
Can you spell '…', please?
How do you say the second word in line 5?
Can you write it on the board, please?
Sorry, I can't find it. What page are we on?

Can I say it in German?
Can you speak louder, please?

Homework and exercises
I've got '…'. Is that right, too?
I can't/couldn't[1] do number 3.
I haven't got my homework.
Sorry, I haven't finished.
I don't understand this exercise.
I don't know./I'm not sure[2].
What's for homework?

Listening and reading
I can't hear the cassette/CD properly[3].
I think the story is nice/interesting[4]/ boring/terrible.
I agree./I don't agree[5].
I like … very much.

You and your partners – you and your teacher
Can we work together, please?
Can I have your ruler/felt-tip/…, please?
It's your turn[6].
Can I read the next sentence?
Can I act Debbie's part?
Can I go to the toilet[7], please?
Can I open/close the window, please?

Was DU im Klassenzimmer sagen kannst

Du brauchst Hilfe
Was heißt „…“ auf Englisch/auf Deutsch?
Was bedeutet „…“?
Können Sie bitte „…“ buchstabieren?
Wie spricht man das zweite Wort in Zeile 5 aus?
Können Sie es bitte an die Tafel schreiben?
Entschuldigung, ich kann es nicht finden. Auf welcher Seite sind wir?
Kann ich es auf Deutsch sagen?
Können Sie bitte lauter sprechen?

Hausaufgaben und Übungen
Ich habe „…“. Ist das auch richtig?
Ich kann/konnte Nummer 3 nicht lösen.
Ich habe meine Hausaufgaben nicht mit.
Entschuldigung, ich bin noch nicht fertig.
Ich verstehe diese Übung nicht.
Ich weiß es nicht./Ich bin nicht sicher.
Was haben wir (als Hausaufgabe) auf?

Beim Zuhören und beim Lesen
Ich kann die Cassette/CD nicht richtig hören.
Ich finde die Geschichte nett/interessant/ langweilig/schrecklich.
Das finde ich auch./Das finde ich nicht.
Ich mag … sehr.

Du und deine Partner/innen – du und dein/e Lehrer/in
Können wir bitte zusammenarbeiten?
Kann ich bitte dein Lineal/deinen Filzstift/… haben?
Du bist dran.
Kann ich den nächsten Satz lesen?
Kann ich Debbies Rolle spielen?
Darf ich bitte zur Toilette gehen?
Kann ich bitte das Fenster öffnen/schließen?

What YOUR TEACHER says

Quiet, please. Sit down.
Open your books at page 24, please.
Close your books.
Look at line 8/at the picture on page 24.
Copy … into your exercise books.
Cut out the …, please.
Stick the … on your posters.
Write down the sentences.
Correct the mistakes.
Fill in/Put in the right words.
Put the words in the right order.
Make notes.
Fill in the chart/the questionnaire.
Read out your answers.
Do exercise 3 for homework, please.
Listen to the cassette/CD, please.
Have you finished?

Was DEIN/E LEHRER/IN sagt

Ruhe bitte. Setzt euch.
Schlagt bitte Seite 24 auf.
Macht eure Bücher zu.
Seht euch Zeile 8/das Bild auf Seite 24 an.
Übertragt … in eure Übungshefte.
Schneidet bitte die … aus.
Klebt die … auf eure Poster.
Schreibt die Sätze auf.
Verbessert die Fehler.
Setzt die richtigen Wörter ein.
Bringt die Wörter in die richtige Reihenfolge.
Macht euch Notizen.
Füllt die Tabelle/den Fragebogen aus.
Lies deine Antworten vor.
Macht bitte Übung 3 als Hausaufgabe.
Hört euch bitte die Cassette/CD an.
Seid ihr fertig?/Bist du fertig?

[1] couldn't ['kʊdnt] [2] sure [ʃʊə] [3] properly ['prɒpəli] [4] interesting ['ɪntrəstɪŋ] [5] agree [ə'gri:] [6] turn [tɜ:n] [7] toilet ['tɔɪlət]